Development Communication Sourcebook

Development Communication Sourcebook

Broadening the Boundaries of Communication

Paolo Mefalopulos

THE WORLD BANK
Washington, D.C.

1818 H Street NW
Washington DC 20433
Telephone: 202-473-1000
Internet: www.worldbank.org
E-mail: feedback@worldbank.org

1 2 3 4 11 10 09 08

ISBN: 978-0-8213-7522-8
eISBN: 978-0-8213-7523-5
DOI: 10.1596/978-0-8213-7522-8

Library of Congress Cataloging-in-Publication Data

Mefalopulos, Paolo.
Development communication sourcebook : broadening the boundaries of communication/ Paolo Mefalopulos.
p. cm.
Includes bibliographical references and index.
ISBN 978-0-8213-7522-8 (print) -- ISBN 978-0-8213-7523-5 (electronic)
1. Communication in economic development. I. World Bank. II. Title.
HD76.M44 2008
338.9001'4--dc22

2008016703

Cover: Patricia Hord Graphik Design

Contents

Boxes

Figures

Tables

Preface

The main reason for writing this book was not simply to gather, organize, and disseminate knowledge on development communication. Rather, it was to make the case for its systematic adoption in development policies and practices. My long experience in the field made me realize that the media-centric conception of communication was not making a significant difference in people's lives. Too often the most important missing element in development programs was genuine (two-way) communication between the decision makers, the experts, and the so-called beneficiaries.

Media, no matter how technologically advanced; messages, no matter how skillfully packaged; and information, no matter how relevant, are not enough to bring about meaningful and sustainable results. These results can only be achieved if the people involved (stakeholders) are part of the process leading to change. This realization shifted my professional focus from media to people, from the products to the process.

My frustration at the frequent misuse of the term "communication for development" has been a major impetus in writing this book. The Sourcebook intends to make clear the seemingly straightforward distinction between "communication *about* development operations and results" and "communication *for* development operations and results." In the first case, communication is used to inform audiences about development initiatives, activities, and results. It is about transmitting information and messages. In the second case, communication is applied to engage stakeholders, assess the situation, and devise effective strategies leading to better and more sustainable development initiatives. *It is more than transmitting information; it is about using communication to generate new knowledge and consensus in order to facilitate change.* Both are important and require a different body of knowledge and different set of skills.

The preparation of the *Development Communication Sourcebook* has been a long dialectical process, where my knowledge and many of my ideas have been challenged by colleagues and by frequent reality checks. Trying to provide a brief but accurate historical overview of this interdisciplinary field, accounting for its most recent conceptual and practical developments, and combining this knowledge with the vast pool of experiences in the World Bank and in many other organizations, has proved to be a highly demanding task. The end product is a publication that can be used as a primer, not only by those in the communication field, but also by development managers, practitioners, and students interested in knowing more about development communication.

In an institution such as the World Bank, which is dominated by economists, a soft science such as communication has often been relegated to the back seat. This has happened despite the fact that past approaches, driven by economic theories, have not always produced significant results and despite the fact that lack of communication has often been identified as a major cause of project failure.

This Sourcebook illustrates how the emerging paradigm in development communication, focused on participation and two-way communication, constitutes a necessary element if we are to avoid the mistakes of the past. It makes the case about the importance of incorporating communication practices into the policies and practices of development. It intends also to offer a broader conception of communication that would take into account other purposes and functions than the usual ones. Communication is not only about raising awareness, informing, persuading, or changing behavior. It is also about listening, exploring, understanding, empowering, and building consensus for change. This should resonate loud and clear for the reader.

Two-way communication, used to understand, assess, explore, and facilitate decision making related to change, combined with the effective use of one-way communication approaches, has been proven to significantly enhance results and the sustainability of development initiatives. This Sourcebook is intended to provide a small contribution in further promoting the understanding and subsequent adoption of such practices, in any sector of intervention.

To sum up, these are the two key messages of this publication: (1) two-way communication, when used from the onset of a development initiative, is not only a useful but also a necessary ingredient to enhance development initiatives and avoid the failures of the past, and (2) two-way communication should be applied professionally by specialists familiar with the rich body of knowledge and the diverse range of methods, techniques, and tools of development communication.

There are many individuals who should be acknowledged and thanked for having contributed to the production of the Sourcebook. The peer reviewers who went through the final draft of the manuscript played a major role. With their knowledge and experiences they raised critical issues and gave constructive suggestions that helped improve and refine the final version of the Sourcebook. They include Grazia Atanasio, Communications Officer, World Bank; Kreszentia M. Duer, Program Manager, New Bank Practices in Civic Engagement, Empowerment, and Respect for Diversity, World Bank Institute; Professor Thomas Jacobson, Sr., Associate Dean for Academic Affairs, Temple University; Sumir Lal, Head, Internal Communications, World Bank; Regina Monticone, Chief, Development Partnerships, Department of Communications and Public Information, International Labour Organization; Rafael Obregon, Associate Professor, School of Media Arts and Studies, and Director of the Communication and Development Studies Program at Ohio University; and Adesinaola Michael Odugbemi, Head of the Communication for Governance and Accountability Program, World Bank.

Other World Bank colleagues should also be acknowledged for their comments on specific parts of the Sourcebook. They include Natalia Kirpikova, Kosta Kostadinova, Leonardo Mazzei, and Irina Oleinik. A number of other individuals have provided valuable insights, sometimes even unknowingly, and assistance that made the completion of this process easier. Among them are Mario Acunzo, Mario Bravo, Daniele Calabrese, Nawsheen Elaheebocus, Eliana Esposito, Manuela Faria, Lucia Grenna, Kafu Kofi Tsikata, Anjali Manglik, Antonietta Poduie, Emanuele Santi, Mohamed Sidie Sheriff, Obadiah Tohomdet, and Stephanos Tsekos. It would be impossible to list all those who contributed in one way or another to this project, but a sincere note of appreciation is extended to all of them.

Abbreviations

AFD	French Development Agency
AfDB	African Development Bank
AKAB	awareness, knowledge, attitudes, and behaviors (or practices)
ALRMP	Arid Lands Resource Management Project
AMARC	World Association of Community Radio Broadcasters
ARRnet	Aceh Reconstruction Radio Network
ASTD	American Society for Training and Development
BCC	behavior change communication
CAS	country analysis strategy
CBA	communication-based assessment
CDD	community-driven development
CDD/R	Departmental Development Committees
CEERD	Civic Engagement, Empowerment, and Respect for Diversity
CEP	Community Empowerment and Local Governance Project (Timor-Leste)
CFSC	Communication for Social Change
CIDA	Canadian International Development Agency
CNA	communication needs assessment
CommGAP	Communication for Governance and Accountability Program
CPR	country portfolio review
CRPD	Convention on the Rights of Persons with Disabilities
DAC	Development Assistance Committee (of OECD)
DevComm	Development Communication Division of the World Bank
DevComm-SDO	Sustainable Development in Operations Unit of DevComm
DFID	Department for International Development (United Kingdom)
DPOs	disabled persons organizations
EXT	External Affairs (World Bank vice presidency)

GTZ	German Agency for Technical Cooperation
HNP	health, nutrition, and population projects
IADB	Inter-American Development Bank
ICT	information and communication technologies
IEC	information, education, and communication
ISN	Information Solutions Network
JRKY	Jaringan Radio Komunitas Yogyakarta (Indonesia)
LFA	logical framework analysis
MDGs	Millennium Development Goals
M&E	monitoring and evaluation framework
NECDP	Nutrition and Early Child Development Project
NGO	nongovernmental organization
NOPS	needs, opportunities, problems, solutions
NWICO	New World Information and Communication Order
OECD	Organisation for Economic Co-operation and Development
PAD	project appraisal documents
PAR	participatory action research
PRA	participatory rural appraisal
PRCA	participatory rural communication appraisal
PRS	poverty reduction strategy
PRSP	Poverty Reduction Strategy Paper
RRA	rapid rural appraisal
SAF	situation analysis framework
SIDA	Swedish International Development Cooperation Agency
SMART	specific, measurable, achievable, realistic, and timely
SMCR	Sender-Message-Channel-Receiver
UNDP	United Nations Development Programme
UNESCO	United Nations Educational, Scientific, and Cultural Organization
USAID	United States Agency for International Development
WCCD	World Congress on Communication for Development
WOPs	Windows of Perceptions
WSIS	World Summit on the Information Society
ZOPP	objective-oriented project planning

Introduction

Why a Sourcebook on Development Communication?

The *Development Communication Sourcebook* aims to provide a clear understanding of the field of development communication and its more recent trends. It illustrates why this field is important and how its methods and tools can be applied effectively to enhance long-term results. The Sourcebook addresses everyone who has an interest in the success and sustainability of development initiatives, from communication practitioners to managers.

Two factors guided the rationale for writing the Sourcebook. First, despite the growing recognition enjoyed by the discipline of development communication, its nature and full range of functions are still not fully known to many decision makers and development managers who tend to identify this field merely with the art of disseminating information effectively. Second, because of the recent shift in the development paradigm (that is, from one-way to two-way communication) and the related changes in the field of development communication, many communication practitioners are not entirely aware of the discipline's rich theoretical body of knowledge and the wealth of its practical applications—which are growing in relevance for the development context.

The Sourcebook is divided into modules that can be read sequentially, to gain a comprehensive overview, or individually, to allow readers to select specific modules for their professional interest or for training purposes. The challenge is to engage readers' different interests while presenting the richness of development communication, which has broadened beyond diffusion to incorporate the more horizontal, dialog-based approaches needed to ensure mutual understanding and to investigate issues before other forms of communication take place.

The Evolution of Development Communication

The initial stages of development communication were characterized by the use of mass media that considered people as audiences ready to be influenced by the messages they received. That communication perspective is rooted in the basic Sender-Message-Channel-Receiver (SMCR) model, which has been widely criticized. This model envisions a sender transmitting a message through the appropriate channel to a receiver (or group of receivers). If done properly, the dissemination of information was viewed as capable of achieving the intended behavior change. This model has been revised a number of times in attempts to strengthen the active role of the "receivers" by including their feedback in the communication model.

The overall effectiveness of this basic model, however, has proved to be limited. Over time, its linear flow has been replaced with a more complex perspective in which communication is envisioned as a horizontal process aimed, first of all, at building trust, then at assessing risks, exploring opportunities, and facilitating the sharing of knowledge, experiences, and perceptions among stakeholders. The aim of this process is to probe each situation through communication in order to reduce or eliminate risks and misunderstandings that could negatively affect project design and its success. Only after this explorative and participatory research has been carried out does communication regain its well-known role of communicating information to specific groups and of trying to influence stakeholders' voluntary change.

It is our hope that by reading this book, practitioners interested in broadening their knowledge of the theory and practice of development communication will become aware that the professional use of this discipline goes beyond the choice of the best channels to disseminate information or the production of media outputs. At the same time, readers better acquainted with the subject will be able to increase their knowledge of concepts, principles, and approaches to be applied in different situations when investigating, conceiving, planning, and implementing a communication intervention.

The field of development communication is a broad but rigorous one: it includes a specific body of research as well as a series of practices to induce change through specific methods and media. While there is a vast literature about planning, production, and strategic use of media in development, there is significantly less material about the "dialogic" use of communication to investigate issues at the beginning of development projects and programs. This Sourcebook intends to close that gap.

Its interdisciplinary nature makes development communication an extremely effective cross-cutting investigative tool that can often make the difference in enhancing project results and sustainability. Engaging stakeholders in assessing key issues helps to mitigate risks and prevent the emergence of problems and conflicts before they arise.

Development Communication at the World Bank

The Development Communication Division (DevComm) of the World Bank was established in 1998. Compared to other international institutions with specific units established as early as the 1960s, DevComm is a relatively new entity in this context. The wide engagement of the World Bank in development and its reputation as a source of knowledge, however, gives DevComm immediate recognition among the major players in this field. The first years of its existence have been spent supporting the Bank's operations and reaching out to clients (both in the World Bank and in client countries) to demonstrate and to promote the value of development communication.

Currently, DevComm is consolidating and strengthening its core of activities on the basis not only of the knowledge and experience gained through these years but also of the constant interactions and active partnerships with other organizations in this field. The role played by DevComm in the ideation and organization of the first World Congress of Communication for Development in 2006 is a further indication of its leading role in this field.

Who Is the Sourcebook's Intended Reader?

The Development Communication Sourcebook intends to address different audiences. Each module has been prepared with a specific purpose and readership in mind. Module 1 concisely presents the emerging concepts and relative applications of development communication and why it is so relevant to operations. This module, while of interest to communication students and practitioners intending to gain a better understanding of the field of development communication, can also appeal to managers of development initiatives who are interested in knowing more about it.

Module 2 addresses communication officers and practitioners who want to become acquainted with the theoretical foundations of this field of study. It deals with conceptual aspects, including a brief overview of the main development paradigms and their influence on the role of communication. In addition, the module presents an integrated model, combining different approaches capable of effectively addressing the diverse needs and situations of project and program design.

Module 3 focuses on the methodological applications of development communication. It is of particular value to all those involved in operational work, especially in the World Bank. This module is divided into four parts, one for each phase of the communication program: communication research or communication-based assessment, strategy design, implementation, and, finally, evaluation.

Module 4 uses a number of articles to illustrate DevComm's role, presenting practical instances and issues of relevance of its work in operations. After a description of DevComm's overall structure and functions, each article addresses a specific issue related to communication, such as the role of community radio or how to assess the impact of development communication. By using World Bank experiences to illustrate the topics, this section is useful for all those who are interested in knowing more about how communication is used by the World Bank.

By adopting a modular structure that addresses specific interests within a broad audience, the Sourcebook allows readers to pick and choose the module that applies best to their situation. At the same time, this approach implies some degree of redundancy among the various modules. For those interested and willing to go through the whole Sourcebook, we have tried to keep such redundancy to a minimum, and we hope that the Sourcebook will be a useful tool to promote a better understanding of the interdisciplinary field of development communication. It can also help to foster a common understanding among various international agencies and contribute to bringing more harmony to their work in this field.

How to Use the Sourcebook

Given its modular structure, the Sourcebook can serve a number of purposes. It is a valuable source of knowledge and practical advice for all those involved in development communication. The materials can be used to gain insight on how to conduct proper communication research, to review the basic steps for designing a communication strategy, or to learn to manage and monitor the communication process effectively.

The Sourcebook can also serve as reference material for courses and workshops in this field. Since the text addresses the rationale for adopting development communication, as well as the practical challenges encountered in its applications, it can constitute a valuable resource for the training of trainers. The brief historical overview of this discipline provides a basic theoretical framework to which trainers and educators can always refer.

Finally, the Sourcebook also can serve as an advocacy piece to promote the discipline to managers and decision makers who have an interest in learning why and when to adopt development communication. Keeping the specific needs of managers and other decision makers in mind, module 1 has been written to make the case and provide a clear understanding of the scope and key functions of development communication while demonstrating its value-added.

MODULE 1

The Value-Added of Development Communication

The newer conceptions of development imply a different and, generally, a wider role for communication.
(Everett Rogers)

Preview

This module introduces the theory and practice of development communication and presents a brief historical survey showing why this field has become so important for development initiatives and instrumental in enhancing sustainability and better overall results. This module not only illustrates the basic features, principles, and methods of development communication, but it also highlights the value it adds to a development project. In a discussion of why it is so important to adopt development communication practices from the start of development initiatives, it shows why failing to do so jeopardizes projects' success and sustainability. The module, a refresher for communication practitioners, also addresses the interests of decision makers and managers of development initiatives, who are among those who can benefit the most by the appropriate use of such approaches.

Contents

1.1 What Communication?

Mass communications, interpersonal communication, and health communication are just some of the specialties that can be found under the communication curricula of major academic institutions in countries around the world. Also included are international communication, speech communication, intercultural communication, communication education, applied communication, organizational communication, and political communication. This list could be expanded even further to include journalism, media production, information and communication technologies, public relations, corporate communication, and development communication, indicating the diversified and multifaceted nature of communication.[1]

Dictionaries, Web sites, and other sources confirm the richness, yet they can cause misconceptions about the term "communication." As noted by Mattelart (1996), this is not a recent development: in 1753 Denis Diderot was already writing in the Encyclopédie, "Communication: a term with a great number of meanings."[2] Rather than being taken as a sign of weakness or confusion, however, this diversity of conceptions and applications should be considered a strength—provided that the different areas are well understood and applied professionally according to their nature and characteristics.

At the outset of this discussion, a point worth clarifying is the correct use of the terms "communication" and "communications," since the two have different connotations. Usually the choice of a singular or plural form indicates merely a quantitative difference, but in this case the difference can be considered one of substance. References to "communications" typically emphasize products, such as audiovisual programs, posters, technologies, Web sites, and so forth. In this respect, it is appropriate to talk of telecommunications or mass communications. The broader field of communication (spelled without an "s") does not describe a single product, but a process and its related methods, techniques, and media. This is the case with development communication, as well as other fields such as research communication, intercultural communication, or political communication.[3] Later in this Sourcebook, the significant difference between everyday communication skills and professional knowledge of communication, another blurred area, will also be discussed.

1.1.1 Different Types of Communication

A challenge for development communication experts is the lack of clarity, and at times the confusion, that many development managers display in their failure to differentiate among the various areas of communication, especially between this field of study and others, such as corporate communication or mass communications. The practical differences are often significant and are rooted not only in the rationale, functions, and applications of the different fields, but also in the theories behind those applications and the methods and techniques being used. Furthermore, the operational implications of the emerging paradigm in development have broadened the scope and function of communication in a way not yet fully understood by all those concerned.

While communication specialists are usually familiar with the different branches of communication, they do not always have the in-depth knowledge to apply each one of these appropriately to different situations. A political communication consultant who has been working for the past 20 years in a New York consulting firm would not likely be the most appropriate person to design a health campaign in a developing country. A journalist who has been working in the corporate communication department of a multinational firm would hardly be the best choice for advice about a communication program for a community-driven development project. Similarly, asking a development communication specialist to write a speech for the director of an institution might be a mistake, since writing speeches is not a required task for such a specialization. Although most specialists possess a number of different skills, they usually master one of those broader areas of communication, and each of those areas requires well-defined professional knowledge, competencies, skills, and specific sensitivities.

Table 1.1 presents the four basic types of communication frequently encountered in the development context.[4] Even though they are highly complementary, the types differ in scope and function, and each can play a crucial role, depending on the situation. Note that the term "conducive environment," used to describe the main functions of development communication, indicates the broader function of two-way communication to build trust among stakeholders, assess the situation, explore options, and seek a broad consensus leading to sustainable change.

Although some functions may overlap to a degree, the different types of communication and the way they are used require different bodies of knowledge and applicative tools. According to the circumstances, each of the types can involve one communication approach or a combination of approaches (for example, marketing, capacity building, information dissemination, community mobilization, and so forth). Different types of communication usually require different sets of knowledge and skills. All the various types of communication, and the related skills, are equally important in general, but they are unequally relevant when applied in specific situations (for example, journalism skills to facilitate community mobilization).

Each type of communication listed in this table, while belonging to the same family and sharing common conceptual roots, requires its own specific set of competencies and knowledge, an idea not yet widely understood in the development community. Too often, a specialist is hired for a communication intervention outside his or her area of expertise, with results that are less than satisfactory. In the world of engineering, for example, the equivalent would be the interchangeable use of different types of engineers, such as hiring an electrical engineer to build a bridge.

Table 1.1 Common Types of Communication in Development Organizations

Type	Purpose/Definition	Main Functions
Corporate communication	Communicate the mission and activities of the organization, mostly for external audiences.	Use media outputs and products to promote the mission and values of the institution; inform selected audiences about relevant activities.
Internal communication	Facilitate the flow of information within an institution/project. Sometimes this area can be included in corporate communication.	Ensure timely and effective sharing of relevant information within the staff and institution units. It enhances synergies and avoids duplication.
Advocacy communication	Influence change at the public or policy level and promote issues related to development.	Raise awareness on hot development issues; use communication methods and media to influence specific audiences and support the intended change.
Development communication	Support sustainable change in development operations by engaging key stakeholders.	Establish conducive environments for assessing risks and opportunities; disseminate information; induce behavior and social change.

Source: Author.

In the medical world, for example, the equivalent would be to ask an orthopedist to treat ear pain.

1.1.2 A Brief History of Development Communication

Awareness of the different purposes and functions of various types of communication is the first step toward a better understanding of the field of development communication and an effective way to enhance necessary quality standards. Being familiar with the origin of this particular discipline and the major theoretical frameworks underpinning it can help achieve a much better understanding. The following pages present a brief overview of the field of development communication (also referred to as "communication for development," "development support communication," and more recently, "communication for social change.")[5] The theoretical models related to this field of work and their implications are presented in more detail in module 2.

The Dominant Paradigm: Modernization

An understanding of the broadening role and practices of development communication is more relevant now than ever, since the old, widely criticized paradigm of modernization has been in part abandoned—and a new paradigm has yet to be fully embraced.[6] This old paradigm, rooted in the concept of development as modernization, dates back to soon after World War II and has been called the dominant paradigm because of its pervasive impact on most aspects of development.

The central idea of this old paradigm was to solve development problems by "modernizing" underdeveloped countries—advising them how to be effective in following in the footsteps of richer, more developed countries. Development was equated with economic growth, and communication was associated with the dissemination of information and messages aimed at modernizing "backward" countries and their people. Because of the overestimated belief that they were extremely powerful in persuading audiences to change attitudes and behaviors, mass media were at the center of communication initiatives that relied heavily on the traditional vertical one-way model: Sender-Message-Channel-Receiver (SMCR). This has been the model of reference for the diffusion perspective, which has often been adopted to induce behavior changes through media-centric approaches and campaigns.

The Opposing Paradigm: Dependency

In the 1960s strong opposition to the modernization paradigm led to the emergence of an alternative theoretical model rooted in a political-economic perspective: the dependency theory. The proponents of this school of thought criticized some of the core assumptions of the modernization paradigm mostly because it implicitly put the responsibility, and the blame, for the causes of underdevelopment exclusively upon the recipients, neglecting external social, historical, and economic factors. They also accused the dominant paradigm of being very Western-centric, refusing or neglecting any alternative route to development.

In the field of communication the basic conception remained rooted in the linear, one-way model, even though dependency theorists emphasized the importance of the link between communication and culture. They were instrumental in putting forward the agenda for a new world information and communication order (NWICO),[7] which was at the center of a long and heated debate that took place mostly in the United Nations Educational, Scientific, and Cultural Organization (UNESCO) in the 1980s (see Mefalopulos 2003). One of the thorny issues was the demand for a more balanced and equitable exchange of communication, information, and cultural programs among rich and poor countries. Although the dependency theory had gained a significant impact in the 1970s, in the 1980s it started to lose relevance gradually in tandem with the failure of the alternative economic models proposed by its proponents.

The Emerging Paradigm: Participation

When the promises of the modernization paradigm failed to materialize, and its methods came increasingly under fire, and the dependency theorists failed to provide a successful alternative model, a different approach focusing on people's participation began to emerge. This participatory model is less oriented to the political-economic dimension and more rooted in the cultural realities of development.

The development focus has shifted from economic growth to include other social dimensions needed to ensure meaningful results in the long run—as indicated by the consensus built in the definition of the Millennium Development Goals. Sustainability and people's participation became key elements of this new vision, as acknowledged also by the World Bank (1994: 3): "Internationally, emphasis is being placed on the challenge of sustainable development, and participation is increasingly recognized as a necessary part of sustainable development strategies."

Meaningful participation cannot occur without communication. Unfortunately, too many development programs, including community-driven ones, seem to overlook this aspect and, while paying attention to participation, do not pay similar attention to communication, intended as the professional use of dialogic methods and tools to promote change. To be truly significant and meaningful, participation needs to be based on the application of genuine two-way communication principles and practices.

That is why communication is increasingly considered essential in facilitating stakeholders' engagement in problem analysis and resolution. Similarly, there is an increasing recognition that the old, vertical, top-down model is no longer applicable as a "one-size-fits-all" formula. While acknowledging that the basic principles behind the Sender-Message-Channel-Receiver model can still be useful in some cases, development communication has increasingly moved toward a horizontal, "two-way" model, which favors people's active and direct interaction through consultation and dialog over the traditional one-way information dissemination through mass media.

Many past project and program failures can be attributed directly or indirectly to the limited involvement of the affected people in the decision-making process. The horizontal use of communication, which opens up dialog, assesses risks, identifies solutions, and seeks consensus for action, came to be seen as a key to the success and sustainability of development efforts. There are a number of terms used to refer to this emerging conception (Mefalopulos 2003); some of the better known are "another development," "empowerment," "participation," and "multiplicity paradigm." This last term, introduced by Servaes (1999), places a strong emphasis on the cultural and social multiplicity of perspectives that should be equally relevant in the development context.

The new paradigm is also changing the way communication is conceived and applied. It shifts the emphasis from information dissemination to situation analysis, from persuasion to participation. Rather than substituting for the old model, it is broadening its scope, maintaining the key functions of informing people and promoting change, yet emphasizing the importance of using communication to involve stakeholders in the development process. Among the various definitions of development communication, the following two provide a consistent understanding of the boundaries that define this field of study and work.

The first is derived from the Development Communication Division of the World Bank (DevComm), which considers development communication as *an interdisciplinary field based on empirical research that helps to build consensus while it facilitates the sharing of knowledge to achieve positive change in development initiatives. It is not only about effective dissemination of information but also about using empirical research and two-way communication among stakeholders.* It is also a key management tool that helps assess sociopolitical risks and opportunities.

The second definition emerged at the First World Congress of Communication for Development, held in Rome in October 2006. It is included in the document known as the Rome Consensus (see the appendix), in which the more than 900 participants of the Congress (World Bank et al. 2007: xxxiii) agreed to conceive it as *a social process based on dialog using a broad range of tools and methods. It is also about seeking change at different levels, including listening, building trust, sharing knowledge and skills, building policies, debating, and learning for sustained and meaningful change. It is not public relations or corporate communication.*

1.2 The Value-Added of Development Communication in Programs and Projects

The history of development has included failures and disappointments, many of which have been ascribed to two major intertwined factors: lack of participation and failure to use effective communication (Agunga 1997); Anyaegbunam, Mefalopulos, and Moetsabi 1998; Fraser and Restrepo-Estrada 1998; Mefalopulos 2003). The same point is emphasized by Servaes (2003: 20), who states, "the successes and failures of most development projects are often determined by two crucial factors: communication and people's involvement."

No matter what kind of project—agriculture, infrastructure, water, governance, health—it is always valuable, and often essential, to establish dialog among relevant stakeholders. Dialog is the necessary ingredient in building trust, sharing knowledge and ensuring mutual understanding. Even a project that apparently enjoys a wide consensus, such as the construction of a bridge, can have hidden obstacles and opposition that the development communication specialist can help uncover, address, and mitigate.

A number of studies have confirmed that a top-down management approach to development is less effective than a participatory one. Bagadion and Korten (1985), Shepherd (1998), Uphoff (1985), and the World Bank (1992) are among those providing data to support this perspective. Development communication supports the shift toward a more participatory approach, and its inclusion in development work often results in the reduction of political risks, the improvement of project design and performance, increased transparency of activities, and the enhancement of people's voices and participation (Mitchell and Gorove, in module 4, 4.6).

1.2.1 Adopting Two-Way Communication from Day One

Communication interventions are often used in ongoing projects, but managers should be aware that their effectiveness is limited by factors that might have emerged since the inception, such as the perceived significance of project objectives, the lack of support by stakeholders, or a number of other potential misconceptions and obstacles that might limit the impact of communication interventions. That communication assessments and strategies can still help when adopted halfway through a project should not affect the recognition that communication initiatives are most effective when applied early in the project cycle.

Even though many practitioners in the new participatory development paradigm advocate the active involvement of local stakeholders from the early stages of an initiative on moral grounds and from a rights-based perspective, participatory approaches have demonstrated their crucial role also in enhancing project design and results sustainability. Hence, participation can be considered a necessary ingredient for successful development, both from a political perspective (good governance and a rights-based approach) and from a technical perspective (long-term results and sustainability of initiatives). Successful communication interventions do not always need to rely on media to engage and inform audiences—they can also rely on more participatory and interpersonal methods, as in the case narrated by Santucci (2005) in box 1.1.

Participation in a project can be conceived in a number of ways—from the most passive (for example, holding meetings to inform stakeholders) to the most active form (for example, collaboration in decision making). Frequently what is often referred to as "participation" in many cases is not, at least not in a significant way. Box 1.2 presents a typology of participation (Mefalopulos 2003) compatible with others, including one used by the World Bank that is presented in module 2.

When not involved from the beginning, stakeholders tend to be more suspicious of project activities and less prone to support them. Conversely, when communication is used to involve them in the definition of an initiative, their motivation and commitment grow stronger. This applies not only in the development context but also in the private sector, as confirmed in a statement by a director of a major private corporation:[8] "It is incredibly irksome and terribly longwinded to get agreement to any action, but it does have enormous benefits—the meetings buy everybody in, and once they get behind the project they'll do anything they can to see it through."

The involvement of stakeholders in defining development priorities has advantages other than just gaining their support. It gives outside experts and managers

BOX 1.1 Getting Results through Interpersonal Communication Methods

The Rural Poverty and Natural Resources Project, implemented by the Panamanian Ministry of Agriculture, was challenged to improve living conditions in the area of operations (556 communities) by devising microprojects relevant to their realities. Most of the project area had poor infrastructure and high rates of illiteracy. Due to this context, to some complexity in the content, and to the need for capacity building, the communication strategy relied mostly on interpersonal and group methods. Owing to the vast area and the size of the population involved, contracts were made with a number of local nongovernmental organizations (NGOs) to provide qualified staff in addition to project personnel. These contracts were very helpful in achieving the expected project results, even though the differences in logos of different NGOs and occasional gaps in coordination generated some confusion among stakeholders.

The project supported the creation of 75 Committees for Sustainable Development, which included 6,000 members, almost one per family. Assisted by NGO and project staff, the committees reviewed and approved 1,216 infrastructure and microprojects. In a number of other cases the committees became involved in seeking additional donors and sources of funding. Overall, the project was considered successful, and the communication strategy based on interpersonal relationships was instrumental in achieving such results, which would have been harder to achieve if adopting a media campaign approach.

valuable insights into local reality and knowledge that ultimately lead to more relevant, effective, and sustainable project design. The next example illustrates what can happen when stakeholders' perceptions diverge, and how major problems can arise because of these perceptions rather than because of actual facts.

According to the experts from the Ministry of Land and Water, the initiative was expected to increase crop yield, thus enabling higher food security, better nutrition, and higher income for poor farmers. Unfortunately, the experts did not involve the farmers in the identification, assessment, and planning phases of the project. This lack of proper communication at the initial stages generated suspicions in the farmers (the so-called beneficiaries) and led to misunderstandings and negative attitudes throughout implementation of the project. The cause of these problems, and ultimately of the project failure, was the lack of two-way communication. The end result was the opposite of what was expected—insecurity and frustration on the side of the farmers instead of increased confidence and a better quality of life, as shown in figure 1.1 (Anyaegbunam et al. 2004).

BOX 1.2 A Typology of Participation in Development Initiatives

The table below illustrates a participation ladder, starting from the lowest form, which is merely a form of token participation, to the highest form, where local stakeholders share equal weight in decision making with external stakeholders.

Passive participation	Stakeholders participate by being informed about what is going to happen or has already happened. People's feedback is minimal or nonexistent, and individual participation is assessed mainly through head-counting and occasionally through their participation in the discussion.
Participation by consultation	Stakeholders participate by providing feedback to questions posed by outside researchers or experts. Because their input is not limited to meetings, it can be provided at different points in time. In the final analysis, however, this consultative process keeps all the decision-making power in the hands of external professionals who are under no obligation to incorporate stakeholders' input.
Functional participation	Stakeholders take part in discussions and analysis of predetermined objectives set by the project. This kind of participation, while it does not usually result in dramatic changes on "what" objectives are to be achieved, does provide valuable inputs on "how" to achieve them. Functional participation implies the use of horizontal communication among stakeholders.
Empowered participation	Stakeholders are willing and able to be part of the process and participate in joint analysis, which leads to joint decision making about what should be achieved and how. While the role of outsiders is that of equal partners in the initiative, local stakeholders are equal partners with a decisive say in decisions concerning their lives.

In summing up the body of evidence that has emerged since the 1980s, Rahnema (1993: 117) concludes, "A number of major international aid organizations agreed that development projects had often floundered because people were left out. It was found that, whenever people were locally involved, and actively participating in the projects, much more was achieved with much less, even in sheer financial terms." Other studies of operations in major organizations (Shepherd 1988), such as the United States Agency for International Development and the World Bank (1992), reported similar findings.

1

Figure 1.1 Windows of Perception in an Agricultural Project

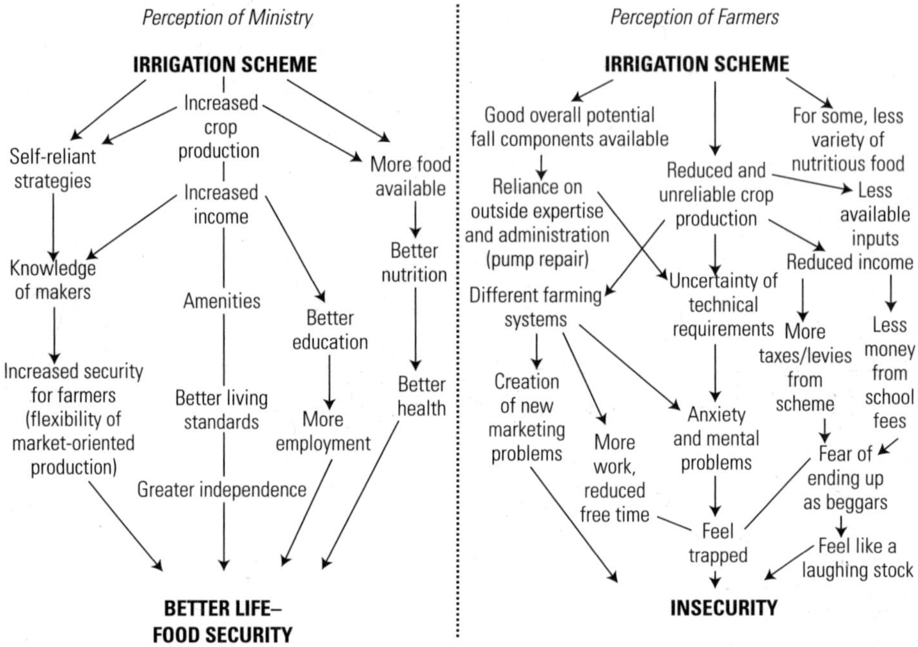

Source: Anyaegbunam et al. 2004.

When adopted from the very beginning of the process, such as in Poverty Reduction Strategy Papers or in projects formulation, communication activities are ideally poised to facilitate dialog and mutual understanding among relevant stakeholders. Early incorporation of communication allows the use of all available knowledge and perspectives in a cross-cutting investigation and analysis of the situation, minimizing both political and technical risks and, most important, enhancing projects planning and results.

With timely information in hand, project managers can refine a project's scope and objectives with a deeper understanding of the environment in which it will be implemented. In doing so, they can avoid most common mistakes, including those that Hornik (1988) characterized as "the political explanation of failures." Through the unveiling of political and other types of risks, and by seeking a broad consensus and mediating among various positions, development communication helps managers to identify the best strategy to support intended change.

United Nations agencies are increasingly acknowledging the key role of two-way communication in assessing the situation, mitigating risks, and building consensus toward change. In the 10th UN Inter-Agency Round Table on Communication for Development (UNESCO 2007: 29), the various agencies proposed to embed the practice of this discipline in all "UN and international standardized program-based approaches and formats for project development."[9]

To use development communication effectively, managers do not need to know the nuts and bolts of this discipline. It is sufficient to understand its scope and basic functions. The most common obstacles to the effective application of development communication are to be found in the inappropriate timing of its inclusion (typically halfway through the project, once a number of preventable problems may have already emerged) and in relying on inappropriate professional expertise (that is, using a specialist with a different communication specialization other then development communication).

Although it is always advisable to involve a development communication specialist at the earliest stage of a project, assistance can be provided also at later stages. In ongoing projects, the strategic use of communication can help mitigate problems and get a project back on track. Therefore, a two-way communication assessment can be applied in two kinds of situations: explorative, to facilitate the appropriate design of development initiatives from the start, and topical, to support the achievement of the set objectives in ongoing projects (Anyaegbunam, Mefalopulos, and Moetsabi 1998).

1.2.2 Development Communication for Communication Programs

The two main communication modes presented later in the module—monologic and dialogic—illustrate the expansion of the scope of communication beyond its well-known dissemination functions to include explorative and analytical cross-cutting features. This distinction is also useful in understanding how communication is of great value, not only in initiatives clearly and explicitly requiring communication components (i.e., those envisioning a specific communication component to disseminate information, carry out media campaigns, or advocate for a reform), but also in those that do not appear to have a need for communication (i.e., initiatives not envisioning specific communication or information activities, such as building a bridge or conducting a feasibility study about a reforestation project).

Projects that include communication components are usually related to the support of predefined development objectives. In such cases, the various phases of the communication intervention (that is, research, strategy design, and so forth) remain within the boundaries set by the scope of the project and its indicated goals. The communication assessment will then be focused on identifying stakeholders' needs, perceptions, and risks on the specific issues of interest for the project. On the basis of the assessment, a strategy will be designed to define the communication program aimed at helping to achieve the project goals.

For instance, an environmental project with the objective of preserving an endangered ecosystem might need a communication component to raise people's awareness and knowledge and encourage local people to adopt certain practices. To be effective, the communication strategy needs to be based on the stakeholders' knowledge, perceptions, and practices toward the ecosystem. Such information would have been collected during the research phase. This kind of research is usually referred to as communication needs assessment (CNA). It investigates exclusively communication-related issues—information gaps, communication needs and capacities, media environment, and so forth. This differs, or better, it has a narrower focus, from what in DevComm is referred to as CBA or communication-based assessment (see box 1.3), which is discussed in the next session.

1.2.3 Development Communication for Noncommunication Projects

Communication for a noncommunication project might seem like an oxymoron, yet this is hardly the case. It basically means that communication is used to investigate, explore, and assess various sectors (health, environment, infrastructure, and so forth), regardless of whether any communication component is envisioned. The dialogical and analytical features of communication are useful for any kind of assessment and for any kind of problem-solving strategy, thus helping managers of development initiatives to prevent conflicts and face unforeseen problems halfway through the project.

For instance, a road-building project might not seem to need the support of communication, yet, contacting the communities involved in the project, listening to their concerns and suggestions, assessing risk and opportunities, or tapping into local knowledge can be of crucial value to the success of the project. Road construction can involve the use of land with special sentimental value to local people (for example, burial grounds) and raising funds for longer-term maintenance, just to mention some issues where communication would make a difference.

Any development intervention involves change of some kind, and as the manager of the Development Communication Division of the World Bank said, "Development is about change and change cannot occur without communication."[10] The limited understanding of communication as a way to disseminate, inform, and persuade fails to embrace the spirit of the new development paradigm, in which communication is used to facilitate participation and generate knowledge.

The interdisciplinary nature of development communication becomes invaluable when conducting comprehensive assessments covering more than a sector. Even when different specialists are able to conduct in-depth assessments for each of the sectors involved (for example, environment, infrastructure, and health), it is often difficult to understand how the issues for each sector are intertwined and what the overall priorities are for different groups of stakeholders. Each specialist can give an accurate representation of his or her specific sector, but there is the need for someone putting together all the pieces in a single consistent frame to avoid the confusion or misrepresentation such as that presented in figure 1.2. In this picture

BOX 1.3 Comparing and Contrasting CNA and CBA

CNAs, or communication needs assessments, are typically carried out to investigate, understand, and determine issues directly related to communication, such as the media environment, infrastructure and policies, institutional communication capacities, information gaps, formal and informal information flows, and networks. They can be effectively used either at the beginning of an initiative or once a project has already begun.

CBAs, or communication-based assessments, on the other hand, are carried out to investigate all relevant issues in any sector. Communication cross-cutting features are used to facilitate the investigation and assessment of key issues in one or more sectors, regardless of their relation to communication. Although a CBA can be used at different stages of the project cycle, its effectiveness is greatly enhanced if it is applied at the beginning of an initiative, since it can link the dots across sectors and compare and contrast different priorities. The following examples serve to clarify the way these two assessments can be adopted most effectively.

As presented by Cabañero-Verzosa (2005), in the Uganda Nutritional and Early Childhood Development Project, a communication needs assessment was carried out to investigate communication issues and understand people's attitudes and practices regarding nutritional patterns relevant to the project objectives. The objective was to identify which communication messages and channels could be applied effectively to induce the desired change. The CNA also included the investigation of the existing communication environment and of the institutional capacity to implement the communication strategy.

In the case of the Bumbuna Hydroelectric Project in Sierra Leone (Hass et al. 2007), instead, the investigation had a broader range and a CBA was conducted to probe stakeholders' perceptions and address negative attitudes and concerns, such as worry about corruption, while addressing some of the long-standing history of conflicts. Two-way communication was used to facilitate the participation of different groups of stakeholders and investigate several issues beyond the boundaries of communication. This helped the project to get back on track while providing communication inputs needed at a later stage to design a proper strategy. Once again, the main difference between the two resides in the communication-centric approach of the CNA, which is about communication issues, versus the use of communication as an investigative tool in the CBA, which uses communication as a two-way tool to explore all kinds of issues.

each mouse draws the cow accurately from its own perspective, but no one is able to fit together all the various pieces in a coherent picture. In a development initiative, communication has the needed cross-cutting features to combine different perspective into a unified frame.

The adoption of two-way communication to involve stakeholders as partners in the problem-analysis and problem-solving processes of development initiatives, rather than treating them as mere receivers of information, is fundamental for making changes effective and sustainable. It also prevents making costly mistakes or investing in solutions that are technically sound but of little use to communities, as the story in box 1.4 illustrates. In this context, communication becomes the best method to investigate and facilitate a "communion of values and experiences" by most stakeholders, needed to achieve sustainable results, no matter what the sector of intervention.

BOX 1.4 When a Perfectly Appropriate Technical Solution Does Not Make Much Sense

During a poverty reduction assessment mission in an Asian country, the team composed of various sector specialists identified a few solutions meant to improve the livelihoods of villagers in the community. Among other issues, the experts noted that women, who were doing a number of heavy chores, had to walk almost an hour to fetch water from the nearby river. If a water well was built by the village, the experts reckoned that women would save time and energy that were now required in the daily walks to the river.

As a result, a technically sound proposal was done, funds were made available and the water well was quickly built. One year later a follow-up mission returned to the same community. To the experts' surprise, the newly built water well was rarely being used by the women. When they asked for the reasons, after some initial resistance from the villagers, the experts learned that the walk to the river was one of the few daily moments in which women could be together and socialize. Taking away that walk meant taking away their only moments of sharing part of their lives and having some relaxed moments away from the other hard chores they carried out individually. If dialog and simple two-way communication had occurred before making the decision to build a well, this aspect would have probably emerged and a more culturally appropriate alternative would have been found.

Figure 1.2 Mice Reconstructing an Image of a Cow

Source: Cartoon by Stefanos N. Tsekos. Used by permission.

1.3 Ten Key Issues about (Development) Communication

The 10 points presented in this section address some of the myths and misconceptions about communication, especially when related to the field of development. These misconceptions can often be the cause of misunderstandings and lead to inconsistent and ineffective use of communication concepts and practices. The first two points on this list are about communication in general, while the others refer to development communication in particular.

1. *"Communications" and "communication" are not the same thing.* The plural form refers mainly to activities and products, including information technologies, media products, and services (the Internet, satellites, broadcasts, and so forth). The singular form, on the other hand, usually refers to the process of communication, emphasizing its dialogical and analytical functions rather than its informative nature and media products. This distinction is significant at the theoretical, methodological, and operational levels.
2. *There is a sharp difference between everyday communication and professional communication.* Such a statement might seem obvious, but the two are frequently equated, either overtly or more subtly, as in, "He or she communicates well; hence, he or she is a good communicator." A person who communicates well is not necessarily a person who can make effective and professional use of communication. Each human being is a born communicator, but not everyone can communicate strategically, using the knowledge of principles and experience in practical applications. A professional (development) communication specialist understands relevant theories and practices and is capable of designing effective strategies that draw from the full range of communication approaches and methods to achieve intended objectives.
3. *There is a significant difference between development communication and other types of communication.* Both theoretically and practically, there are many different types of applications in the communication family. In this publication, we refer to four main types of communication, which are represented significantly in the work of the World Bank: advocacy communication, corporate communication, internal communication, and development communication. Each has a different scope and requires specific knowledge and skills to be performed effectively. Expertise in one area of communication is not sufficient to ensure results if applied in another area.
4. *The main scope and functions of development communication are not exclusively about communicating information and messages, but they also involve engaging stakeholders and assessing the situation.* Communication is not only about "selling ideas." Such a conception could have been appropriate in the past, when communication was identified with mass media and the linear Sender-Mes-

sage-Channel-Receiver model, whose purpose was to inform audiences and persuade them to change. Not surprisingly, the first systematic research on the effects of communication was carried out soon after World War II, when communication activities were mostly associated with a controversial concept—propaganda. Currently, the scope of development communication has broadened to include an analytical aspect as well as a dialogical one—intended to open public spaces where perceptions, opinions, and knowledge of relevant stakeholders can be aired and assessed.

5. *Development communication initiatives can never be successful unless proper communication research is conducted before deciding on the strategy.* A communication professional should not design a communication campaign or strategy without having all the relevant data to inform his or her decision. If further research is needed to obtain relevant data, to identify gaps, or to validate the project assumptions, the communication specialist must not hesitate to make such a request to the project management. Even when a communication specialist is called in the middle of a project whose objectives appear straightforward and clearly defined, specific communication research should be carried out if there are gaps in the available data. Assumptions based on the experts' knowledge should always be triangulated with other sources to ensure their overall validity. Given its interdisciplinary and cross-cutting nature, communication research should ideally be carried out at the inception of any development initiative, regardless of the sector or if a communication component would be needed at a later stage.
6. *To be effective in their work, development communication specialists need to have a specific and in-depth knowledge of the theory and practical applications of the discipline.* In addition to being familiar with the relevant literature about the various communication theories, models, and applications, development communication specialists should also be educated in the basic principles and practices of other interrelated disciplines, such as anthropology, marketing, sociology, ethnography, psychology, adult education, and social research. In the current development framework, it is particularly important that a specialist be acquainted with participatory research methods and techniques, monitoring and evaluation tools, and basics principles of strategy design. Additionally, a good professional should also have the right attitude toward people, being empathic and willing to listen and to facilitate dialog in order to elicit and incorporate stakeholders' perceptions and opinions. Most of all, a professional development communication specialist needs to be consistently issue-focused, rather than institution-focused.
7. *Development communication support can only be as effective as the project itself.* Even the most well-designed communication strategy will fail if the overall objectives of the project are not properly determined, if they do not enjoy a broad con-

sensus from stakeholders, or if the activities are not implemented in a satisfactory manner. Sometimes communication experts are called in and asked to provide solutions to problems that were not clearly investigated and defined, or to support objectives that are disconnected from the political and social reality on the ground. In such cases, the ideal solution is to carry out field research or a communication-based assessment to probe key issues, constraints, and feasible options. Tight deadlines and budget limitations, however, often induce managers to put pressure on communication experts to produce quick fixes, trying to force them to act as short-term damage-control public relations or "spin doctors." In such cases, the basic foundations of development communication are neglected, and the results are usually disappointing, especially over the long term.

8. *Development communication is not exclusively about behavior change.* The areas of intervention and the applications of development communication extend beyond the traditional notion of behavior change to include, among other things, probing socioeconomic and political factors, identifying priorities, assessing risks and opportunities, empowering people, strengthening institutions, and promoting social change within complex cultural and political environments. That development communication is often associated with behavior change could be ascribed to a number of factors, such as its application in health programs or its use in mass media to persuade audiences to adopt certain practices. These kinds of interventions are among the most visible, relying heavily on communication campaigns to change people's behaviors and to eliminate or reduce often fatal risks (for example, AIDS). The reality of development, though, is complex and often requires broader changes than specific individual behaviors. Module 2 explains this in more detail.
9. *Media and information technologies are not the backbone of development communication.* As a matter of fact, the value-added of development communication occurs before media and information and communication technologies (ICTs) are even considered. Of course, media and information technologies are part of development communication, and they are important and useful means to support development. Their application, however, comes at a later stage, and their impact is greatly affected by the communication work done in the research phase. Project managers should be wary of "one-size-fits-all" solutions that appear to solve all problems by using media products. Past experience indicates that unless such instruments are used in connection with other approaches and based on proper research, they seldom deliver the intended results.
10. *Participatory approaches and participatory communication approaches are not the same thing and should not be used interchangeably, but they can be used together, as their functions are often complementary, especially during the research*

phase. Even if there are some similarities between the two types of approaches, most renowned participatory approaches, such as participatory rural appraisal (PRA) or participatory action research (PAR), do not usually assess the range and level of people's perceptions and attitudes on key issues, identify communication entry points, and map out the information and communication systems that can be used later to design and implement the communication strategy. Instead, these are all key activities carried out in a participatory communication assessment.

1.4 Understanding the Scope and Uses of Development Communication

To fully understand the way development communication can be effectively applied in operations, it is necessary to have clearly in mind how its scope has broadened. Even the media-centric MacBride report (1980)[11] indicated that the communication role was not restricted to media and dissemination—that it should also be concerned with "involving people in the diagnosis of needs and in the design and implementation of selected activities." To be effective in that task, and to be true to the interdisciplinary nature of communication, a specialist in this field should be familiar not only with communication do's and don'ts but should have broad analytical skills and be able to use communication methods to assess the cultural, political, and social context.

A communication specialist, when called in to assist in development projects and programs, should always ask why a certain issue is occurring and what kind of communication is needed to address it effectively. Is communication mostly used to inform and promote project activities and objectives? Or is it to engage stakeholders in the investigation and assessment of priorities for change, thus enhancing the design of the initiative? As stated by Quarry (2008), managers and decision makers want communication, but too often it is the first kind of communication, which in this Sourcebook is referred to as monologic, and they tend to neglect the importance of the other type of communication, here referred to as dialogic.

The typology adopted in this Sourcebook divides development communication into two basic modes, or families of approaches: the "monologic" mode, based on the classical one-way communication model associated with diffusion, and the "dialogic" mode, based on the interactive two-way model, associated with participatory approaches. Being familiar with these two modes helps one to better understand which to apply under what circumstances. They serve different purposes, but they are not mutually exclusive and can often be used in a complementary way, as explained in module 2.

1.4.1 Monologic Mode: One-Way Communication for Behavior Change

The monologic mode is linked to the development communication perspective known as "diffusion." It is based on the one-way flow of information for the purpose of disseminating information and messages to induce change. Its main intentions can be divided into two different types of applications: (1) communication to inform (or simply "information," as Latin American scholars such as Pasquali [2003] and Beltrán Salmón [2000] refer to it); and (2) communication to persuade.

"Communication to inform" typically involves a linear transmission of information, usually from a sender to many receivers. It is used when raising awareness or providing knowledge on certain issues is considered enough to achieve the intended goal (for example, informing a community about the activities of a project or informing the public about a reform coming into effect). In other instances, the dissemination of information is only a temporary stage to be reached in a longer process aimed at achieving behavior changes. This modality can be labeled "communication to persuade."

Approaches in communication for behavior change use methods and media to persuade individuals to adopt specific practices or behaviors. These approaches are frequently used in health initiatives. The Family Health International Web site (www.fhi.org) states that communication for behavior change aims to foster positive behavior; promote and sustain individual, community, and societal behavior change; and maintain appropriate behavior. Its underlying assumption is that individual attitudes and behaviors can be changed voluntarily through communication and persuasion[12] techniques and the related use of effective messages. Since the approaches, methods, and media used for this modality rely mostly on the one-way model, the mode of reference is monologic communication.

In many cases, approaches to persuade still rely on the classic notion of one-way communication. The primary objective is for the sender to be able to persuade the receivers about the intended change. In this model the feedback is a sort of tune-up, allowing the sender to refine its persuasive message (Beltrán Salmón 2000). A common approach closely associated with this communication mode is strategic communication, which is often used in development initiatives to support management objectives.

1.4.2 Dialogic Mode: Two-Way Communication for Engagement and Discovery

On the other hand, the dialogic mode is associated with the emerging participatory paradigm. It is based on the horizontal, two-way model of communication, creating a constructive environment where stakeholders can participate in the definition of problems and solutions. The main purposes of this model can be divided into two broad types of applications: (1) communication to assess; and (2) communication to empower.

This categorization helps one to understand the way in which the ultimate scope of the communication interventions shapes the choice of communication approaches, methods, and models of reference. Both of these types of applications take a radical turn away from the common conception of communication, since they do not involve any dissemination of information or messages. Even if these two types of communication cannot be easily positioned in a sequence because their scope is often closely intertwined, the use of dialogic communication to ensure mutual understanding and explore a situation often becomes the best tool to facilitate empowerment.

"Communication to assess" is used as a research and analytical tool that, thanks to its interdisciplinary and cross-cutting nature, can be used effectively to investigate any issue, well beyond those strictly related to the communication dimension. The power of dialogic communication is applied to engage stakeholders in exploring, uncovering, and assessing key issues, opportunities, and risks of both a technical and political nature.

As an illustration, take an initiative that at the surface does not appear in need of communication, such as building a bridge to link two areas and their communities separated by the river. A communication-based assessment prior to the project would probe the knowledge, perceptions, and positions of local stakeholders on the intended initiative. Unless probed through two-way communication, the identified technical course might neglect important aspects that could lead to problems or conflicts, for example by local fishermen who see their livelihoods endangered.

This use of two-way communication engages experts and local stakeholders in the problem-analysis and problem-solving process leading to change. Active listening becomes as important as talking. In a way, it could be said that dialogic communication is not used to inform but to truly "communicate"—that is, to share perceptions and create new knowledge.

Dialog should be understood not as a broad form of chit-chat, but as a process where "participants come together in a safe space to understand each other's viewpoint in order to develop new options to address a commonly identified problem." This assertion is put forth by Pruitt and Thomas (2007: 20) in a publication on the virtue of dialog in development, commissioned jointly by the Canadian International Development Agency (CIDA), the International Institute for Democracy and Electorate Assistance (IDEA), Organization of American States (OAS), and United Nations Development Programme (UNDP). The same publication states, "In dialog, the intention is not to advocate but to inquire; not to argue but to explore; not to convince but to discover."

The same notion is also included in the other typology of the dialogic mode, that is, "communication to empower." When used to facilitate the active engagement of stakeholders, the dialogic feature of communication enhances the capacities of all groups, especially the most marginalized ones, and addresses the issue of poverty as explained below.

Dialogic communication is not only effective as a problem-solving tool, but it also builds confidence, prevent conflicts, and addresses the issue of poverty by engaging the poorest and most marginal sectors in the process concerning issues of relevance to them. Amartya Sen (1999), a Nobel Prize winner in economics, highlights how the poverty dimension goes beyond the notion of lacking sufficient income to address basic needs. Poverty is also about capabilities deprivation and social exclusion. By involving the poor in the assessment of problems and solutions, by engaging them, and not just the experts, in the decision-making process, and by making the voices of the poor heard, the dialogic mode can address and reduce one key dimension of poverty: social exclusion.

The overall goal of the dialogic mode is to ensure mutual understanding and to make the best use of all possible knowledge in assessing the situation, building consensus, and looking for appropriate solutions. By facilitating dialog with key stakeholders, this type of communication enhances the analysis and minimizes risks. On the other hand, the primary scope of the monologic mode emerges especially when information needs to be packaged and disseminated to address specific needs and gaps. Table 1.2 provides a further clarification of the two approaches by contrasting their scope, basic functions, and main differences.

Development is about change and about people. Each of the communication types presented in table 1.2 is a means to bring about change. Methods to achieve change, however, may vary according to the perspective, situation, and overall scope of the initiative. Even if past experiences indicate that the mere dissemination of information seldom achieves the intended change, properly packaged message dis-

Table 1.2 Basic Features of Communication Modes

	Monologic Mode		Dialogic Mode	
Compare and contrast	Communication to inform	Communication to persuade	Communication to assess	Communication to empower
Main purpose	To raise awareness or increase knowledge of key audiences	To change attitudes and behaviors of key audiences	To assess, probe, and analyze the situation	To involve stakeholders in decisions over key issues
Model of reference	One-way model (monologic)	One-way model (monologic)	Two-way model (dialogic)	Two-way model (dialogic)
Preferred methods and media	Predominant use of mass media	Predominant use of media	Wide range of methods to investigate issues	Use of dialog to promote participation

Source: Author.

semination may be effective in a number of cases, such as the prevention of the spread of pandemic illnesses or for explaining the benefits of a public reform. On the other hand, two-way communication is more indicated in achieving mutual understanding, building trust, and uncovering and generating knowledge, leading to better results.

1.4.3 Misconceptions about Development Communication

Attitudes of development managers and decision makers toward communication were studied in a survey commissioned by the Development Communication Division of the World Bank (Fraser, Restrepo-Estrada, and Mazzei 2007). The findings indicated that while many managers and decision-makers are fully aware of the importance of communication in development programs, most of them use it in a broad and at times confused way. They usually conceive communication mostly in terms of public relations, media production, information dissemination, or corporate communication. The study clearly indicates the need for positioning and clarifying the scope, body of knowledge, and practical applications of the field of development communication.

Since the use of communication in development has been associated historically with information dissemination and one-way persuasion, it is not surprising that many managers and decision makers involved in development focus primarily, or even exclusively, on these aspects. This leads many of them to seek communication interventions only halfway through the project cycle, rather than as part of the project's initial conception when it is more strategic and cost-effective.

When discussing persuasion, it should be noted that in addition to the commonly conceived one-way modality, which often carries a negative connotation, there is also a wider conception, where persuasion is used in two-way communication among two or more parties who are exchanging opinions and knowledge in order to uncover and agree on the best option. Jacobson (2003), for instance, refers to the philosopher Jurgen Habermas's concept of communicative action to address this issue at different levels of scale. He claims that persuasion can also take place in dialogic/participatory communication as "large-scale political discourse requires mass media, whereas interpersonal and small-group communication do not. Nevertheless, the principles of reciprocity, the equal distribution of opportunities to contribute, and the freedom to raise any proposals are common to participatory communication at both levels" (108).

Distinguishing development communication from other areas of communication is essential—failure to do this leads to misconceptions and wrong expectations. Its analytical focus and its embrace of a number of principles from other disciplines, such as anthropology, sociology, adult education, and marketing, are signature features. The interdisciplinary nature of development communication is defined by its dialogical focus, which becomes a crucial feature to explore and uncover risks and opportunities. It is important to remember that the concept of "dialog," when used in the context of development communication, refers to more than just engaging people in a conversation or discussion. It is about the professional facilitation of dialogic methods among stakeholders to explore and identify priorities and best alternatives leading to change.

Another prevalent misconception in this context equates discussion with dialog. When engaged in a discussion, the goal is usually to prove the superiority of one's point of view, and at the end, winners and losers emerge. Alternatively, in a genuine dialog, nobody is trying to win. As Bohm (1996: 7) states, "Everybody wins if anybody wins. In genuine dialog there is no attempt to gain points, or to make one's particular view prevail. Rather, whenever any mistake is discovered on the part of anybody, everybody gains." Conceived in this way, dialog becomes instrumental in setting the groundwork for any successful development initiative. It becomes a heuristic method, striving to seek and to sustain the best possible solution or change. When all parties involved feel that their contribution is part of the solution, it is more likely that everyone will put forth their best effort to support the initiative.

A further misconception surrounds the qualifications for development communication work. Once the scope, range of functions, and multifaceted nature of a project are fully understood, the depth of the communication discipline needed becomes apparent. At this stage, it is difficult to support the argument that anyone who "communicates" well can be considered a communication specialist, without specific studies or in-depth expertise on the subject (an assertion that is implicitly and tacitly accepted too often in development circles). To be applied effectively, especially in the complex development context, communication strategies and approaches require a specialist's in-depth knowledge, at both the theoretical and applicative levels.

1.4.4 Two-Way Communication-Based Assessment: First Step to Mutual Understanding and Strategy Design

The first step in a communication intervention always should be based on empirical research through the use of two-way communication investigative methods. In order to assess and minimize risks, DevComm stresses on-site research as the basis of any communication intervention and consequently as the basis for the success of any development intervention.

Depending on the scope of the intervention, the various communication approaches presented in the Sourcebook can be adopted to address a given situation. Yet, accurate measuring of the effectiveness of specific communication approaches can vary considerably. Assessing if and how much the level of awareness and knowledge of a certain issue has increased is not a particularly difficult matter; the same applies when measuring changes in attitudes and behaviors. Evaluating the impact of dialog, empowerment, joint analysis, and consensus, however, is a much more complex issue—one that some argue cannot be accurately measured, at least in a rigorous quantitative manner.

The question of whether such "preventive functions" can be measured or accounted for is not an easy one to answer. Maybe it should be acknowledged that, given the complexity of the human dimension, not everything can be accurately measured. Or perhaps measurements can be carried out in more creative ways, such as assessing projects that have failed because of the lack of communication intervention at the initial stages. This would measure the costs of noncommunication,[13] which in many cases are evident and easy to quantify.

Moreover, people's participation has gradually become a pillar of the current development conception, and a number of studies, including some by the World Bank, demonstrate the positive impact of participation in development projects. And participation cannot occur without two-way communication. There is a growing international consensus considering participation not only as a means, but also as an end in itself (Sen 1999). UNDP (1993: 21) asserts that "Participation, from the human development perspective, is both a means and an end." Nonetheless, the debate on this issue, while extremely valuable, is beyond the scope of this Sourcebook. For the purposes at hand, participation is treated primarily as a means, a valuable element to meet development objectives.

Communication is not only considered as a necessary ingredient for meaningful stakeholders' participation in development initiatives, but it is often paired with the term "strategy." An effective strategy based on two-way communcation increases a development project's success and sustainability. Communication strategies need to be professionally designed and prepared to avoid some of the problems found most frequently in projects and programs: inadequate diagnosis, flawed or ill-conceived design, or inappropriate timing (Hornik 1988).

When designing a strategy, communication professionals should be clear about the specific objectives and the communication mode required for the intervention. The temptation to jump into the design of messages or into the production of audiovisual materials without carefully assessing what is really needed or what the benchmark is to assess the intervention should be resisted. To be effective, a communication strategy should always be based on the findings of a two-way assessment.

Whenever the term "communication strategy" is used, managers' attention almost automatically goes to the search for a solution—what do we need to do or say to achieve the intended change? The focus, instead, should be first on the search for the root of the problem, on what different stakeholder groups think, and on what elements impede the desired change. Since most of the causes are usually created by or related to people, communication is the best and perhaps the only tool to investigate them comprehensively and effectively. There are a number of met[h]... providing guidelines to follow, usually starting from the causes of the prob...

the outputs needed for addressing the situation successfully, the Logical Framework[14] approach probably being the most renowned of these methods.

1.5. The Operational Framework of the Development Communication Division

In 1998 the World Bank established the Development Communication Division, or DevComm. Unlike in other institutions, where such entities are often positioned within operational departments, DevComm has been placed within the World Bank's External Affairs Vice Presidency, in the company of Media and Corporate Communication. This positioning might have contributed to some of the difficulties in differentiating the role of development communication from the other types of Bank communication. To be sure, these other types of communication, among their various functions, include support to operations. The field of development communication, however, does not simply support operation, but is engaged in operations (dealing with operational issues of projects and programs beyond aspects regarding communicating information), and this is its main scope.

DevComm's mission is to incorporate communication into World Bank operations in order to improve development results, helping to achieve set objectives and strengthen long-term sustainability. DevComm functions are not limited to the design of effective communication strategies. The value-added of its work is most evident in the initial phase of development initiatives, where communication is used as a research and analytical tool. Using its full range of resources, development communication supports operations not only through dissemination and outreach activities, but also by exploring and analyzing project issues on the ground.

DevComm operations are carried out along three business lines: (1) polling and opinion research, (2) learning and capacity building, and (3) operations. The bulk of activities carried out by DevComm are aimed directly at working in projects and programs in client countries. DevComm's services in polling and opinion research provide the basis needed to inform further research and to understand how institutions, reforms, or other key issues are perceived by key groups.

The Learning and Capacity Building Unit provides a number of services aimed at strengthening the knowledge and skills of the participants in relevant areas and strengthening key institutional capacities. The bulk of DevComm services, however, are in operations, and they cover a wide range of communication applications, from empirical research for engaging stakeholders, exploring their perceptions, and assessing risks and opportunities, to the dissemination-of-information media campaigns to promote behavior change, or the use of two-way-based approaches to facilitate social change. A detailed explanation of the scope and range of activities within each business line is presented in module 4.

Figure 1.3 DevComm Methodological Framework

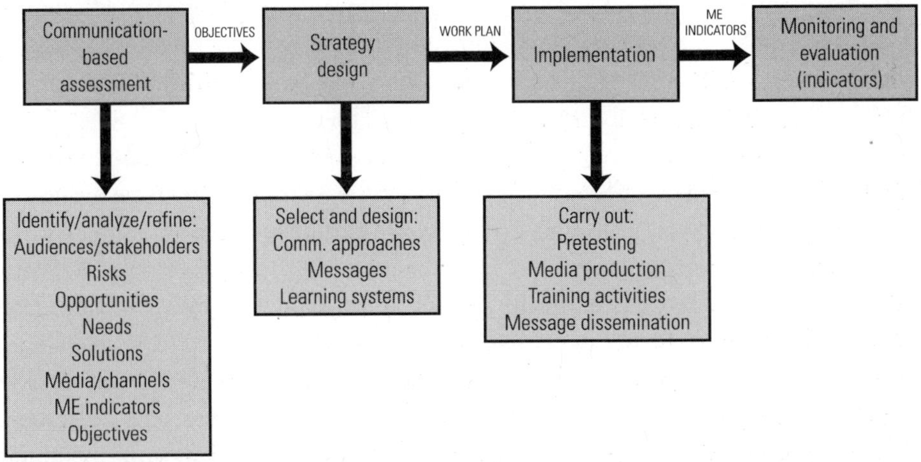

Source: Author.
ME: monitoring and evaluaton

DevComm's methodological framework is divided into four main phases. Figure 1.3 illustrates the overall process/cycle of the development communication intervention, highlighting the key functions for each phase. The first phase involves research and is often referred to as communication-based assessment, or CBA. This phase provides the inputs for the strategy design, which makes up the second phase. The next phase concerns the production of the materials and implementation of the planned activities. Finally, the fourth phase is concerned with evaluation. Proper evaluation of the impact of the communication intervention requires the definition of monitoring and evaluation (ME) indicators during the initial research phase.

1.5.1 Communication-Based Assessment

Communication-based assessment is a flexible and relatively rapid way to conduct an initial investigation, usually followed by more extensive research. For any communication intervention to be effective, it must be rooted in research. In addition to exploring the situation and the perceptions of the various stakeholders, this analysis also produces data for the design of subsequent communication strategy. When carrying out a CBA, DevComm specialists study the cultural, political, and social context; identify and interview opinion leaders and relevant stakeholders; assess risks (such as opposition and potential conflict); seek solutions; and, finally, define the objectives to support the intended change.

As indicated previously, the term "communication-based" indicates that this phase uses communication as a way not only to assess communication needs, but also to explore and probe all kinds of issues through communication methods and tools. The results of the interaction adopted in this type of assessment usually provide a better understanding of different stakeholders' positions, minimizing risks and facilitating the search for a broader consensus toward the needed change. Communication-based assessment provides an overview of the whole socioeconomic context, which is always needed to properly frame technical issues, regardless of their operational sector. Without a proper communication-based assessment, projects are more vulnerable to unforeseen problems. such as misunderstanding, conflicts, opposition, and other obstacles because of stakeholders' divergent views and their lack of support.

The communication-based assessment defines, refines, or validates (if already identified by specialists in specific sectors) the project's objectives, and it also outlines the needed communication objectives. The emphasis on empowerment and dialog brings the CBA in line with the emerging development paradigm. Yet, its relative novelty requires it to be "marketed" assertively to policy makers and decision makers. In addition to its use in specific projects, DevComm has demonstrated CBA's value in several other areas, including sectorwide approaches and other analytical work, such as country analysis strategy (CAS) activities and Poverty Reduction Strategy Papers (PRSPs).

1.5.2 Strategy Design

The second phase of the DevComm methodological approach is strategy design. Here DevComm staff assist in transforming the findings of CBA into usable data to inform the design of effective strategies. The main output of this phase is the definition of a strategy and relative action plan. These indicate the budget and time required, the communication approaches needed, and the related media and messages identified for each audience. DevComm has developed a template, known as the Five Management Decisions, to simplify the management and monitoring of activities in instances that require straightforward communication interventions (e.g., media campaigns).

This tool is a particularly useful for managing and monitoring straightforward communication strategies that have clear objectives requiring changes in knowledge or behaviors. It is not a rigorous planning tool, however, nor is it appropriate for strategies with diversified objectives requiring more complex changes at a social level. In such cases it is advisable to draw multipronged communication strategies based on the sequence illustrated in the section on strategy design in module 3.

1.5.3 Implementation

The third phase is implementation. Usually the activities in this phase are carried out by local firms or consultants, with some advice by DevComm, when requested. Communication activities are prepared and executed according to the agreed strategy and plan of action. They include training of relevant staff, media design and production, information dissemination, and a host of other activities.

1.5.4 Monitoring and Evaluation

The final phase, monitoring and evaluation, is about both examining the process (formative evaluation) and measuring the final outcomes (summative evaluation). Given the Bank mandate and the timing cycle of operations, DevComm is seldom involved in the impact evaluation.[15] Nevertheless, at the beginning of the communication intervention, its staff advises project managers how to set up indicators to monitor the communication progress and measure to what degree the set objectives have been achieved.

Module 3 presents in greater detail the communication functions, methods, and tools that can be effectively used in each phase. Even if communication should be adopted at the very beginning to be most effective, it can also be applied with some success at a later stage in specific points of the project cycle. Evidence at hand suggests that, when professionally applied, communication impact greatly enhances project results, but more significantly it also indicates that lack of or poor adoption of communication often results in problems and project failure.

Summary of Main Points in Module I

- There are different types of communication, each of which requires a specific body of knowledge and a well-defined set of competencies.
- In the World Bank, as well as in many other international organizations, the most common types of communication are corporate communication, internal communication, advocacy communication, and development communication.
- The three main development paradigms that have influenced the role of communication are the modernization paradigm, the dependency theory, and the participation paradigm.
- The current conception of development communication is based on the two-way model, which is used first of all to involve stakeholders and investigate issues, before starting to design and implement a communication strategy. Two basic definitions of development communication are presented in section 1.1.
- Development communication approaches are often significantly participatory in nature and, to be most effective, should be adopted from the very beginning of the initiative.
- Development communication approaches can be used to support projects with specific communication components, as well as to enhance the overall design and sustainability—even in projects that do not have a specific communication component.
- Communication needs assessment (CNA) and communication-based assessment (CBA) are two substantially different applications. In the first case, the assessment focuses on communication needs and capacities, while in the second, it implies the use of two-way communication as a tool to investigate and assess the broader situation beyond its strict communication dimension.
- Ten key points have been presented to emphasize the broader role of the current communication paradigm and clarify some recurrent misconceptions.
- To facilitate the understanding of its concepts and practices, development communication scope has been divided into two basic modes: monologic, associated with the diffusion model, and dialogic, linked to the participatory model.
- The monologic mode, based on the one-way model of communication, is mostly used to disseminate information and transmit messages that persuade audiences to change.
- The dialogic mode, based on the two-way model of communication, seeks to engage stakeholders' knowledge and perceptions in assessing the situation and in defining priorities leading to change.
- The last section presents an overview of the main functions and services offered by the Development Communication Division—DevComm. It also provides an introduction to its methodological framework, which will be dealt with in more depth in module 3.

Notes

1. A renowned communication scholar, Fiske (1982: 1), addressed this issue, the difficulties in defining such a diverse and multifaceted area, as a subject of study and stated that, "Communication is not a subject, in the normal academic sense of the word, but a multidisciplinary area of study."
2. The Encyclopédie, one of the renowned works of the Enlightenment, was edited by Denis Diderot and Jean d'Alembert.
3. Communication, by its very nature, can be considered always to be political in the Aristotelian sense, since as a process it can hardly be separated from the political community in which it takes place. The discipline of political communication, however, refers specifically to the use of communication for political purposes, such as to support the election of a candidate.
4. Although internal communication can be considered to be included in corporate communication, here it is treated separately for purposes of clarity.
5. The main reason for adopting the term "development communication" has been that of keeping the original two terms delineating the field's scope (that is, "communication" and "development") while addressing some of the shortcomings of other similar terms. The term "development support communication" has been criticized for considering communication as an add-on component used only to support other projects' components, while the term "communication for development" reinforces the wrong idea that any kind of communication used in the development context (for example, corporate communication) shares the same theoretical and methodological features.
6. This discussion will be treated in more depth in module 2.
7. Naturally, the NWICO was closely linked with the broader debate on a new international economic order.
8. Alan Bishop, former chairman of Saatchi & Saatchi in New York, as quoted in "Dream teams can be a nightmare." *The Financial Times,* April 16/17, 2005.
9. The statement is contained in the final report of the 10th UN Inter-Agency Round Table on Communication for Development, which took place in Addis Ababa, Ethiopia, in 2007.
10. Paul Mitchell, DevComm manager, in the opening speech at the 9th United Nations Round Table on Communication for Development, held by the Food and Agriculture Organization of the United Nations in Rome, September 2005.
11. The studies for the MacBride report were carried out under UNESCO auspices and are some of the most comprehensive studies done on the role of communication in society at the national and international level.
12. Even if in this section persuasion is associated with the monologic mode, persuasion can also be part of a dialogic process. A dialogic use of persuasion implies an honest dialog on different positions and a quest for the best possible option that would offer the most advantages for the various actors.

13. This issue is dealt with in more detail in the section on monitoring and evaluation in module 3.
14. The Logical Framework Approach, or LFA, is an analytical tool for project design and planning based on objectives. It is widely applied by international organizations and often required by donors as a way to monitor and evaluate project results in a quantifiable manner.
15. Advice is usually given for the assessment and the subsequent design of the communication strategy, even if the ultimate entity responsible for the strategy and its implementation is always the client country. Not being involved directly in this phase, DevComm specialists cannot directly get involved in the evaluation, except in those cases where specific advice is requested and proper baseline studies have been carried out at the beginning of the initiative.

References

Agunga, R. A. 1997. *Developing the Third World: A Communication Approach.* Commack, NY: Nova Science Publishers.

Anyaegbunam, C., P. Mefalopulos, and T. Moetsabi. 1998. *Participatory Rural Communication Appraisal: Starting with the People.* Harare, Zimbabwe: FAO/SADC.

———. 2004. *Participatory Rural Communication Appraisal: Starting with the People* (2nd ed.). Rome: FAO and SADC.

Bagadion, B. U., and F. F. Korten. 1985. "Developing Irrigators Organization: A Learning Process Approach." In *Putting People First,* ed. M. M. Cernea, 2nd ed., 73–112. New York: Oxford University Press.

Beltrán Salmón, L. R. 2000. *Investigacion Sobre Comunicacion en Latinoamerica: Inicio, Trascendencia y Proyeccion.* La Paz, Bolivia: Plural Editors.

Bohm, D. 1996. *On Dialog.* London: Routledge.

Cabañero-Verzosa, C. 2005. "Counting on Communication: Uganda Nutritional and Early Childhood Development Project." Working Paper No. 59, World Bank, Washington, DC.

Fiske, J. 1982. *Introduction to Communication Studies.* London: Methuen.

Fraser, C., and S. Restrepo-Estrada. 1998. *Communicating for Development: Human Change for Survival.* London: I. B. Tauris.

Fraser, C., S. Restrepo-Estrada, and L. Mazzei. 2007, August 2. "What do they think? Policy Makers and the Role of Commmunication for Development." *Glocal Times* 7. http://www.glocaltimes.k3.mah.se/archive.aspx.

Hass, L., L. Mazzei, and D. O'Leary. 2007. "Setting Standards for Communication and Governance." Working Paper No. 121, World Bank, Washington, DC.

Hornik, R. C. 1988. *Development Communication: Information, Agriculture, and Nutrition in the Third World.* Lanham, MD: University Press of America.

Jacobson, T. L. 2003. "Participatory Communication for Social Change: The Relevance of the Theory of Communicative Action." In *Communication Yearbook* 27, ed. P. Kalbfleisch, 87–124. Beverly Hills, CA: Sage Publications.

Mattelart, A. 1996. *The Invention of Communication.* Minneapolis, MN: University of Minnesota Press.

Mefalopulos, P. 2003. "Theory and Practice of Participatory Communication. The Case of the FAO Project 'Communication for Development in Southern Africa'," PhD diss., University of Texas at Austin.

Mefalopulos, P., and C. Kamlongera. 2005. *Participatory Communication Strategy Design, A Handbook: A Training and Reference Guide for Designing and Implementing Communication for Development Strategies for Field Projects,* 2nd ed. Harare, Zimbabwe: SADC/FAO.

Pasquali, A. 2003. *18 Ensayos sobre Comunicaciones.* Caracas, Venezuela: Random House/Mondadori.

Pruitt, B. and P. Thomas. 2007. *Democratic Dialog—A Handbook for Practitioners.* Stockholm, Sweden: CIDA, IDEA, OAS, and UNDP.

Quarry, W. 2008. "Decision Makers Do Want Communication—But They May Not Want Participation." In *Glocal Times* 10, http://www.glocaltimes.k3.mah.se/archive.aspx.

Rahnema, M. 1992. "Participation." In *The Development Dictionary,* pp. 116–31, ed. W. Sachs. London: Zed Books.

Santucci, F. 2005. *Strategic Communication for Rural Development.* Washington, DC: World Bank.

Sen, A. 1999. *Development as Freedom.* New York: First Anchor Books Edition.

Servaes, J. 1999. *Communication of Development: One World, Multiple Cultures.* Cresskill, NJ: Hampton Press.

———. 2003. "By Way of Introduction." In *Approaches to Development: Studies on Communication for Development,* ed. J. Servaes, 1–22. Paris: UNESCO.

Shepherd, A. 1998. *Sustainable Rural Development.* New York: St. Martin's Press.

UNDP. 1993. *Human Development Report.* New York: Oxford University Press.

UNESCO. 2007. *Achieving the Millennium Development Goals.* Report of the 10th UN Inter-Agency Round Table on Communication for Development. Paris: UNESCO.

Uphoff, N. 1985. "Fitting Projects to People." In *Putting People First,* ed. M. Cernea, 2nd ed., 467–511. New York: Oxford University Press.

World Bank. 1992. *World Development Reports.* New York: Oxford University Press.

———. 1994. *The World Bank and Participation.* Washington, DC: World Bank, OPD.

World Bank, Food and Agriculture Organization of the United Nations, and the Communication Initiative. 2007. *World Congress on Communication for Development: Lessons, Challenges, and the Way Forward.* Washington, DC: World Bank.

MODULE 2

Reflections on the Theory and Practice of Development Communication

Words do not only define reality, they create it. Hence, to speak true words is an act of transforming the world.
(Paulo Freire)

Preview

This module is intended primarily for an audience composed of development practitioners, students of social sciences, and everyone interested in understanding the principles, models, and conceptual evolution of the interdisciplinary field of development communication. It provides an overview of the main theoretical frameworks and illustrates the role communication plays in the development context. It also presents an innovative model, the "multitrack communication approach," which combines different communication perspectives.

Contents

Development Communication Theoretical Trajectory

In order to frame this discipline in the broader development context, this module presents a historical overview of development communication, its origin, theories, and current applications. To ensure a consistent understanding, the first section discusses the concepts, applications, and overlapping boundaries among some key terms intrinsically linked with development communication. The second section provides an overview of the theoretical paradigms that played a major role in the development scenario in the last decades, highlighting the role assigned to communication in each of them. The third section also explores in more detail the current boundaries of the two main modalities of communication, monologic and dialogic, discussing their scope, main approaches, and the role of media and new communication technologies. Finally, the fourth section introduces a practical approach named "multitrack communication," combining the scope, features, and strengths of each of the two main communication perspectives into a homogeneous and integrated model.

2.1 Setting Common Ground on Key Terminology

"Development" and "communication" are two terms heavily loaded with different conceptions and a richness of uses and functions shaped by their various theoretical underpinnings. Such richness often leads to ambiguities and a lack of clarity that affects the field of development communication. The wide range of interpretations of key terminology and the rapid evolution of some concepts have led to inconsistencies in the way basic terms are understood and used. This section intends to address and clarify some of those inconsistencies. The differences and similarities of the key terms selected are discussed to ensure a common and clearer understanding for the readers. The terms presented are "information," "communication," "participation," "consultation," "capacity building," "empowerment," and "dialog."

Information—This term is often and erroneously used as a synonym for communication or as its predominant function. Rather, information should be considered as one of the outputs of communication, but not the only one, and in many instances not even the main one. Information can always be considered part of communication, but not vice versa. Pasquali (2005), one of the social scientists and researchers who has done extensive work in this field since the 1960s, has extensively studied the difference between communication and information. Even though Pasquali (2006) considers them closely intertwined, he emphasizes the importance of understanding how information and communication differ from one another.

While communication can denote an open interactive process among various actors, information is usually related to causality intents: using messages (the cause) to affect or change knowledge, attitudes, or behaviors (the effect) of the receiving individuals. Information denotes the transmission of data apt to influence or change specific knowledge and attitudes or behaviors. A campaign aimed at preventing the spread of HIV/AIDS is just such an example. Information remains linked to a model where "talking is equated with persuading, and hearing with understanding and accepting" (Beltrán Salmón 2006a [1979]).

The difference between information and communication, therefore, is not simply a matter of different theoretical models: one-way vertical flow versus two-way horizontal flow. The difference is also of scope: a transmitter trying to cause changes in others' behaviors versus an equal opportunity to exchange knowledge and shape the process among individuals who are transmitters and receivers at the same time. In conclusion, information can be seen as part of communication (but not vice versa), and understanding the implications of this is especially valuable when making decisions and selecting the best possible courses of action in the design of communication strategies.

Communication—The concept of communication, with its different types and functions, is treated extensively throughout this Sourcebook. Within the emerging paradigm of development communication, the model of reference has acquired a stronger horizontal connotation, including dialogic functions in addition to the most common dissemination ones. Doubtless, owing to its long tradition of theoretical studies and practical applications, "communication" can be considered a comprehensive term, encompassing all forms of human interactions, from the interpersonal to the mediated ones, and from the one-way linear flow to the two-way dialogic processes.

Communication as a process denotes a circular communicative flow (that is, dialog), in which the specific outcomes and the results are not necessarily predetermined. According to Pasquali (2006), "Authentic communication, then, is only that which is based on a symmetrical relational scheme, with parity of conditions between sender and receiver, and the possibility of one hearing or giving ear to the other, as a mutual will to understand one another." In other words, communication, especially when used for research and analytical purposes, is more effective when making full use of its dialogic features, enhancing stakeholders' voices, knowledge, and participation.

Participation—Another key term of the current development paradigm is "participation," which is discussed extensively in another section of this module. Clearly, participation is not an absolute concept—a choice between having full participation in development projects and programs and having no participation at all. There are a number of different shades or levels of participation, as noted throughout this module. Sometimes participatory approaches, mistakenly, are considered to be equivalent to participatory communication approaches. Even if both have a "participatory soul," they also have significant differences.

Participatory communication methods and tools are used in a project's assessment phase not only to investigate the overall situation but also to research communication-related issues (for example, media systems, available capacities, and so forth) and to provide inputs needed to design the appropriate communication strategy. However, participation, conceived at its fullest extent, is seldom adopted in practice, since its genuine application in the current development context is unfeasible. Most current development policies and practices (for example, project cycle, approval process, procurement procedures) would have to be modified to allow for the flexibility and for other key features of genuine participatory approaches.

As with most social concepts, such as freedom and democracy, however, participation is not an absolute condition. There are various degrees to which participation can be applied. When using this term, it is important to be clear about what kind of participation is referenced. In general, when referring to participation, some degree of sharing and an exchange capable of influencing decisions should be made. Even if the ideal form of participation is not easily achievable given the current structure of development, participation remains a desirable and crucial ingredient in most development initiatives.

Consultation—Given the discussion so far, it is evident that consultation is not the same as participation and communication, but it is closely related and can be considered a subset of both. Consultation can be regarded as an imperfect form of participation. In genuine participation the stakeholders are equal partners, while in consultation the decision-making control rests with the few who are in charge of the consultation and decide if and how to take into account the inputs collected during the consultation.

Consultation is a form of communication, but it is different from the dialogical process. Though the main scope of consultation is listening, the information does not flow freely from the stakeholders, but rather it is conceived as a feedback on predefined topics intended for the experts. Consultation does not intend to change specific behaviors at the outset. While there are different ways to conduct consultations, the rationale is usually to reveal new information (for example, opinions of different groups) or to triangulate that which is already available. There are two crucial ingredients for the successful implementation of an effective consultation: the review and preparation of the issues of interest before the consultation and the neutral position on those issues during the consultation (because the primary mode of communication in this case is not engaging in dialog but listening).

Capacity building—This frequently used term, increasingly referred to as capacity development, presents a number of complexities. There is a broad consensus in the international community that capacity refers to the ability of individuals, institutions, and communities to analyze and assess problems and take part in relevant decision-making processes. One of the overall goals of development aid is to strengthen capacities in developing countries, because this is likely to enhance the chances of success and long-term results of development initiatives.

Capacity building for communication is often associated with training, adult education, learning, and participation and empowerment. In this sense, capacity building means enhancing specific knowledge and skills, both at an individual and institutional level, especially when the educational model of reference is the experiential one. In this approach participants have the opportunity to share their knowledge and experiences, learning from each other, while the instructor facilitates the process, ensuring that the final outcome will enhance the intended capacities.

According to a World Bank working paper (Siri 2002: vi), to be effective, capacity-building should "be demand-driven" and must "transfer quality operational skills and knowledge." It is achieved, not only through knowledge transfer and formal training, but also through experience, in a learning-by-doing mode, and through dialog and collaboration in the various phases of an initiative. Regardless of which area of intervention or which sector needs strengthening, communication remains a key ingredient in achieving the intended capacity-building objectives.

Empowerment—Many of the elements discussed in the definitions of the previous terms can also be found in the concept of "empowerment," a term of growing relevance in the current development scenario. A more detailed discussion on empowerment is presented later in this module. Here it is important to note that, in contrast to power as the degree of control exercised over others, empowerment is more of an inner condition or, as stated by Cornwall (2000: 33), "it is not something that can be done to people, but something people do by and for themselves."

Development communication, with its dialogical and explorative connotation, can facilitate empowerment through specific training or by creating the space for working cooperatively on specific initiatives at an individual, institutional, or community level. By taking part in decisions concerning their own lives, even the most disenfranchised and marginalized individuals tend to gain confidence and feel more empowered. Whenever communication is applied to facilitate dialog, knowledge exchange, and joint assessment of the situation, stakeholders' participation and empowerment grow. Consequently, the chances for setting and achieving sustainable projects' objectives increase as well.

Dialog—This last term is also the most crucial one in the current communication paradigm. In the context of this publication, dialog is to be understood as the professional use—and the word "professional" cannot be stressed enough in this context—of dialogic methods and approaches meant to engage stakeholders in the definition and investigation of relevant issues for the development initiative. The role of communication specialists consists in facilitating the creation of a safe public space and an enabling environment where stakeholders, even the most marginalized ones, can air their points of view and knowledge in search of the best course of action for improving the situation.

In this context, dialog is not simply about discussing issues or communicating information, but about generating knowledge. Bohm (1996) makes the point that, in contrast to a discussion where one party tries to win by convincing the others about the superiority of his/her point of view, in dialog there is a cooperative mode of discussion where nobody wins, or, better, where everybody wins if anyone wins. In sum, dialog, in the context of development communication, should be considered as the professional application of interactive methods and techniques to engage stakeholders in exploring the situation and uncovering risks and opportunities that can benefit the development initiative and make it more successful and sustainable.[1]

2.2 Development and Communication: An Overview

Although Worsley (1984) states that the history of development is as old as human history, the current conception of international development is usually traced back to soon after World War II. In his January 1949 inaugural speech, President Truman stated, "We must embark on a bold new program for making the benefits of our scientific advances and industrial progress available for the improvement and growth of underdeveloped areas." Truman's speech is considered to mark the beginning of the modern conception of development (Esteva 1992), and it synthesized the emerging vision of the world divided between richer and poorer countries.

Since then, the issue of development has been highly debated—a debate with many different perspectives and voices, broadly classified until recently into two opposite camps. In one camp, there were those who viewed development as an effort, and as a mission, under the guidance of the richer countries, to defeat poverty and ignorance. The scope was to help poorer countries achieve steady economic growth in order to emerge from their "underdeveloped" condition. This perspective became the dominant position in development.

In the other camp, there were thinkers and practitioners highly critical of such a conception of development. Even though they were not unified under a single alternative model, they tended to consider the dominant approach to development as an attempt by the rich countries to maintain a dominant position through political and economic predefined models, often ignoring local knowledge, needs, and realities in the poorest countries.

Whatever the perspective embraced, development was, and still remains, among the top priorities of the international political agenda. It continues to involve great financial and human resources at the local, national, and international level, as shown by the statistics of major international development organizations. For example, data from the Organisation for Economic Co-operation and Development (OECD; www.oecd.org) indicate that in 2005 official development assistance by member countries rose by 32 percent to a record high of over US$106 billion. In 2006 the lending commitment of the two entities of the World Bank Group (IBRD and IDA) increased to over US$23 billion (www.worldbank.org). Of even more interest, the *Global Development Finance* report of the World Bank (2006) indicated that net private capital flows to developing countries had reached a record high of US$491 billion, highlighting the growing relevance of developing markets.

To understand better why and how such great amounts of resources are devoted to development initiatives, one should be familiar with the sociopolitical frameworks that shape decisions to influence the allocation and the use these resources. The following pages provide a brief overview of the main paradigms that characterize the field of development and the role attributed to communication by each of them. It should be noted that, in this context, the term "paradigm" is used in its general sense to denote a set of theoretical beliefs that, by trying to explain the world around us, shapes the practical applications in the everyday struggle toward betterment (Guba 1990).

Since World War II, there have been three theoretical approaches dominating the development context and, consequently, the field of development communication: (1) the modernization paradigm, also referred to as the dominant paradigm; (2) the dependency theory, including the subset of world-system theory; and recently, (3) the participatory paradigm, referred to by a number of different terms.

2.2.1 The Modernization Paradigm

The modernization paradigm arose soon after World War II, along the lines traced in Truman's inaugural speech of 1949. It envisioned development as a challenge to bring the "underdeveloped countries" out of their conditions of poverty by modernizing them and by promoting economic growth spurred by free-market approaches. The best way, if not the only way, to achieve these goals consisted in the diffusion and adoption of the values, principles, and models that ensured the success of the way of life in wealthier countries.

The origin, principles, and applications of this paradigm should be considered within the historical context of the postwar years, also known as the Cold War period, when world influence was polarized by two superpowers: the United States and the Soviet Union. Their influence reached every sphere of the international scenario, including development. In this context, the modernization paradigm promoted by political scientists and scholars of Western countries became so strong and so pervasive in every dimension of social life that it became also known as the "dominant paradigm."

At the cultural level, modernization advocated for a change in the mindset of individuals in poor countries who had to abandon traditional beliefs, considered an impediment toward modernization, and embrace attitudes and behaviors favorable to innovation and modernity (Lerner 1958). At the technocratic level, modernization required people with inquisitive minds who were guided by faith in the scientific method and rooted in the principles of enlightenment. At the political level, it required staunch advocates of the doctrine of liberalism based on political freedom and the adoption of democratic systems. Finally, at the economic level, it required blind faith in the virtues and power of the free market, with no or minimal government intervention.

Within this paradigm, the conception of development is a linear one based on trust in science, reason, technology, and the free market. The main role of communication was to persuade people to embrace the core values and practices of modernization. Among the merits of this paradigm, in addition to a certain number of successes in specific instances and projects, there was the establishment of a more systematic and rigorous approach to development initiatives. Overall, however, this theoretical approach to development, with its related bag of practical tools, did not deliver the expected results. By the end of the 1980s, it became evident that the promises of the modernization paradigm had not materialized and that poor peoples' conditions across the world had failed to improve significantly.

Critics of this paradigm attacked its predominant, if not exclusive, economic focus. In its quest to develop, modernization neglected to consider the relevance of other social dimensions and failed to take into account a number of historical and broader sociopolitical factors (Servaes 1991) that impeded the autonomous development of many developing countries. By providing ready-made recipes emphasizing what a country should do to develop itself, modernization's proponents overemphasized the power of individual countries and ignored elements, such as colonization, past exploitation of resources, and, more recently, globalization, all of which greatly affect and limit the individual capacities of countries in the political and economic arena.

Gradually, the criticisms of this paradigm became so intense that even some of its stronger supporters began revisiting some of its theoretical assumptions and practical underpinnings. For instance in the mid-1970s, Rogers (1976), a renowned scholar associated with modernization, was already announcing "the passing of the dominant paradigm." In reality, this passing never materialized completely, because the principles of this paradigm still permeate many of the theories and concepts of current development practices.

The decade of the 1970s did not witness the expected outcomes, and optimism, based on the scientific and pro-innovation approaches of scholars, practitioners, and leaders around the world (Burkey 1993). In the 1980s, things got even worse as large numbers of people in many developing countries experienced a significant decline in their living standards (Chambers 1997). This decline gave new fuel to the criticisms of the dominant conception of mainstream development practices, which came under fire for being culturally insensitive, theoretically flawed, and methodologically inadequate (Servaes 1991).

In the communication field, modernization theory led to the first systematic and rigorous attempts to research communication applications in the development context. A few scholars started to devote increasing attention to communication processes and effects, among them Lasswell (1948), Katz and Lazarfeld (1955), and Klapper (1960), while others, such as Lerner (1958), Rogers (1962), and Schramm (1964), became particularly interested in studying how communication could be used to foster national development, which at that time was conceived predominantly in economic terms. Communication was expected to help modernize people's attitudes and ways of thinking, which would be conducive to support of the economic model already adopted successfully by the West, in accordance with the belief that individuals had to change before development could truly take off (Melkote and Stevens 2001).

Communication in the dominant paradigm is basically associated with the linear, mass media model aimed at transmitting information and messages from one point to another or many others, usually in a vertical or top-down fashion. This idea was rooted in the strong belief in the persuasive power of media, especially until the 1970s. Development communication was associated with the use of media to persuade people to achieve, maintain, and strengthen development goals, and media's role was paramount. UNESCO, for example, considered media to be a crucial means for promoting change,[2] and in the 1960s, it provided guidelines about a country's desirable per capita consumption of television sets, radio receivers, newspapers, and cinema seats.

This heavy emphasis on media was owing to the belief that this form of communication, when used properly, was capable of changing people's mindsets and attitudes. In 1948 Lasswell provided a blueprint to decision-makers and managers on how to use communication to persuade audiences to change behaviors. Its model can be summarized in the following five questions: WHO, says WHAT, in WHICH channel, to WHOM, with what EFFECT. Over time this basic model was refined and changed by other communication specialists, but it did not lose its linear flow from a central source to many (passive) receivers, as indicated by the renowned Berlo's formula (1960) that illustrated the process of communication as Source-Message-Channel-Receivers, or SMCR. The common conception of strategic communication is also rooted in this theoretical framework.[3]

The failures attributed, directly or indirectly, to modernization caused a rethinking of the theoretical models of reference for communication. As it became increasingly evident that media alone could not change people's mind-sets and behaviors, theories such the "the hypodermic needle theory" or "the bullet theory,"[4] which overemphasized the power of media over people, lost their relevance. With time, it became progressively more evident that media impact was not as direct and as paramount as commonly believed, and that audiences were not as passive, either.

Even though communication studies reviewed and downgraded the influence of media, giving more relevance to the role of interpersonal communication, the model of reference remained the same. None of the newly emerging theoretical approaches questioned the overall validity of the one-way, and usually top-down, flow of information. Although it would be unfair to label them as propaganda, it is not difficult to see the manipulative potential of many communication applications within the modernization paradigm.

Until the late 1980s, most development institutions conceived and applied communication primarily for the dissemination of information and adoption of innovations. The emphasis placed on tangible communication products neglected the potential of communication as a dialogic, cross-cutting investigative tool. This emphasis was so pervasive that the medium appeared to be more important than the content itself, echoing Marshall McLuhan's famous slogan, "The medium is the message." Unfortunately, the available data indicated that the most important message was that media were not the answer to development problems, at least not in the way they were being used.

It was only during the late 1970s and early 1980s that new perspectives in development communication began to grow stronger. The Latin American school of thought was very influential in promoting the new communication conception, based on the two-way horizontal model. Luis Ramiro Beltrán Salmón (2006a [1979]) and Juan Díaz Bordenave (2006 [1977]) were some of the most influential scholars working on this idea.

2.2.2 Dependency and World-System Theories

Latin America was also the place where, at the beginning of the 1970s, the dependency theory originated. This is another example of a major alternative theoretical framework that is rooted in a political-economy perspective. One of its founding fathers, A. G. Frank (1969), reflected critically on the assumptions of modernization, which placed full responsibility and blame on developing countries for their conditions of underdevelopment. On the basis of a structural analysis of the international capitalist system, he considered development and underdevelopment as two faces of the same coin, shaped by specific historical, economic, and political factors. Hence, neither the causes nor the solutions of underdevelopment should be sought exclusively, or even mostly, within the poorest countries, but within the broader international scenario and forms of exploitation such as the richest countries' colonial past.

Dependency theory claims that the imbalances in the world's state of affairs were mainly owing to the international division of labor and to the continuation of past patterns of domination. The world was separated into two blocs: the core, composed of a few rich countries, and the periphery, composed of many poor countries. According to this perspective, core countries took advantage of their technological knowhow, superior infrastructure, and economic power to strengthen their lead. The main role of the peripheral countries was restricted to that of supplying raw materials and cheap labor to the richer ones, making it impossible for them to ever catch up.

To address this problem, dependency advocates proposed a plan that works on two levels. Nationally, developing countries on the periphery were to become economically self-reliant and less dependent on foreign imports. Internationally, they would form alliances among themselves to create a stronger political presence. The ultimate goal would be to change the overall international set of relationships by forming a bloc of many countries with similar aspirations.

Dependency theory had a significant impact in the economic and development policies of a number of Third World countries, especially in the 1970s and early 1980s, resulting in the adoption of import-substitution policies by many of those countries (Escobar 1995). This strategy aimed to protect national industries from outside competition by subsidizing them and putting high tariffs on imported products. The main idea was to stimulate growth of domestic industrialization (McMichael 1996) and to reduce or sever dependent ties with richer countries. However, the overall results of import-substitution policies have been rather unsatisfactory (Jaffee 1998).

Even though this strategy appeared to be partially successful in a few countries (for example, Brazil), it failed to achieve its goals in most countries. Protecting and supporting local industries did not produce the expected objectives, and it often resulted in poor-quality products and inefficient processes. Many poorer countries were forced to borrow more, a situation that led to a refined version of financial and political dependency (Servaes 1991).

Its oversimplified division of the world into core and periphery levels is blamed for the dependency theory inadequacy to fully explain the causes of underdevelopment and for its limited effectiveness in proposing successful alternative models of development. By ascribing causes of underdevelopment exclusively to the centers of international capitalism, dependency theorists failed to consider relevant internal causes contributing to the problem (Worsley 1984), such as the role played by national elites.

These elites often form strategic alliances with those of the developed world, and they play a significant role in shaping, often in negative ways, the development process of their countries (Servaes 1991). Dependency theories are also criticized for how little attention they pay to the differences in political-economic status among developing countries, resulting in big and potentially rich countries such as Brazil or India being put in the same category as much smaller and poorer ones. Wallerstein's world-system theory, while remaining within the dependency perspective, addresses this key concern and provides a more appropriate representation of international relations.

Wallerstein, the main thinker behind this world-system theory, addresses and refines the major flaws of the theoretical model of dependency by adopting a more holistic approach, encompassing national and international dynamics within a unified world system. His historical analysis puts the origin of the modern world system in the 16th century (Hopkins and Wallerstein 1982). This world system, based on capitalism, is divided into a core, dominated by a few rich countries; a periphery, inhabited by the many poorer countries in Africa, Asia, and Latin America; and a semi-periphery, including major countries such as Egypt, Mexico, Brazil, India, and others, with higher levels of resources than the majority of developing countries. This intermediate layer, the semi-periphery, addresses the criticisms received by dependency theorists for the oversimplified division into two spheres of rich and poor countries.

The three levels (that is, core, periphery, and semi-periphery) are contained in a unified world system, the mechanisms of which are those of capitalism operating at national and international levels. Wallerstein acknowledges that the system can take various forms in different places and settings; he states, however, that once deprived of its different attributes, the essence of that system remains the capitalist one. In other words, he claims that because of the overwhelming power of capitalism at the global level, each relationship—social, political, or economic—occurs within the capitalist system. Hence, all the causes for development and underdevelopment can be considered internal to the capitalist system, on the basis of the international division of labor and the control of raw resources.

The major contribution of the world-system theory consists in elevating the unit of analysis from the national to the international level, thus allowing a better comprehension of the global scenario. However, it does not provide practical recipes to successfully address development challenges. Moreover, similar to its antagonist modernization models, world theory has been accused of being too economically focused and of not paying enough attention to social and cultural factors. Communication is not given more attention than in dependency theory, which is still focusing on the key but narrow role of media and information flows in the overall international scenario.

Among the main issues on top of the international agenda in the 1970s and 1980s were the demands for a new international economic order put forward by developing countries. Linked to those demands, communication and information issues also ranked high on the international agenda. The "nonaligned movement," an alliance formed by 77 developing countries, was a key player in demanding a new world information and communication order, commonly referred as NWICO. Such demand gained high visibility in the international scenario because of the debate that took place at UNESCO. The heated debate on communication resulted in the renowned report, "Many Voices, One World," published by UNESCO in 1980. Despite the influence it had on political and academic circles, the report did not have a significant impact on the conception and operations of development communication.

The main focus of the report was on freedom of information and how media and communication technologies should be used to promote a fair and balanced flow of information. Developing countries complained about the uneven flow of media programs and information coming from the richer countries, especially the United States, which had a dominant position in the production and distribution system worldwide. They believed this imbalance to be a form of cultural imperialism and wanted some regulations to address this situation.

The United States and its allies considered such requests to be a form of undue interference, even censorship, on "the free flow of information." They considered the media world as a marketplace that should be ruled by supply and demand without other external interferences. In the 1980s, the battle over NWICO reached its climax, leading to the withdrawal from UNESCO of the United States and Great Britain. This and other political events in the following years weakened the bargaining power of the nonaligned movement, and finally, with the fall of the Soviet Union, many of the issues raised by NWICO lost much of their relevance in the international scene.

The proponents of the dependency theory vigorously supported rethinking the communication agenda along the lines of a more balanced flow of communication at the international level. Yet, at the national level, they often neglected to consider the horizontal component of communication within countries and failed to give proper attention to the potential of privately owned media and community media. While arguing against the "free-flow" argument proposed by the United States and its allies, the "dependentistas" remained rooted in the classic media-centric conception of communication, mostly from the state perspective.

Ideally, the state is expected to represent the wider public's interest, but reality shows that this has seldom been the case. Dependency theories did not consider and support the wider role that "freer" communication systems, and not just media, at different levels could play in creating spaces and actively engaging broader sectors of society in development. Despite significant differences between modernization and dependency theories, their communication model was basically the same: a one-way communication flow, with the main difference between the two theories being who was controlling and sending the message and for what purpose.

2.2.3 The Emerging Participatory Paradigm

The search for a different and better vision in development practices is currently linked to people's participation and empowerment. Participation is a concept that has been gaining increasing recognition and prestige in the development discourse and its practices. Participatory approaches require a shift in the way individuals are considered, from passive recipients to active agents of development efforts. There are a number of reasons for this shift, a major one of which is presented by Ascroft and Masilela (1994: 282), "If peasants do not control or share control of the processes of their own development, there can be no guarantee that it is their best interest that is being served."

Nowadays, most development programs seem to carry the participatory mark, as a sign of purification from the mistakes of the past. The wide convergence in participatory approaches, nonetheless, has not resulted in a unified paradigm. Rather, it has generated a number of theoretical approaches still seeking a unified and consistent common framework. The following are some of the most renowned: the multiplicity paradigm (Servaes 1991); the empowerment approach (Friedmann 1992); another development (Melkote 1991; Jacobson 1994), derived from the conception of former UN Secretary General Dag Hammarskjold and further promoted in the Cocoyoc Declaration;[5] the autonomous development (Carmen 1996); and other conceptions of participatory, people-based development.

In contrast to the proponents of modernization and dependency theories, most of the advocates of the participatory theoretical perspective do not seem particularly interested in defining a grand theory to provide a universal analysis and interpretation of the world. They seem more interested in identifying and analyzing drawbacks and limitations of current development practices, especially at project and community level, and in attempting to identify normative approaches that could provide operational guidelines in the field. Common features of this perspective are the emphasis on people, the endogenous vision of development, and the attention to power and rights issues.

Development efforts have been refocused to increasingly engage stakeholders and pay attention to aspects of social life previously neglected (culture, education, and so forth). The new priorities, well beyond the economic dimension, are reflected in the Millennium Development Goals, or MDGs, adopted in the 1990s by the United Nations and other development organizations as key challenges to be addressed successfully. In addition to poverty reduction, they include objectives in education, gender equality, and health issues. Most development priorities are outlined within political frameworks based on the adherence to good governance and democratic principles (for example, freedom and human rights), and people's participation is also key in this context.

There are many reasons for the adoption of participation in development, some of which relate directly to the enhancement of project results. As early as 1982, White (as cited in McKee 1994: 215) summarized the major reasons for the adoption of this approach in development initiatives, maintaining that (1) services can be provided at a lower cost; (2) participation has intrinsic values for participants, alleviating feelings of alienation and powerlessness; (3) participation is a catalyst for further development efforts; (4) participation leads to a sense of responsibility for the project; and (5) participation ensures the use of indigenous knowledge and expertise.

Despite these and other benefits, participation has remained a highly praised term, but a poorly adopted one. This is probably owing to the concerns that managers may experience when not in total control of a project, as well as participation's multifaceted conception and the many sensitive issues involved in its application.

Many development practitioners and managers have their own understanding of participation, leading at times to divergent views on what it truly entails and how it should be applied.

The richness, or "broadness," of the concept of participation is not considered a problem by everybody. Servaes argues that in dealing with participation, rigidly defined theoretical structures are neither feasible nor desirable (Servaes, Jacobson, and White 1996). He claims that participation's strength derives from its flexibility in adapting its strategic approach according to the situation. Other scholars tend to differ: they believe that this adaptability constitutes a major weakness of participatory approaches, which can be easily modified and used in a number of ways, often not consistent with a genuine participatory philosophy.

Huesca (2000: 75) confirms this point: "Indeed, participation has been embraced by development scholars who have incorporated this notion into modernization practices, such as message development and social integration. The pluralistic spirit of the participatory turn in development communication has had the ironic effect of redeeming the dominant paradigm from its critics." This statement is a further indication of the complexity and ambiguity that this concept implies.

That participation is not an absolute concept, and that it can be conceived and applied in different degrees, is part of the problem. Pretty devised a typology that includes seven different types of participation as interpreted and applied by various development organizations (Pretty et al. 1995). This taxonomy ranges from passive participation, where people are simply told what is happening and their participation is conceived as a mere head-counting, to self-mobilization, where people not only have the power to make decisions but can also initiate the process. In between these two extremes, there are other kinds of participation with varying degrees of people's involvement. The full categorization, starting from the least participatory, includes passive participation, participation in information giving, participation by consultation, participation for material incentives, functional participation, interactive participation, and self-mobilization.

The World Bank (1995) identified four types of participation: (1) information sharing, (2) consultation, (3) collaboration, and (4) empowerment. Information sharing and consultation are considered low-level forms of participation, while the other two are considered high-level forms. These types are consistent with others, such as the classification derived by a literature review by Mefalopulos (2003), which includes (1) passive participation, when stakeholders attend meetings to be informed; (2) participation by consultation, when stakeholders are consulted but the decision making rests in the hands of the experts; (3) functional participation, when stakeholders are allowed to have some input, although not necessarily from the beginning of the process and not in equal partnership; and (4) empowered participation, when relevant stakeholders take part throughout the whole cycle of the development initiative and have an equal influence on the decision-making process.

Despite the wealth of experiences and studies on participation, many development experts still fail to understand what genuine participation is. When looked into closely, studies presenting the pitfalls of participatory programs reveal that they are actually discussing, unknowingly, the pitfalls of applying participatory approaches in a partial and often insufficient manner. Assessing the value of participation conceived as people reacting to certain information or as their involvement in activities designated by the experts, without recognizing the limited participatory degree of such applications, is not methodologically valid—or relevant. And yet often this is what is being done.

Historically, the terminology related to participation entered the development discourse in the 1950s (Rahnema 1992). The trend started to catch up only in the 1970s when new approaches, aimed at giving people a bigger role in development efforts, emerged to address the causes of past failures. In particular, participatory research methods allowed a growing role for local stakeholders and indigenous knowledge in the problem-analysis and problem-solving processes of development initiatives. A confirmation of this can be seen in the U.S. Foreign Assistance Act that in 1973 called for American aid to involve intended beneficiaries in the planning and implementation phases of development projects (Cornwall 2000).

In the family of participatory approaches, participatory rural appraisal, PRA, is probably the best known. It started to become popular in the 1980s as a research method trying to reach a balance between researchers' needs to be scientific in their approach and the communities' rights to participate in activities concerning their own well-being (Chambers 1993). By spending extended periods of time in the community, PRA researchers were expected to better understand and pay closer attention to the needs and problems identified and defined by the community.[6]

Thanks also to Chambers' work, participatory rural appraisal gained increasing relevance at the international level. Starting from the consideration that the rural poor are some of the most disadvantaged, often illiterate, members of society, Chambers uses and promotes a number of participatory techniques and tools that require no literacy skills. In this way, his methodology encourages all individuals to express their knowledge and ideas openly.

This approach facilitates people's involvement in the problem-analysis process, and it stimulates the "reversal of learning" from the rural poor to the experts. As he often states in his experiential workshops, "Everyone is ignorant, only in different fields." His work in many ways is consistent with Freire's (1997) approach. They both share a sincere concern for the empowerment of the poorest and the most disadvantaged sectors of society, which often tend to be in rural areas or on the periphery of urban agglomerates.

The strengths and weaknesses of participation and empowerment are also evident in another well-known approach that originated in the 1970s—participatory action research, or PAR. It is an approach that strongly opposes the basic theoretical and practical assumptions of the dominant positivist-scientific paradigm, since it claims that participatory research should not be neutral but should always side with the poor and the marginalized (Fals-Borda and Rahman 1991).

PAR and other participatory approaches are frequently used in community-driven development (CDD) initiatives. These approaches aim at putting communities and local stakeholders in the driving seats of development efforts. Unfortunately, while, on one hand, PRA, PAR, and other CDD approaches highlight the importance of actively involving stakeholders and employing their wealth of knowledge and experience in the decision-making process of development initiatives, on the other hand, these approaches have often neglected to include communication in a systematic and dialogic way. That has made it more difficult to actively achieve meaningful participation and effectively benefit from it.

The emphasis on participation in development also implies increased attention to communication, because there can be no participation without communication, at least without a certain type of communication. In other words, the added emphasis on participation helps to mainstream communication in many initiatives, and at the same time promotes a more dialogic and two-way conception of communication. The model of reference is significantly different from the traditional one, since it is now characterized by dialog and by a horizontal flow, enabling the balanced sharing of perceptions and knowledge. In this perspective, the top-down features rooted in the modernization paradigm get diluted, and communication acquires a more interactive connotation aimed at facilitating participation and empowerment. Even when using mass media, messages can be expected to originate from people themselves rather than from "outside experts" (Mody 1991).

Because genuine participation in development implies having the opportunity and the power to take part in decisions concerning one's own well-being, participatory communication models need to take the issues of power and empowerment into account. Furthermore, once adopted, participation can hardly remain contained within the realm of development projects. It often transcends its scope to enhance projects' results and sustainability and become a capacity-building element of a broader social dimension. The United Nations Development Programme (UNDP) Annual Report (1993: 21) confirms this: "Since participation requires increased influence and control, it also demands increased empowerment—in economic, social, and political terms."

This notion is particularly relevant since UNDP has been one of the main United Nations agencies trying to broaden the conception of development beyond the strict boundaries of the economic dimension. UNDP was among the first to promote the idea that stakeholders should be engaged in development initiatives from the very beginning and play an active role throughout the process. This meant that local people should have the power to take part in the decision-making process, since power can be conceived as the ability to shape social context (Wilkins 2000).

Power is a major factor that needs to be considered, especially at the macro level. Cultural, political, and economic powers greatly influence development structures, policies, and institutions, affecting also the way in which people's participation takes place. However, while keeping such considerations in mind, given the scope and focus of the Sourcebook, in this context "empowerment" might be a more appropriate concept to consider rather than "power." The difference between the two concepts is not always clearly distinguishable, but it is significant.

Narayan (2002: 14) conceived empowerment "as the expansion of assets and capabilities of poor people to participate in, negotiate with, influence, control, and hold accountable institutions that affected their lives." This definition is consistent with others found in the literature. Freire (1997) has been one of the most renowned scholars, practitioners, and activitists who have significantly shaped this notion. According to him, people's empowerment can be achieved through a process of awareness or "conscientization" that requires the poor to become aware of their conditions through a totality of reflection and action. The key to achieve this kind of empowerment is communication through dialog.

For Freire, dialog is an act of creation, and the act of naming the world is in many ways equivalent to creating the world. He asserts: "to say the true word . . . is to transform the world, saying the word is not the privilege of some few persons, but the right of everyone" (1997: 70). Ensuring that everybody says the word is a task of dialog, which is needed to empower stakeholders, enabling a meaningful change. Thus, a genuine and sustainable change, aiming at a better and more just society, can be achieved and legitimized only through an empowered dialog.

Finally, the participation mode also addresses poverty, or at least one of its key dimensions, in a direct way. Poverty is not simply the deprivation of basic material needs; it concerns other significant dimensions of people's life. Amartya Sen, the winner of the Nobel Prize for Economics, introduced the concept of capability deprivation to illustrate how poverty is not simply an income issue, but also and especially a social issue. He considers income poverty and capability poverty to be two closely related dimensions because income greatly affects the capabilities of an individual, and vice versa.

Social exclusion is one of the elements contributing to the overall poverty dimension. Eliminating or significantly reducing social exclusion, through the dialogic use of communication, is a step toward a world without poverty. The deprivations deriving from feeling excluded from relevant decisions and from seeing limited available options can be successfully addressed through communication, since it is by communicating that individuals perceive and define their conditions and construct their reality in social networks.

By engaging stakeholders who often have been excluded from any form of decision making in their lives and allowing them to engage in the decision-making process, development communication not only reduces poor people's "capability deprivation" but also facilitates the process of empowerment, going well beyond the specific initiative in question. Using dialog to engage stakeholders in probing and assessing the situation can help break the broader vicious circle of poverty, where income cannot be earned without a proper level of individual capabilities, and individual capabilities cannot be improved while the individual remains in conditions of poverty.

At this juncture, the relationship between participation, empowerment, and communication should be clearer. The newly appreciated horizontal model of communication opens up new spaces for dialog among stakeholders and facilitates the exchange of knowledge, empowering people to participate actively in the process affecting their own lives. In this perspective, media are no longer the central element of communication, but one of the tools to be used according to the circumstances. The linear communication model loses part of its pervasive dominance and is complemented by a simpler, at the same time also more complex, two-way circular model where the sender is at the same time the receiver and vice versa. The combination of these elements in the emerging development paradigm is shifting the focus from media to people, from persuasion to participation.

2.2.4 Current Boundaries of Development Communication: Diffusion and Participation

The discipline of development communication, as currently conceived, was significantly shaped by Erskine Childers, considered by some to be the founding father of this field (Fraser and Restrepo-Estrada 1998). Childers was a researcher, author, and broadcaster of international affairs, as well as an occasional consultant with the United Nations. In the 1950s and 1960s, development was all about economic growth. Because of his experiences in developing countries, however, Childers witnessed firsthand how some of the major obstacles to successful development did not have an economic cause but were due to the lack of communication between decision makers and beneficiaries. The need for communicating with stakeholders to ensure long-term results was clear to him: "This seems so crashingly obvious that one can only shake one's head at how neglected it has been" (Fraser and Restrepo-Estrada 1998: 43).

Even if his approach did not constitute a total break from modernization models, Childers was one of the first to advocate the systematic use of communication to involve and inform people in the planning and implementation of development projects. He used his high-level network of social relations to vigorously promote the mainstreaming of communication in development organizations. As a result UNDP, later followed by other UN agencies, required that their projects pay specific attention to communication factors.

Unfortunately, many development managers and decision makers did not (and, unfortunately, continue not to) understand the implications of the theoretical and operational differences between "communicating information" and the broader scope and nature of communication. Hence, the newly established units of development support communication, as the units were often called, were frequently underutilized, and their use was mostly limited to the production of audiovisual and other information materials designated to inform specific audiences, rather than opening flows of communication with stakeholders.

The many efforts to change the way communication has been conceived and applied in development has led to an increasing recognition of the importance of establishing two-way flows to share knowledge, opinions, and perceptions among stakeholders. The report of the 8th UN Inter-Agency Round Table on Communication for Development[7] discussed this field along three main strands (UNFPA 2002): behavior change communication, or BCC; communication for social change,[8] and advocacy communication.

Behavior change communication is probably the most renowned strand because it has been used in many development projects and programs. Its conception and applications are rather controversial, since it is typically considered by some to promote voluntary change in attitudes and behaviors based on informed choices. In this respect, behavior change and social change are seen as two faces of the same coin. However, this strand has also been widely criticized for giving too much emphasis to the role of persuasion played by communication through the traditional one-way model and for the focus on individual change that usually neglects wider social factors and often makes it difficult to scale up the intended change.

Communication for social change is the strand closer to the newly emerging paradigm in development, since it emphasizes the importance of two-way communication and the need to facilitate stakeholders' participation and empowerment. Change is now expected to be defined with the people and not for the people, making communication for social change closely aligned with the participatory communication perspective. Finally, advocacy communication involves the use of communication to influence specific audiences, policies, and programs on key development issues.

Notwithstanding the relevance of the above classification, this Sourcebook adopts a different classification resembling one often found in the literature that compares, contrasts, and defines development communication approaches within two broad families: diffusion and participation. The tension between these two kinds of approaches has characterized much of the field in recent years; Morris (2005) carried out a study on how these two modes differ, and also on how they are increasingly being applied jointly in development projects.

The diffusion model is rooted in the modernization paradigm, characterized by the intent to use communication media and methods to persuade people to change specific behaviors. The participatory approach is based on a two-way model of communication whose primary goal is to involve and empower people in the definition, design, and implementation process of development initiatives. Despite their differences, the two conceptual models are not antithetical: elements of each can be combined in a hybrid approach, as will be illustrated later.

To maximize the potential of each communication approach, it is important to be fully acquainted with the theoretical underpinnings and practical implications underlying both conceptual models. Even if theories are often detached from practical applications, they serve to provide insightful and rigorous ways to understand reality and act, or react, accordingly.[9] Familiarity with the basic ontological (that is, the nature of the knowable/reality), epistemological (that is, the relationship between the knower and the known), and methodological (that is, the best way to obtain knowledge) principles of the two major families of communication approaches can certainly assist in understanding the way they can be best applied.

Set in the modernization theoretical paradigm, diffusion approaches believe progress is achieved by inducing change in individuals' attitudes and behaviors. At the ontological level, the assumption is that by using the correct (that is, scientific) methods, the only and true reality will be revealed. On the epistemological level, the researcher is expected to detach him- or herself from the object of the study, hence ensuring an objective perspective. Methodologically, quantitative methods are preferred, and all methods adopted in this perspective are expected to be in line with positivist/scientific dogma in order to get to the truth. As a consequence, if one party has the truth, all other parties with different perspectives must be wrong. It is easy to see how such an assumption can have profound implications in development initiatives.

Approaches linked to the participatory model, instead, acknowledge that there can be different constructions of the same reality. No one single party has the ultimate truth; rather, there are a number of realities that often need to be reconciled through communication. This theoretical framework grows out of the constructivist perspective and carries a number of implications.

Ontologically, reality is considered socially constructed through intersubjective agreements among individuals or groups of individuals. It means that there is not necessarily "one true reality," but several constructions of a certain situation. Different groups are likely to define and view reality in different but equally valid ways, which need to be reconciled. This issue is particularly significant for the role of development communication, since in a number of instances, failures of development initiatives have been ascribed to different understandings and perceptions about the nature of a problem, rather than to the problem itself (Mefalopulos 2003).

On the epistemological level, there is no clear distinction between the researcher and what is being studied, as the two belong to the same reality. The researcher does not need to be separated from the issue investigated; on the contrary, he or she can and should be part of the context in which the investigation takes place in order to better understand it. Finally, at a methodological level, the researcher can use a number of qualitative and quantitative methods, not following a predetermined priority order, but according to the required needs.

Table 2.1 highlights some of the basic differences between the modernization and participation paradigms and relative communication perspectives. By comparing and contrasting basic differences on a practical level, this table illustrates the main features of each mode and its purposes, highlighting the rationale for selecting one over the other. A development communication specialist needs to be familiar with both modalities and be able to select the most appropriate approaches according to the scope of the initiative.

The diffusion mode is more media- and message-oriented, while the participation mode is more about dialog, investigation, and analysis. By necessity, the development communication specialist needs to be conversant with research methods of both modalities. In the initial phases of development projects and programs—inception, preparation, and design—familiarity with empirical investigation techniques and approaches often becomes more important than familiarity with communication media and messages.

The elements presented in the table help to identify which approaches might be most suitable in a given situation. Social marketing, media campaigns, information dissemination, lobbying, awareness raising, and persuasive and strategic communi-

Table 2.1 Basic Differences in the Two Communication Modes

Elements	Modernization/ Diffusion/Monologic	Participation/ Participatory/Dialogic
Main scope	Disseminate information and/or persuade audiences to change attitudes/ behaviors	Ensure proper dialog for sharing knowledge and perceptions to achieve broad consensus leading to change
Model of reference	One-way, linear, often top-down	Two-way, horizontal, and circular
Model orientation	Output-oriented, with the outputs defined at the outset	Process-oriented, with the outcome determined by and through the process
Basic conception of development communication	Communication methods and media applied in the development context	Professional use of dialogic methods to assess and ensure stakeholders' involvement
Main role of the communication specialist	Decide, design, and use methods and media products to persuade audiences to change	Facilitate dialog, analyze the situation, and propose the appropriate strategy for change
Timing of the communication intervention	Usually at the implementation stage when objectives have already been decided	Best used at the beginning of the project, before objectives have been defined

Source: Author.

cation are all approaches commonly associated with the diffusion perspective. The approaches often adopted in the participation perspective are community mobilization, conflict resolution, nondirective communication, and other dialog-based approaches. Depending on how they are being applied, approaches such as education or institutional strengthening can fall in either of the two perspectives.

None of the approaches related to the two perspectives are universally applicable, nor are they necessarily mutually exclusive. Each approach should be applied selectively according to the objectives of the communication intervention. In many cases, approaches of both families can be used in the same initiative. An analysis of the four phases of a typical communication program (see module 3) reveals that, even though each phase is closely intertwined with the others, each has a different purpose and function that might need different communication approaches.

2.2.5 The Role of Media, and Information and Communication Technologies in Development Communication

There are many publications dealing extensively with media and information and communication technologies (ICTs; the Internet, satellites, mobile phones, wireless computers, and so forth). Even if these technologies often play a major role in development communication initiatives, it is not within the scope of this publication to discuss in detail the functions and practical challenges faced by media and ICTs in development. However, given the importance and the potential of current communication technologies, this topic deserves a brief presentation.

The use of media in development can be treated at two levels: mass media, often using television, radio, and print media in campaigns aimed at inducing the adoption of innovations or other changes in behaviors; and community media, mainly using radio and other folk expressions such as theater, concerned with giving voice and representation to the various segments of local communities. An increasing number of scholars focus their attention on the ownership patterns of media. In "Broadcasting, Voice and Accountability: A Public Interest Approach to Law and Regulation," Buckley et al. (2007) classify media within a country into three groups: private, public, and community. Such a classification seems to better reflect the different nature, scope, and range of functions included within the broader media system.

In the past, media systems were considered key elements in supporting the national development of poorer countries. During the 1980s the role of communication and, especially, media was at the center of a heated debate that reached its highest level of visibility and controversy at UNESCO. The impact of this debate, while having a number of implications for media policies and international relations, affected the field of development communication and its on-site applications only in a limited way.

There can be little doubt that media are instrumental in increasing knowledge and influencing attitudes and behaviors, but this influence is not as strong as originally believed, especially if it does not take the local context into account. For instance, the vibrant world of community radio (see module 4, 4.3) that has emerged in recent years is often more empowering and influential than the more celebrated medium of television, at least at the local level.

The blind faith placed on media in the past as a means to push or even leapfrog development in poorer countries resembles the current hype for ICTs. The rise of more sophisticated communication and information technologies, such as satellites or the Internet, has opened new horizons and opportunities. The potential of the new technologies has not only increased the penetration of mass media, for instance, through satellites, but it has also created new opportunities to enhance communication at the local level utilizing technologies such as the Internet or mobile telephones. The establishment of "telecenters" in rural areas is spreading in many countries as a way to support local development in the social and economic dimension.

New media and ICTs are gaining increasing attention in development and are considered of great help in achieving some of the main challenges, such as the Millenium Development Goals.[10] Whenever information is part of the solution, they become crucial. However, to avoid past mistakes, media and ICTs, powerful as they are, should always be considered as tools to be used within the context of the broader social and communication environment.

Communication technologies are still looked upon by some with suspicion, probably because of past experiences when media were often used to "spin" arguments and impose change on people. The effectiveness and value of ICTs and other new communication technologies are determined by the way they are selected and utilized. Even if technologies are not the panacea for every communication problem, they are valuable tools to address specific needs, especially when used in a way compatible with and relevant to specific local needs, as illustrated in the example in box 2.1. Once more, the research element of the communication strategy is crucial in determining the best and most effective use of media and ICTs.

Even if the Internet, satellites, mobile phones, and wireless computers appear to constitute the new frontier in communication, there are some critical factors to consider before adopting them. These factors can be divided in three basic categories: economic, technological, and cultural. From an economic point of view, there are high costs associated with the software and the hardware components of ICTs for individuals in developing countries, placing these commodities outside the reach of most people. In the case of the Internet, there are also access and connectivity costs to consider.

Other costs related to ICTs include the establishment and maintenance of reliable infrastructure for telecommunications. It should also be noted that the wave of

BOX 2.1 The Importance of the First Mile

The First Mile Project in Tanzania promoted the use of communication technologies, and especially mobile phones, to provide information about market prices to farmers. Thanks to this information, farmers significantly improved their income. Before the project farmers could get about US$100 per ton of rice; after the project started farmers were able to get around US$600. This project combined communication technologies and a learning environment where farmers' experiences and knowledge were shared and their capacities enhanced, which helped the long-term sustainability of the project (World Bank, CI, and FAO 2007).

liberation and privatization taking place in this sector in many developing countries can be a limiting factor for marginalized sectors of society, as noted in the First World Congress on Communication for Development (World Bank, CI, and FAO 2007: 104): "The development of ICTs by the private sector fails in bridging the gap between the rich and the poor. The poor who are marginalized—and in some cases physically isolated—remain disconnected from the rest of society and what development opportunities there might be."

From a technological point of view, it is difficult to ensure the proper operation of such technologies in places where there are no phone or electric lines. Even where those services are guaranteed, regular maintenance and updates, and issues of compatibility among different standards, become major issues. Technical support is a necessity for individuals in richer countries and would be even more necessary in countries where people are less technology-literate. In many countries, users need basic training in computer use, and prior to that, literacy skills to communicate effectively on the Internet.

From a cultural point of view, there are also a number of constraints. The language in which most of the information is available on the Internet can pose a barrier. In 1999, a survey concluded that about 86 percent of all Web pages are in English (Thussu 2000), thus precluding access to information for many users. Additionally, given the high illiteracy rate of many areas of developing countries, many potential users are excluded from the start. Even when language barriers are overcome, often cultural issues remain crucial in gaining fundamental knowledge and the needed frame of mind in order to take full advantage of the power of these technologies.

The concept of cultural capital (Straubhaar et al. 2006) draws attention to what shapes the use of information and communication technologies by groups of individuals with different backgrounds. It is not easy to predict how poor farmers in a rural village in Africa will use and eventually benefit from having access to a computer that allows them to connect with the rest of the world. This is not to say they will not benefit, but it should not be considered as a given that they will.

The debate about the digital divide—the division between those who have access to modern information technologies and those who don't—has become a hot one in recent years. Many development workers believe that ICTs can be the right answer to leapfrog developing countries toward a better future. The enthusiasm for these technologies is reflected in the demand for universal connectivity (Sachs 2005), but connectivity and access are only some of the issues that need to be addressed.

Many studies on the digital divide show that the information poverty gap between the have and have-nots is still a wide one (Thussu 2000), and it does not seem to be decreasing in any significant way. The optimism of the 1990s regarding ICTs and related expectations has not been justified so far. As recognized in the report of the 9th UN Round Table on Development Communication (FAO 2005: 17), "There is a very long way to go for the new ICTs to even begin to approach a level of universal service or access."

Despite such shortcomings, however, media and ICTs can and do play a major role in development communication. In addition to the widely used information dissemination functions, technologies such as the Internet also have the potential to support the horizontal processes of communication. The same potential has been demonstrated by other less technologically sophisticated media, such as community radio and even participatory video, in promoting people's participation and empowerment, as presented in box 2.2. The challenge in these instances is to effectively promote and use communication technologies to facilitate local stakeholders' participation within the broader process of development.

The interest of international organizations in ICTs is also reflected in the World Summit on the Information Society (WSIS), a two-phase summit aimed at exploring how best to use ICTs to support development goals. Even though the WSIS has been criticized for its excessively technological orientation, it is certainly a significant attempt to incorporate multiple actors' views on how to use information and communication technologies, in what is referred to as a multistakeholder approach (Servaes and Carpentier 2006).

With their quantifiable and fast exchange transmission flows of information and their capacity for overcoming time and space, there is no doubt that ICTs and media can have a stronger appeal than participatory processes, which appear more complex to manage and require longer and closer interactions. Yet, the lessons of the past teach that communication technologies are more effective when used within proper cultural frameworks and in processes that engage stakeholders in the selection of the objectives, key issues, and appropriate channels. ICTs and media can certainly play a key role in development communication, but they are not a panacea capable of solving all problems and of filling all gaps related to knowledge and perceptions.

BOX 2.2 A Different Use of Video

The use of video for giving people a voice rather than a message has been adopted in a number of instances, especially in Latin America and in Africa. A coastal livelihoods project in Tanzania became one of the first in the region to use video in a participatory way. The project convened a week-long workshop among the fishermen of the area and facilitated the video recording of the meetings in an unobtrusive way. After a couple of days, some of the fishermen were able to do their own recordings and watch the playback. They realized how the process and the content of what was being discussed could be controlled. After this workshop, six of the participants started touring the more than 40 villages of the coast and incorporated many of the comments of those communities in their video.

Thanks to the flexibility of digital technology, the fishermen were able to edit their video. Then some project officers brought it to Dar Es Salaam and showed what the people were saying to a number of high-ranking officials of relevant ministries. After viewing the video the ministries' staff replied to the issues raised, by recording their comments, which were later shown to the fishermen on the coast. This kind of "policy dialogue" led to a better understanding and a more open interaction among communities, local officials, and representatives of the central government. The entire project narrative changed in that it was defined or largely shaped by inputs of the villagers themselves, and their involvement started to grow beyond activities related to the coastal livelihoods project (Farmesa 1996).

2.3 A Different Take on Development Communication Applications

As it has been presented in this Sourcebook, development communication is often defined along two different, at times antithetical, perspectives or families of communication approaches (Morris 2005; Servaes 2003; Waisbord 2000): diffusion and participation. This differentiation is not a mere theoretical exercise to be indulged in academic circles—it implies a number of practical consequences in the daily operations of development projects and programs. It addresses two basic factors that should be present in any initiative: the stakeholders' needs and rights to be fully informed about development initiatives (monologic mode) and their needs and rights to have their voices heard and to play an active part in the initiatives' decision-making process (dialogic mode).

To underline the substance of the main functions of each and to make clearer the implications of their conceptual differences, the two main communication modes or families of approaches are defined and contrasted according to their basic scope. The diffusion mode is identified with monologic communication, reflecting the most common conception of communication, or better, information. It is concerned with disseminating information and sending messages to specific audiences. On the other hand, the participatory mode is associated with dialogic communication, based on the horizontal two-way model of communication. The basic features of the two modes are outlined below:

Monologic mode—The monologic mode is broadly equivalent to the diffusion perspective and is based on the transmission model. It adopts one-way communication to send messages, disseminate information, or impart knowledge aimed at increasing awareness of knowledge or changing attitudes and behaviors. In the monologic mode, the scope of the communication program is set from the beginning of the process; it is expected to inform and persuade people to adopt innovations or change behaviors. An example of this mode is represented by a communication initiative to provide support for a public sector reform due to take place in the near future, or a health campaign aimed at persuading people to adopt certain behaviors in order to eliminate the risks of infection.

Dialogic mode—The dialogic mode is closely associated with the participation perspective and based on the communicative[11] *or horizontal model.* It primarily uses two-way communication methods and techniques to build trust, exchange knowledge and perceptions, achieve mutual understanding, and assess risks and opportunities. In a dialogic mode, the scope of a communication application is not usually predetermined in a rigid way because it intends to explore the situation and weigh possible options. Two-way communication is used to engage stakeholders in investigating the situation, helping to uncover and minimize potential risks, generating new knowledge, and identifying viable options. This mode seems to adapt perfectly to a key communication feature defined by Jaspers (2000: 297) as the "openness to the knowability of what is not yet known."

The difference between these two modes is also reflected in how each perspective defines or conceives a communication objective and the relative implications for evaluating the impact of the intervention. In monologic or diffusion approaches, the communication objective is something that requires changes at the level of awareness, knowledge, attitude, and, ultimately, behaviors or practices of specific groups of people. The impact of the communication intervention can be assessed by carrying out a baseline study before the intervention, and then a similar survey after the intervention. The difference between the pre- and post-survey[12] should provide the measurement of the impact, or change, that is due to the communication intervention.

In dialogic, participatory approaches, the main scope relates to the engagement of stakeholders in assessing risks, identifying opportunities, preventing problems, and identifying or confirming the needed change. In other words, in most cases the objectives cannot be specifically defined beforehand because they are the results of a heuristic process that provides new knowledge and valuable inputs for better strategy design.

Clearly, the impact of such an open-ended and process-oriented use of communication is much harder to measure accurately. The question of how to measure trust, empowerment, better project design, consensus seeking, and problem prevention is still an unresolved issue. A number of methods have been proposed (some of which are discussed in module 4, 4.6), but at the moment there does not seem to be a broad consensus on any of them.

As illustrated in table 2.1, the two basic communication modes are subdivided into communication to inform and communication to persuade, in the monologic mode, and communication to assess and communication to empower, in the dialogic mode. This further subdivision has been done to make the rationale for the selection of communication approaches even more evident. Based on the findings of the research phase, it is the communication's ultimate scope that determines the types of approaches most suitable in a given situation.

2.3.1 Communication to Define and Design Development Projects

If the main causes of many past failures are to be ascribed to the insufficient, or the absence of, stakeholders' engagement in the problem analysis of social, political, and cultural environments, there can be little doubt that dialog and the professional use of two-way communication are the best remedies to successfully address this issue. The dialogic functions of communication, in addition to its more informative functions, have become crucial to rectify past mistakes and to enhance projects' design and sustainability. The dialog-based approach can define priorities and project objectives in a more reliable and effective way, thus shaping and improving the overall design of the initiative.

Another factor influencing the growing role of communication in the current context of international development, a factor increasingly embraced by major national and international organizations, resides in the rights-based approach as a key element for development. In this regard, development communication not only leads to better and more sustainable results but also promotes people's participation in accord with the ethical and democratic principles of the current development paradigm. In sum, while providing the inputs for better and more sustainable design of development initiatives, communication also enhances the application of the rights-based approach, facilitates people empowerment, and supports transparency and accountability, key elements of good governance.

In an issue of the magazine of the World Bank Institute devoted to human rights and development, Daniel Kaufmann highlights the link between human rights governance and development. Kaufmann (2006: 19) states that "civil liberties, voice, and participation mechanisms are thus not only very important because of their fundamental value but also due to their instrumental value as key to socio-economic development outcomes." The key role of two-way communication for the rights-based approach and for the empowerment of individual stakeholders is only partially addressed in this Sourcebook, which instead focuses on the value-added of communication to enhance projects' design, effectiveness, and sustainability.

The literature review indicates that the failure of development projects and programs is attributable to a number of causes (Hornik 1988; Mefalopulos 2003), from poor design and lack of people's support to open opposition to the projects' objectives and related activities. Often, these problems could have been addressed and avoided if relevant stakeholders' inputs, perceptions, and knowledge were taken into account when the initial investigation and assessment of the situation were conducted. Using dialog and other empirical research methods to involve stakeholders and to probe risks and opportunities would avoid most of these failures.

Despite the sophisticated research methods developed in different sectors and fields, the most "commonsensical" approach often is also the most effective—talking and listening to local stakeholders. Maybe this simplicity is what has prevented dialog from becoming the method of reference in identifying, defining, and designing development initiatives in a reality that often tends to overemphasize complexity and technocratic knowledge. Empirical research based on dialog and two-way communication can generate a large number of findings that can be difficult to manage effectively. How to interpret, prioritize, and transform the large amount of data into usable inputs is one of the main challenges a communication specialist may face in the initial phases of any initiative.

The act of listening to different voices and of exploring risks and opportunities is crucial for the effective overall design of the project as well as for that of the communication strategy. Communication specialists are facilitators of the process, rather than playing the role of experts in specific content issues. Communication should be used to validate the knowledge of sector specialists and compare it with that of local stakeholders, to ensure that critical factors are not being overlooked.

The reverse of the statement that everybody is ignorant, only in different fields, is that everybody can be considered an expert—only in different areas. No matter how many PhDs in agriculture one might have acquired, one's specific knowledge about African crops of a certain area might never match the practical knowledge of an illiterate farmer living in that area for all of his or her life. The richness and diversity of local knowledge and perspectives has been too often neglected in the past, and dialogic communication is the best way to address and correct that negligence.

2.3.2 Communication to Inform and Promote Behavior Changes

The most widely known functions of communication are undoubtedly the ones associated with the use of media for purposes of dissemination and persuasion.[13]

With the limited success of development initiatives in the last decades, however, the role and influence of mass media and the relative transmission communication model is being rethought.[14] There are instances of such approaches used successfully in sectors such as family planning, health, and agriculture, but overall they have not succeeded in providing systematic solutions to key problems, and, in many cases, they have proved inadequate to address broader development needs, especially in the area of planning (Melkote and Stevens 2001).

Over time it has become increasingly evident that behavior change through media cannot be achieved without considering and facilitating broader social transformations. Most communication approaches[15] aimed at informing or persuading individuals to change behaviors are usually associated with the diffusion family (that is, linear transmission of data and messages), and these can include approaches such as social marketing, advocacy, campaigns, or edu-tainment.[16] Such models, while praised by some as cost-effective and persuasive ways to promote change with large audiences, have also been criticized by others for their linear, deterministic, top-down approach, often overemphasizing the influence of media and neglecting the bigger social framework in which change occurs.

Through the years, diffusion models have been reviewed and refined to make them more appropriate and effective in the development context. Once an issue has been investigated and the design of a project or program completed, there is still a major role for communication. If used professionally as part of a broader effort, communication methods and media can play a key role in informing stakeholders and promoting specific changes in the level of awareness, knowledge, attitudes, or behaviors of key audiences, as indicated in the examples in box 2.3.

The scope of the development initiative and the findings of the initial assessment define the strategic design, determining which communication approach to use, to what avail, and with what audience. When used in ongoing projects, communication approaches are often linked to the monologic mode, to inform and change behaviors, but on certain occasions other approaches can be used as well. Communication specialists need to select and combine different communication modalities, approaches, methods, and media in relation to the intended objectives. The power of information and proper persuasion can be instrumental in inducing behavior and social change, but only when the broader cultural and social context are taken into account.

2.4 Combining Theory with Practice: The Multitrack Model

Many scholars and practitioners, despite certain differences in theoretical perspectives, agree in considering development communication as a specific discipline in its own right or, better, as an interdisciplinary field of study. It is certainly related to the broader communication family, but it has its own theoretical body of knowl-

BOX 2.3 Communication to Inform and Change Behavior

The following are two examples that demonstrate the successful use of communication to inform or persuade people to change behaviors. The first concerns information dissemination in which data transparency and ease of availability for the public leads to significant results in a relatively short time. In Uganda, a public expenditure tracking survey in primary education revealed that only small portions of the grants made were received by schools (Reinikka 2001). Various reasons were given, but it was evident that a major problem consisted in the "secrecy" of the information about the disbursements that were not made public. Furthermore, the grants-releasing process was seldom audited or monitored and this aggravated the problem.

This situation, affecting mostly the poorest schools in the country, was addressed successfully through a communication initiative that first raised public awareness about this issue. Once out in the open, the central government took a series of actions to address it, including publishing regular updates on the dispersal of funds in local newspapers, broadcasting this information as news on local radio, and requiring primary schools to post grant information in places accessible to the public. Simply making the information available was largely responsible for greatly decreasing waste and inefficiency in the system and seriously reducing the problem overall. The amount of funds reaching the schools grew from 13 percent in the early 1990s to 80 percent in 2001.

The second instance, also in Uganda, was the application of communication approaches and methods in the Nutrition and Early Child Development Project (NECDP) aimed at improving children's nutrition and health. The primary audience addressed by the communication was parents, and the objective was to induce voluntary changes in their behaviors that would be beneficial to the children. The NECDP followed basic steps to create conditions leading to change and utilized a multimedia approach to increase parents' knowledge and to achieve specific behavior changes to improve children's health and nutrition standards. The communication campaign adopted by the project applied a mix of media and methods that resulted in the intended changes. Evaluation studies confirmed that the project achieved significant results in the targeted health and nutrition areas (Cabañero-Verzosa 2005).

edge, its own methodologies, and its own analytical, investigative, and communicative toolbag, which in a number of instances differs significantly from those of other communication areas, such as journalism, public relations, or corporate communication. The two dominant perspectives described above (diffusion/monologic and participation/dialogic) greatly define the field of development communication, the primary focus of which should always be on people and not on media, as highlighted in the first World Congress on Communication for Development held in Rome in October 2006.

The model proposed in the following pages belongs to the discipline of development communication and combines different approaches within a flexible framework that is particularly effective in development projects and programs. Its theoretical roots are grounded in the two-way dialogic mode, but it also incorporates monologic approaches and methods. This integrated and project-oriented model is named the "communication multitrack approach," and it borrows ele-

BOX 2.4 The World Congress on Communication for Development (WCCD)

The World Congress on Communication for Development (WCCD) that took place in Rome, Italy, in October 2006 originated from the realization that despite the increasing formal recognition that was attributed to communication in the development context, there was the need to promote and clarify the scope and value of this discipline. The initial concept was developed by the Unit of Sustainable Development in Operations of the Development Communication Division (DevComm-SDO) at the World Bank, in partnership with the Food and Agriculture Organization of the United Nations, the pioneer of this discipline in the UN family, and the Communication Initiative, which provides the most popular online space where practitioners, scholars, and institutions can share knowledge and ideas about the use of communication and media to support economic and social development.

In organizing the Congress, the three partners' main objectives were to (1) facilitate the exchange of valuable experiences in development communication from across the world, and (2) make the case with policy makers about the value and need to incorporate development communication policies and practices in development initiatives. To this purpose, three key audiences that rarely interact were brought together: practitioners, academicians, and policy makers and decision makers. The Congress was organized around four streams considered of particular interest in the current context. They are communication and governance, communication and health, communication and sustainable development, and communication labs, where different topics and themes related to development communication have been presented and discussed.

The organization of the Congress has been a challenging task, since the goal was to make it as open and participatory as possible. The Steering Committee was composed of 19 organizations, including UN organizations, donors, academic centers, and NGOs from various parts of the world.

BOX 2.4 (continued)

The Advisory Body was established to provide more feedback to the process and involve a number of organizations that expressed their interest in participating actively in the preparation of this event. Finally, there was the Scientific Committee, composed of 23 members, which was instrumental in collecting, evaluating, and compiling a huge number of presentations and papers, many of which were part of the Congress.

The Congress was deemed a major success in that it brought together a large number of professionals and decision makers from different parts of the world, with different responsibilities, experiences, and perspectives. The sharing of challenges, knowledge, and applications resulted in a series of recommendations highlighting actions for mainstreaming communication for development and putting it at the core of the development initiatives. Equally important, more than 900 participants of the WCCD also agreed on a document titled "The Rome Consensus" (included in the appendix of this book), which broadly defines the boundaries of this field and provides clear indications of the way forward. A book titled *World Congress on Communication for Development: Lessons, Challenges, and the Way Forward,* has been published by the World Bank.

Source: World Bank, Communication Initiative, and Food and Agriculture Organization of the United Nations 2007.

ments from each of the two main modes according to the needs and the timing of the intervention in the project cycle.

The multitrack approach requires that dialogic features of communication be used during the initial stages of an initiative, no matter what the purpose or the sector of the intervention. It is only after this initial phase that this approach becomes truly multitrack, using a variety of approaches appropriate to the situation. The various approaches, such as information dissemination, social marketing, lobbying, edu-tainment, community mobilization, and others, are considered tracks and are intended as courses of actions or paths to be followed (hence the name multitrack). This model is not simply a sum of different communication approaches; it has a consistent theoretical and methodological framework, which is capable of containing the major differences of the two opposing paradigms without incurring basic contradictions.

The new communication paradigm does not call for a replacement of the basic communication functions associated with information dissemination, but rather it broadens boundaries to include more interactive ways of communicating. This new conception contains functions of both communication modes: the monologic and the dialogic. When the two are fully understood and properly applied according to the situation and, if needed, combined, development communication is at its best.

The theoretical conception of the multitrack model considers communication fundamentally as a horizontal and participatory process, at least in the crucial initial stages, where issues and priorities are assessed and defined. It also acknowledges that in development there are information gaps and areas of needed change that can be effectively supported by approaches linked to the linear flow of monologic models. In the multitrack model, the monologic approaches, or communication tracks, are to be used only after the horizontal communicative process occurs and determines the objectives of the intervention in a participatory way. As the Greek philosopher Aristotle realized more than 20 centuries ago, the beginning is more than half of the whole!

When dealing with the challenges of each individual phase of a communication program (that is, research or CBA, strategy design, implementation, and evaluation), it is easier to see what type of communication to apply for which purpose. The research phase, based on two-way communication methods, is used to create a sort of public space where stakeholders (including outside experts) are engaged in investigating, assessing, and uncovering key issues. This kind of dialogic assessment greatly reduces the possibility of relying on incorrect assumptions and avoids the risk of alienating relevant stakeholders by leaving them out of the decision-making process. After this phase, approaches of both modes can be used according to the needs and scope of the initiative.

Unlike others, the multitrack model selects and combines different kinds of communication into a unified grand approach. The differences between the two modalities remain significant, but those differences, when used in an integrated and purposeful way, become an asset rather than an impediment. Selecting monologic/diffusion tracks such as social marketing, edu-tainment, or IEC (information, education, and communication) based on the findings of a dialogic/participatory assessment can be very effective in addressing issues related to relevance, participation, effectiveness, persuasion, sustainability, and, ultimately, results.

To conclude, the multitrack approach combines the theoretical potential of the two main communication perspectives with their great range of practical applications. It uses two-way communication in the research phase to engage stakeholders who are investigating key issues and defining objectives. From the next phase this approach envisions the use of monologic or dialogic approaches, or a combination of the two, according to the circumstances. DevComm's experiences in a number of projects confirm the value-added of this approach; however, more long-term and systematic studies are needed to accurately assess its effectiveness.

Figure 2.1 illustrates the model. The single arrow linking the research phase with the strategy design phase indicates the requirement of always using the dialogic mode at the beginning. From the second phase a number of different approaches in any (or a combination) of the two modes can be applied based on the situation—hence the additional arrows. Monitoring and evaluation, while positioned as the last phase, should also be considered at the start to be effective—as indicated by the peripheral arrows at the top and bottom.

Figure 2.1 The Multitrack Communication Model

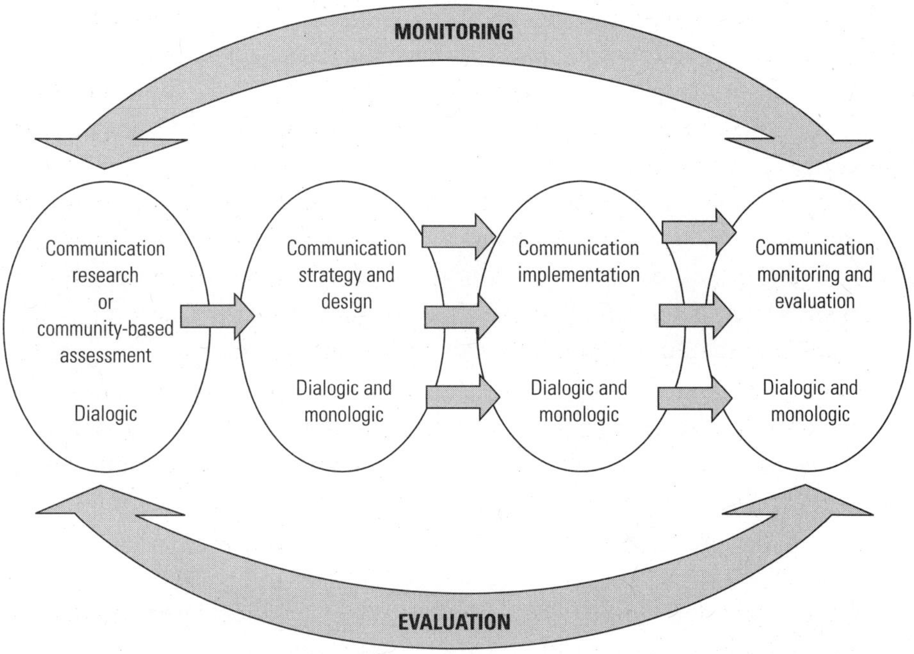

Source: Author.

Summary of Main Points in Module 2

- This module provides some basic definitions of terms frequently used in development communication: information, communication, participation, consultation, capacity building, empowerment, and dialog. The intention is to ensure a common understanding for readers.
- A brief history of the main development theories and the related communication models is presented, from the modernization paradigm to the dependency theory, closing with the emerging paradigm of participation.
- Two divergent conceptions or modes of development communication have been dominating the practices of this field in recent years. Diffusion is heavily rooted in the monologic, one-way model of communication. On the other hand, participation is based on the dialogic, two-way model. Each mode contains a number of different approaches, which can also be combined in an integrated strategy when needed.
- Even though this publication does not focus specifically on media and ICTs (information and communication technologies), their role in development communication is discussed, highlighting how they should be adopted within the broader sociopolitical context.
- The importance of dialogic communication in defining objectives and designing effective strategies cannot be overemphasized. Without efforts to engage stakeholders in key decisions, the risks of conflicts and failures increase exponentially.
- The relevance of monologic communication used to inform and promote change was noted, and a number of successful instances were presented.
- An innovative model called multitrack communication was introduced. It uses two-way dialogic communication to engage stakeholders in the research phase. Subsequent phases can include monologic or dialogic approaches, or a mix of the two types. Such approaches are considered to be communication tracks, hence the term "multitrack communication."

Notes

1. Clearly, dialog constitutes part of the investigation, which is then probed and validated by a number of empirical research methods and tools.
2. UNESCO, in its 1978 General Conference, openly recognized the importance of media at a national and international level.
3. In the literature, the term "strategic communication" is usually associated with the idea of the linear use of communication to persuade individuals to change behavior. It is also being used in the corporate sector to indicate how to achieve its objectives and even in the military sector, where some claimed this term originated.
4. These theories attributed a strong causal and direct effect of media on people's behavior (that is, people would watch television, and it would have a direct influence on what they would think and do).
5. The Cocoyoc Declaration on Self-Reliance was the result of a conference held in Mexico City in 1974 attended by social and natural scientists of many countries.
6. Until the beginning of the 1990s the institutions that developed and adopted the less participatory method of RRA, or rapid rural appraisal, were mostly universities, while the ones developing and adopting PRA were mostly nongovernmental organizations (Chambers 1993).
7. The United Nations Inter-Agency Round Table on Communication for Development was first introduced in the late 1980s as a mechanism to bring together UN agencies and their international key partners to discuss and deliberate on how to best promote the principles and practices of this field of work.
8. A pioneering role in this perspective is played by the Communication for Social Change Consortium (CFSC), which defines communication for social change (www.communicationforsocialchange.org) as "a process of public and private dialogue through which people themselves define who they are, what they need, and how to get what they need in order to improve their own lives. It utilizes dialogue that leads to collective problem identification, decision-making, and community-based implementation of solutions to development issues."
9. Kaplan (1964) considers a theory to be a way of making sense of an unwanted situation so as to allow us to deal with it and change it in a desired manner.
10. These are goals agreed to by all countries and major international lending institutions as a way to address successfully the major challenges faced in development. They range from reducing poverty to providing basic education for all and improving a number of key health issues.
11. In this sense, the term "communicative" is closer to Jaspers' conception of the intersubjective communication among individuals as the way to improve one's consciousness and existence, rather than Habermas's conception of communicative action, which is largely addressing issues related to rationality. In sum, in this context "communicative"

stands for an open system of interactions where individuals are equally able to explore and exchange meanings and knowledge, eventually leading to change.

12. Of course, other variables that interfere with the communication process should be taken into account and their roles weighed out of the communication impact.
13. Once again, in this context persuasion is to be understood as the use of one-way communication initiatives aimed at changing audiences' behaviors. However, this does not exclude the acknowledgment that persuasion can also be part of a dialogic process, where two or more parties debate, compare, and identify viable options based on the best arguments.
14. The transmission model can be summarized in the classic formula Sender-Message-Channel-Receivers.
15. Mefalopulos and Kamlongera (2004) conceive a communication approach as a focused way of using communication techniques, methods and media to address specific issues effectively.
16. As the term indicates, edutainment is a way of applying educational messages in popular forms of entertainment, such as television soap operas, radio programs, and even music.

References

Ascroft, J., and S. Masilela. 1994. "Participatory Decision-Making in Third World Development." In *Participatory Communication: Working for Change and Development,* ed. S. White with K. S. Nair and J. Ascroft, 259–94. New Delhi, India: Sage Publications.

Beltrán Salmón, L. R. 2006a. Excerpt from "Communication: Forgotten Tool of National Development." In *Communication for Social Change Anthology,* ed. A. Gumucio-Dagron and T. Tufte, 36–37. Communication for Social Change Consortium. (Original work published in 1979).

———. 2006b. "A Farewell to Aristotle: Horizontal Communication." In *Communication for Social Change Anthology,* ed. A. Gumucio-Dagron and T. Tufte, 157–73. Communication for Social Change Consortium. (Original work published in 1967).

Berlo, D. K. 1960. *The Process of Communication: An Introduction to Theory and Practice.* San Francisco: Rinehart Press.

Bohm, D. 1996. *On Dialog.* London: Routledge.

Buckley, S., K. Duer, T. Mendel, and S. Ó. Siochrú. 2008. *Broadcasting, Voice and Accountability: A Public Interest Approach to Policy, Law and Regulation.* Washington, DC: World Bank and University of Michigan Press.

Burkey, S. 1993. *People First: A Guide to Self-Reliant Participatory Rural Development.* London: Zed Books.

Cabañero-Verzosa, C. 2005. *Counting on Communication: The Uganda Nutrition and Early Childhood Development Project.* Washington, DC: World Bank.

Carmen, R. 1996. *Autonomous Development.* New York: Zed Books.

Chambers, R. 1983. *Rural Development: Putting the Last First.* London: Longman.

———. 1993. *Challenging the Professions: Frontiers for Rural Development.* London: Intermediate Technology Publications.

———. 1997. *Whose Reality Counts: Putting the First Last.* London: Intermediate Technology Publications.

Cornwall, A. 2000. *Beneficiary, Consumer, Citizen: Perspectives on Participation for Poverty Reduction.* Gothenburg, Sweden: Sida Studies n.2.

Díaz Bordenave, J. 2006. Excerpt from "Communication and Rural Development." In *Communication for Social Change Anthology,* eds. A. Gumucio-Dagron and T. Tufte, 133–141. United States: Communication for Social Change Consortium. (Original work published in 1977).

Ehrlich, E., L. H. Ehrlich, and G. B. Pepper, ed. 2000. *Karl Jaspers: Basic Philosophical Writings.* Amherst, NY: Humanity Books.

Escobar, A. 1995. *Encountering Development: The Making and Unmaking of the Third World.* Princeton, NJ: Princeton University Press.

Esteva, G. 1992. "Development." In *The Development Dictionary,* ed. W. Sachs, 7–17. London: Zed Books.

Fals-Borda, O., and M. A. Rahman, eds. 1991. *Action and Knowledge: Breaking the Monopoly with Participatory Action-Research.* New York: Apex Press.

FAO. 2005. *9th United Nations Development Communication Roundtable Report.* Rome: FAO.

Farmesa. 1996. *Engaging Participation: The Use of Video as a Tool in Rural Development.* Workshop Proceedings, Bagamoyo, Tanzania. Harare, Zimbabwe: Farmesa.

Frank, A. G. 1969. *Capitalism and Underdevelopment in Latin America.* New York: Monthly Review Press.

Fraser, C., and S. Restrepo-Estrada. 1998. *Development Communication: Human Change for Survival.* London: I. B. Tauris.

Freire, P. 1997. *Pedagogy of the Oppressed* (Rev. ed.). New York: Continuum.

Friedmann, J. 1992. *Empowerment: The Politics of Alternative Development.* Cambridge, MA: Blackwell.

Guba, E. G., ed. 1990. *Paradigm Dialog.* Newbury Park, CA: Sage Publications.

Hopkins, T. K. and I. Wallerstein. 1982. *World-Systems Analysis.* London: Sage Publications.

Hornik, R. C. 1988. *Development Communication: Information, Agriculture, and Nutrition in the Third World.* Lanham, MD: University Press of America.

Huesca, R. 2000. "Communication for Social Change among Mexican Factory Workers on the Mexico-United States Border." In *Redeveloping Communication for Social Change: Theory, Practice, and Power,* ed. K. G. Wilkins, 73–87. Lanham, MD: Rowman & Littlefield.

Jacobson, T. 1994. "Modernization and Post-Modernization Approaches to Participatory Development Communication." In *Participatory Communication: Working for Change and Development,* ed. S. White with K. S. Nair and J. Ascroft, 60–75. New Delhi, India: Sage Publications.

Jaffee, D. 1998. *Levels of Socio-Economic Development Theory.* Westport, CT: Praeger.

Kaplan, A. 1964. *The Conduct of Inquiry.* San Francisco: Chandler.

Katz, E., and P. F. Lazarfeld. 1955. *Personal Influence.* New York: Free Press.

Kaufmann, D. 2006. "Human Rights, Governance, and Development: An Empirical Perspective." In *Development Outreach,* October 2006. Washington, DC: World Bank Institute.

Klapper, J. 1960. *The Effect of Mass Communication.* New York: Free Press.

Lasswell, H. 1948. "The Structure and Function of Communication in Society." In *The Communication of Ideas,* ed. L. Bryson, 37–51. New York: Harper.

Lerner, D. 1958. *The Passing of Traditional Society.* New York: Free Press.

McKee, N. 1994. "A Community-based Learning Approach: Beyond Social Marketing." In *Participatory Communication: Working for Change and Development,* ed. S. White with K. S. Nair and J. Ascroft, 194–228. New Delhi, India: Sage Publications.

McMichael, P. 1996. *Development and Social Change: A Global Perspective.* Thousand Oaks, CA: Pine Forge Press.

Mefalopulos, P. 2003. "Theory and Practice of Participatory Communication: The Case of the FAO Project 'Communication for Development in Southern Africa'." PhD diss., University of Texas.

Mefalopulos, P., and C. Kamlomgera. 2004. *Participatory Communication Strategy Design.* 2nd ed. Rome: FAO/SADC.

Melkote, S. R. 1991. *Development Communication in the Third World: Theory and Practice.* New Delhi, India: Sage Publications.

Melkote, S. R., and H. L. Stevens. 2001. *Development Communication in the Third World.* New Delhi, India: Sage Publications.

Mody, B. 1991. *Designing Messages for Development Communication.* New Delhi, India: Sage Publications.

Morris, N. 2005. "The Diffusion and Participatory Models: A Comparative Analysis." In *Media and Global Change,* ed. O. Hemer and T. Tufte, 123–44. Buenos Aires, Argentina: CLACSO.

Narayan, D., ed. 2002. *Empowerment and Poverty Reduction: A Sourcebook.* Washington, DC: World Bank.

Pasquali, A. 2005. *18 ensayos Sobre Comunicaciones.* Caracas, Venezuela: Random House/Mondadori.

———. 2006. Excerpt from "Communication Theory: the Sociological Implications of Information on Mass Culture." In *Communication for Social Change Anthology,* eds. A. Gumucio-Dagron and T. Tufte, 5–25. Communication for Social Change Consortium, Inc.

Pretty, J. N., I. Gujit, J. Thompson, and I. Scoones. 1995. *Participatory Learning and Action: A Trainer's Guide.* London: International Institute for Environment and Development.

Rahnema, M. 1992. "Participation." In *The Development Dictionary,* ed. W. Sachs, 116–31. London: Zed Books.

Reinikka, R. 2001. "Recovery in Service Delivery: Evidence from Schools and Health Centers." In *Uganda's Recovery: The Role of Farms, Firms, and Government,* ed. R. Reinikka, and P. Collier. Kampala, Uganda: Fountain Publishers.

Rogers, E. 1962. *The Diffusion of Innovations.* Glencoe, IL: Free Press.

Rogers, E. M., ed. 1976. *Communication and Development: Critical Perspectives.* Beverly Hills, CA: Sage Publications.

Sachs, J. D. 2005. "Information and Communication Technologies for Development." In *Harnessing the Potential of ICT for Education,* ed. B. Bracie and T. Culver. New York: UNICT Task Force.

Schramm, W. 1964. *Mass Media and National Development.* Stanford, CA: Stanford University Press.

Sen, A. 1999. *Development as Freedom.* New York: Anchor Books.

Servaes, J. 1991. "Toward a New Perspective for Communication and Development." In *Communication in Development,* ed. F. L. Casmir, 51–86. Norwood, NJ: Ablex.

———. 1999. *Development Communication: One World, Multiple Cultures.* Cresskill, NJ: Hampton Press.

———. ed. 2003. *Approaches to Development Communication.* Paris: UNESCO.

Servaes, J., and N. Carpentier, eds. 2006. *Towards a Sustainable Information Society.* Bristol, UK: Intellect Book.

Servaes, J., T. L. Jacobson, and S. White, eds. 1996. *Participatory Communication for Social Change.* New Delhi, India: Sage Publications.

Straubhaar, J., M. Fuentes-Bautista, V. Rojas, and J. Pinon. 2006. "Still Divided: Ethnicity, Generation, Cultural Capital and New Technologies." Paper presented at the annual meeting of the International Communication Association, New York.

Thussu, D. K. 2000. *International Communication: Continuity and Change.* London: Oxford University Press.

UNDP (United Nations Development Programme). 1993. *Human Development Report.* Oxford, UK: Oxford University Press.

UNESCO (United Nations Educational, Scientific and Cultural Organization). 1980. *Many Voices, One World.* Paris: UNESCO.

UNFPA (United Nations Population Fund). 2002. *VIII Communication for Development Roundtable Report.* New York: UNFPA.

Waisbord. S. 2000. *Family Tree of Theories, Methodologies and Strategies in Development Communication.* New York: Rockefeller Foundation. http://www.comminit.com/pdf/familytree.pdf.

Wilkins, K. G., ed. 2000. *Redeveloping Communication for Social Change: Theory, Practice, and Power.* Lanham, MD: Rowman & Littlefield.

World Bank. 1995. "Social Development Notes." No. 13, World Bank: Washington, DC.

———. 2006. *Global Development Finance 2006 (Complete Print Edition): The Development Potential of Surging Capital Flows.* Washington, DC: World Bank.

World Bank, Communication Initiative, and Food and Agriculture Organization of the United Nations. 2007. *World Congress on Communication for Development: Lessons, Challenges, and the Way Forward.* Washington, DC: World Bank.

Worsley, P. 1984. *The Three Worlds.* Chicago: University of Chicago Press.

MODULE 3

Development Communication Methodological Framework and Applications

For the beginning is thought to be more than half of the whole.
(Aristotle)

Preview

This module is directed to communication practitioners, both in the World Bank and other organizations, public and private, and all those interested in development communication practices. It presents the methodological framework adopted by the Development Communication Division (DevComm) and its application in the programs and projects around the world. The methodological process is divided into four phases: communication research, strategy design, implementation, and monitoring and evaluation. Each phase is treated in a sort of mini-module, or component, of its own in which the scope, functions, and basic tools to support operations are outlined.

Contents

Principles and Methodology Fundamentals of the Four-Phase Framework

The scope and functions of different types of communication have been discussed in the previous modules, but it is important to remember that each of these different types require different skills and competencies. When dealing specifically with operational issues in the field, it could be stated that almost any type of communication (for example, corporate, internal, advocacy, public relations) supports operations by "communicating" information about projects and programs and by promoting their objectives. However, when (development) communication is an integral part of operations, it contributes to define the objectives of the project and enhancing the overall project design and its sustainability. In this way communication scope and functions go beyond the ones related to the creation of messages and the dissemination of information.

To review DevComm's setting and role in operations, it is important to remember that four basic functions categorize communication in the World Bank. *Corporate communication* uses media and other methods to communicate the organization mission and its activities, expanding knowledge of its work to external audiences and furthering the global development agenda. *Internal communication* keeps the staff informed on issues relevant to the institution and ensures the efficient exchange of information among the various units, departments, and staff. At times internal communication is combined with corporate communication.

Advocacy communication effectively promotes key issues to raise awareness and to win support with the public or to influence relevant policy-making processes. Finally, *development communication* explores and assesses operational situations, building wider consensus among stakeholders and using communication approaches, methods, and media to promote change and enhance project effectiveness and sustainability.

This module addresses the wide range of methodological and practical applications of development communication. Rather than presenting what it is and why it should be adopted (topics discussed extensively in previous modules), this section illustrates when and how to apply development communication throughout the different phases of the project or program cycle. It also presents the basic steps to follow when designing and managing a communication strategy and discusses which methods and tools are most appropriate according to the circumstances.

The methodology of development communication programs can be divided into four stages, or phases, each of which builds on the previous one but maintains its own specific scope, methods, and set of tools. The module is subdivided into four parts, or components, one for each phase: communication-based assessment; communication strategy design; implementation; and monitoring and evaluation. They are described in varying degrees of detail, according to their relevance to DevComm's mission and the scope of work.

The first, communication-based assessment (CBA), is the research phase, which illustrates how to select and use appropriate communication research methods and techniques, as well as how to engage stakeholders in the investigation of the sociopolitical context before examining specific technical issues. Regardless of the sector of intervention, DevComm's work facilitates achieving sustainable results through the preliminary assessment of the situation. Naturally, empirical research is most effective when performed during the initial phases of the intervention. Nevertheless, even when it is included halfway through the project cycle, CBAs can play a significant role in supporting the project's objectives.

In the second phase of the communication program, communication strategy design, DevComm staff assist in transforming the findings of the communication-based assessment into valuable inputs for the strategy design. The design of the strategy is followed by the third phase, which is the implementation of the activities. An action plan is usually drawn up to organize and monitor their implementation. Finally, the fourth phase involves monitoring the process and evaluating the impact of the communication intervention. The pyramid in figure 3.1 illustrates the four phases of development communication and represents not only their sequence but also their relevance in achieving the expected results. The physical area in the pyramid also represents the importance, workload, and time needed for each phase within the overall methodological process. The foundation of the pyramid, or the research phase, constitutes the broadest and most important part of the whole; it is from this base that the strategy is rooted and, subsequently, all activities are imple-

Figure 3.1 The Process Pyramid

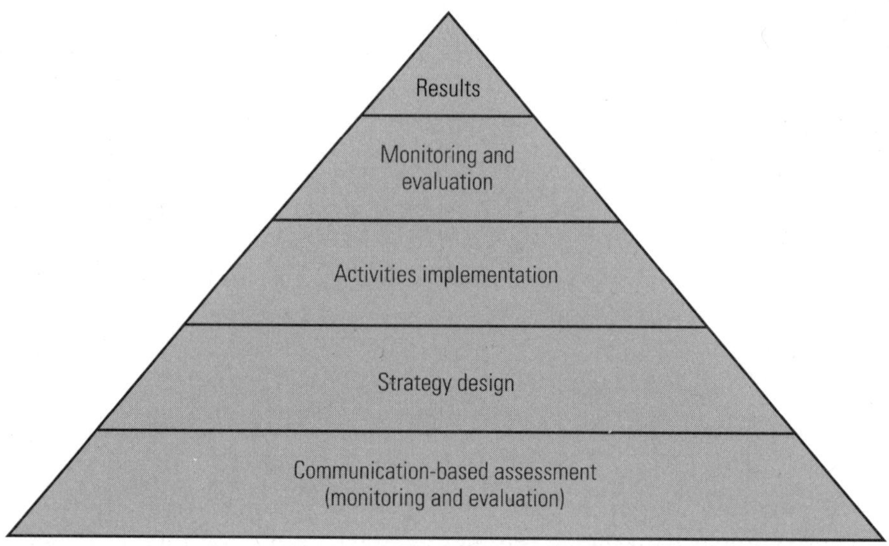

Source: Author.

mented and evaluated. The amount of work and resources invested in the research phase is a significant factor in the achievement of the communication objectives at the top of the pyramid.

Although the monitoring and evaluation process is almost at the top of the pyramid, the term "monitoring and evaluation" in brackets also appears at the base to emphasize that monitoring and evaluation indicators should be identified and defined from the beginning of the intervention, even though the specific measurements are usually carried out at the end. Monitoring is an important mechanism that should be incorporated throughout the development process to guarantee the proper implementation of activities. Its incorporation creates a real-time alert system, which allows prompt intervention and relative corrections whenever something goes wrong.

Before previewing the four phases of the methodological process, a reminder of development communication and its two modes of communication approaches or "grand-modes," treated extensively in modules 1 and 2, is in order. The first mode is referred to as the monologic mode, closely associated with diffusion and rooted in the one-way transmission model whose scope is communicating messages and information to "sell a product" or to induce needed change. The second mode, referred to as the dialogic mode, is based on the two-way model, using professional facilitation of dialog as part of the process to engage key stakeholders in uncovering perceptions, risks, and opportunities while building a wider consensus leading to change. Awareness of these two different perspectives leads to a better understanding and use of the approaches discussed in the next pages.

Phase 1, communication-based assessment, or CBA, offers a comprehensive investigation of a situation and should be the first step of any development initiative, regardless of the sector. Given its interdisciplinary and cross-cutting nature, communication-based assessment is of particular value in exploring and assessing the overall circumstances, building trust, and minimizing sociopolitical risks. CBA addresses the what, who, and why of each situation investigated by involving all relevant stakeholders. It utilizes the principles and tools of the DevComm methodological framework, facilitating dialog, building trust, analyzing political risk, and assessing conditions to identify entry points for the communication strategy. These steps minimize possible risks and enhance projects' chances for success and sustainability.

CBA is, most of all, a type of field research. It is often preceded by a desk review, or secondary sources review, which can highlight key issues and provide useful background to investigate the perceptions and knowledge held by the various stakeholder groups. Country reports and client surveys are two of the useful sources to consult when preparing for a communication-based assessment.

Those familiar with the current development communication applications understand that the greatest value-added of a communication-based assessment resides in its use at the very beginning of a development initiative, to ensure the appropriateness and relevance of the project design in the eyes of all stakeholders. Unfortunately, too frequently, development managers and decision makers limit themselves and their projects to the traditional concept of using communication as a tool only after projects begin—to inform or to persuade specific audiences or to help defuse a crisis. Of course, communication can still assist in these circumstances, but this scenario limits its power as a strategic methodology.

To design an effective communication strategy, a CBA is always necessary. Even if the project is already halfway through its implementation, the communication research phase cannot be skipped unless all relevant information about the problem, its causes, and the stakeholders' perceptions are already available—a situation rarely encountered. A CBA identifies, refines, or validates the causes and differences in the positions and perceptions of the groups relevant to the development initiative. This crucial information can address and prevent possible problems and diffuse potential crises through appropriate channels, messages, or methods, contributing to successful outcomes.

A CBA is a flexible instrument that can be used in various ways, according to the situation on the ground. The goal is to identify, refine, or validate both project and communication objectives. The definition of specific objectives is usually the main output of this phase, and it becomes the main input for the next phase. In some cases, two or three weeks are sufficient to conduct a communication-based assessment and to identify the needed objectives in order to define the communication strategy. Most cases however, because of their complexity, require additional weeks of in-depth empirical research. DevComm staff carry out the shortest version of the CBA, but they take more of an advisory role when an in-depth, extended research component is required; this is a task usually performed by local consultants or firms.

Phase 2, strategy design, refers to the problem-solving or strategic thinking that designs the best way to achieve the objectives identified in phase 1. This phase defines the type of change needed and helps to select the most appropriate communication approach for each initiative, such as social marketing, advocacy, diffusion of information, or capacity building. These approaches are not mutually exclusive and can stand alone or in combination with each other (see the multitrack model in module 2). The planning done in this phase emphasizes the strategic selection and application of methods, techniques, and media resulting from research-based findings and objectives.

For example, when the objective is to inform policy makers about the findings of an opinion poll or an environmental assessment, the communication approach could focus on disseminating this information. Questions like the following would be asked: "Should this be considered enough to achieve the goal?" or "Should we adopt a more 'aggressive' advocacy approach to win policy-makers' support for the reform?" Answers to questions like these determine whether the communication design should be different and more strategically focused. How different will depend on the objectives and the audiences or stakeholders involved. The work done during the communication research phase is crucial. It is important not only to know what change to achieve but also to know the perceptions, knowledge, and attitudes of primary audiences and other relevant background information on the issue of interest.

Phase 3, implementation, concerns the implementation of the communication approaches and activities selected in the strategy and defined in the action plan. This phase also includes the activities needed to produce or to ensure the results of the strategic design, such as writing a script for a radio program or strengthening the capacities of the extensionists before a rural sector reform. Other common activities carried out at this stage include the design and production of communication materials (print, radio, video), their pretesting, and the training of the relevant staff.

In Phase 4, monitoring and evaluation are crucial for the success of any project. Monitoring the process of the intervention is known as "formative evaluation," while evaluation of the final impact of the intervention is referred to as "summative evaluation." The first is necessary to ensure that the communication activities are being carried out as planned and are achieving the intended results effectively. By monitoring the intervention closely, staff can perform any adjustment as needed to support the overall success of the initiative. Summative evaluation, on the other hand, is necessary for considering the impact of the intervention and assessing if and how its objectives were achieved.

To be most effective, development communication specialists should be involved at the onset of a development initiative, when they can identify and define indicators for monitoring and evaluation, among other things. Indicators serve for measurements at the end of the intervention, but they should always be established at the beginning. This crucial aspect is neglected in many instances, making it impossible to assess the communication impact. Another problem related to this is that since managers and other decision makers often do not see the need for communication at the initial stage, there are no specific budget lines dedicated to communication, and, more specifically, dedicated to communication-based research needed to identify indicators. As illustrated in the following pages, communication's greatest asset resides in its analytical and assessment power. Hence, the systematic incorporation and effective application of CBA as a critical tool in the initial as well as in the implementing phases of World Bank projects and programs greatly depend on the establishment of a dedicated budget line.[1]

Methodology Fundamentals

Figure 3.2, also used in module 1, provides a graphic illustration of the four phases framing DevComm's methodology and of the main functions addressed by each

Figure 3.2 DevComm Methodological Framework

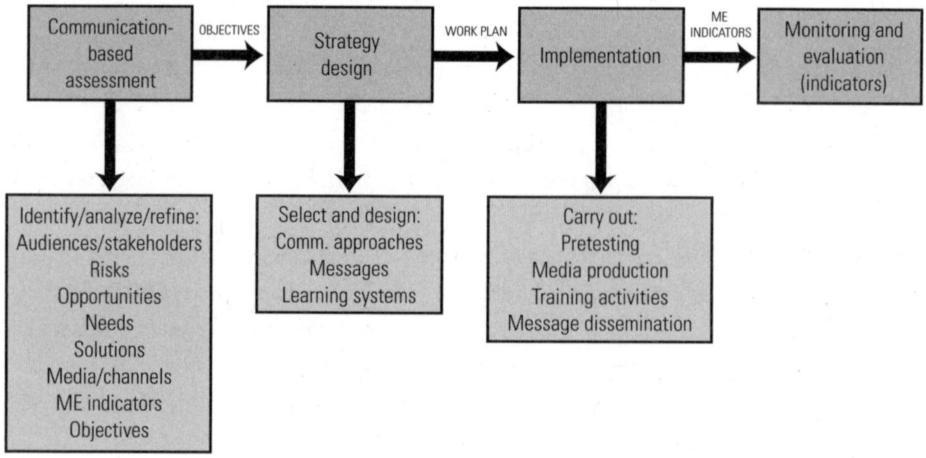

Source: Author.

phase. Another figure in module 4 (figure 4.1) illustrates the specific communication outputs expected in each phase and how they relate to the project-cycle phases of the World Bank. All the applications in the various phases are rooted in a sound theoretical framework, needed to interpret reality and induce change accordingly.

Theories are ways of making sense of reality, and Kuhn (1970) defines paradigms as "universally recognized achievements that for a time provide model problems and solutions to a community of practitioners." To be effective and credible, development practices need to be rigorously rooted, if not in a paradigm, at least in a theoretical framework, which ensures the soundness and effectiveness of the development communication methodology.

Theory is generated and refined primarily in academic institutions. Academic programs devoted specifically to development have been, and still are, a rare commodity. This is one of the main factors allowing many self-appointed specialists to operate in this field, often without a consistent body of knowledge and expertise, and frequently with less than satisfactory results. Of course, education is not the sole way to learn and impart knowledge; practical experiences can be as valuable. Nevertheless, academic or other types of educational centers are very useful in collecting knowledge and helping to set and maintain quality standards.

No discipline in the social realm can afford to perform its daily practices effectively without the support of a recognized body of knowledge. In recent years, academic programs dedicated to development communication have been established in universities around the world. In addition, the increasing relevance of this discipline has created more venues where scholars and practitioners could debate and exchange ideas, models, and experiences—thus strengthening development communication's theoretical and conceptual understanding. This theoretical conception has evolved significantly in the last decades, but many managers and officials in development are not aware of the conceptual basis, and they persist in considering communication as a means to disseminate messages and persuade audiences, rather than a specialized interdisciplinary field with a broader analytical and communicative scope.

There is a growing consensus that development communication's theoretical framework is based on a constructivist perspective (that is, it does not matter if there is an "objective" reality, because reality is socially constructed through shared interpretations of relevant groups of individuals).[2] This explains why a situation can be perceived, assessed, and prioritized differently by different groups of people. The difference is not just in the way reality is perceived, but in the way it is constructed. It is evident that communication is instrumental in assessing, probing, and reconciling those different realities. This use of communication also encompasses the understanding and analysis of the political dimension of those realities.

Despite some differences in the way the discipline of development communication is conceived among practitioners and scholars, it enjoys a wide consensus about some of its basic principles, as indicated in events such as the first World Congress on Communication for Development, held in Rome in October 2007. The following principles constitute the foundation of the emerging paradigm in development communication and are closely associated with DevComm's work. It is in the research phase, or communication-based assessment, that their relevance is especially evident. In subsequent phases, communication can adopt various approaches for diverse purposes, and, in some cases, the relevance of the following principles may be reduced.

Basic Principles of Development Communication

Dialogic—Dialog is the heart of the new communication paradigm. The professional application of dialog, the two-way model of communication, is widely endorsed by most development institutions and should be the basis of any initiative. Development communication should foster dialog to facilitate mutual understanding, to assess the situation, and to seek wider consensus. Dialogic approaches guarantee that relevant stakeholders have their voices heard and that project priorities are aligned with people priorities. Professionally directed, dialog is an invaluable research tool and is absolutely to build trust, optimize knowledge, minimize risks, and reconcile different positions. To facilitate dialog professionally and effectively, a communication specialist must be conversant with proper communication skills, including principles of active listening.

Inclusive—Inclusion is a first step in any situation analysis, whereby DevComm identifies, defines, hears, and understands relevant stakeholders. In this respect, inclusiveness is one of the basic principles of the DevComm methodological framework, even if the appropriate strategy might focus only on selected groups of stakeholders. Omitting a group from the assessment on a basis that might not seem relevant can cause problems further along and can increase the risk factors in the successful achievement of the intervention. Two-way communication should always pay special attention to groups that are marginalized or at a disadvantage in society. Gender issues are always a primary concern in this context, as well as issues related to the poor, or any other vulnerable group.

Heuristic—The investigative use of communication to discover or solve problems during the initial phases of a development initiative is essential. Communication is often defined as a way of sharing meanings or "as a process in which two or more people share information and converge toward mutual understanding, mutual agreement, and collective action" (Yum 1989). This definition denotes the sharing of information and knowledge, which usually generates more knowledge that in turn can lead to effective collective action. The heuristic and explorative scope of development communication, strengthened by its analytical and dialogic features, constitutes its main value-added in addressing and rectifying the past failures in development.

Analytical—Going beyond communicating could be a DevComm motto; a large amount of its work, such as the assessment of political risks and opportunities, is analytical. In this context, the communication function is not about relating messages but about uncovering and generating knowledge to design better projects and programs that lead to sustainable change. The effectiveness of diffusion and dissemination activities depends significantly on how appropriately the analytical work is conducted and how effectively people are empowered to voice their perceptions and opinions.

Participatory—While rarely employed in practice to its ideal and fullest extent, participation is applied in different degrees according to the intervention. Its relevance is echoed in virtually all development organizations and communities, at the national and international levels. Only genuine communication can facilitate effective participation, especially in its most advanced forms. As discussed in depth in module 2, participation can be applied in different degrees, and there are several classifications describing the different types of participation. The World Bank classification illustrated in table 3.1 is in line with many others in this context and identifies four levels of participation (Aycrigg 1998): information sharing, consultation, collaboration, and empowerment.

While the most common mode of operation in development practices can be categorized as "participation by consultation," DevComm also operates at a higher level, by collaboration. This occurs specifically in the research phase, where dialog with relevant stakeholders is sought and promoted and their input valued, especially in community-driven development projects. This application is adopted according to the circumstances; although it is a main feature in communication-based assessments, participation is not always a feature of communication

Table 3.1 Levels of Participation and Communication

Participation Level	Basic Features Related to Communication
Information sharing	One-way communication—basically, people are included by informing them about what is being done.
Consultation	Primarily one-way communication with a stronger emphasis on feedback—stakeholders provide their input but do not have a significant say in the decision-making process.
Collaboration	Two-way communication supporting open interaction in decision making—input in decision making is balanced.
Empowerment	Transfer of control over decisions and resources—two-way communication ensures shared decision making.

Source: Aycrigg 1998.

approaches in subsequent activities, such as a campaign to raise awareness about how to react to an avian flu pandemic.

Contextual—There is no precooked universal formula applied a priori in development communication. In its recent adoption of the Comprehensive Development Framework, the World Bank acknowledged "country ownership" as one of the main principles of development and as a basis for all of the Bank's work. This means "encouraging participatory processes" that are necessarily rooted in the cultural context of specific countries and their socioeconomic reality. In employing communication-based assessment around the world, DevComm staff are fully aware of the implications of this principle. While investigating a local context and assessing needs, problems, risks, and opportunities, DevComm specialists tap local resources to obtain a better understanding of the relevant situation and to triangulate their findings. Even if the overall process of a communication intervention (that is, executing communication-based assessment, designing communication strategies, and implementing and evaluating related activities) is consistently similar, the tools, content, and modes of applications vary significantly according to the specific situation.

Interdisciplinary—To be effectively applied, a development communication body of knowledge includes a number of principles borrowed from other disciplines. In addition to specific expertise in the theory and practices of development communication, the specialist in this field is often required to be familiar with other disciplines, such as ethnography, sociology, political economy, adult education, and marketing. The specialist might be asked to assess political risks, conduct negotiations to reduce conflicts, or mediate between opposing views. While sector experts could address each of these areas with a specific and narrower focus, the cross-cutting nature of communication makes it an easier and more effective tool to acquire a comprehensive overview of the situation.

Strategic—The principle of strategy, which contains many of the previous elements, emphasizes the professional and timely application of communication techniques and methods to achieve intended objectives. At the risk of oversimplification, a strategy could be defined as a plan to achieve set objectives with available resources in a given time frame. It is surprising how often the basics of a strategy are overlooked, not only by communication specialists, but by all sorts of decision makers. Often this occurs when practitioners jump into strategy design without making sure that the objectives are technically sound, well understood, and relevant to most stakeholders. If the project objectives do not meet all these criteria, no matter what strategy one adopts, the initiative is bound to fail—like building a house on a faulty foundation. The principles of "strategic" imply that all parts of the process, from setting the objectives to selecting the media, are carefully assessed, triangulated, and, if needed, modified to allow the design and implementation of an effective strategy. The strategic use of development communication should not be confused with "strategic communication," the narrower use of communication to persuade individuals to change behaviors.

Persuasive—At times this term has a negative connotation, mostly due to past uses of persuasion techniques taken to an extreme and often associated with manipulation and propaganda. Persuasion per se should not be thought of in negative terms. The renowned Greek philosopher Aristotle considered it as an effective way to communicate. In development communication, persuasion can be used to induce voluntary changes in individuals. The legitimacy for its use is derived from this rationale and the definition of change. To avoid the manipulation connotations of the past and be ethically appropriate, persuasion should be based on accurate information and within a context of two-way communication. Each party can present its points of view with the intention of achieving the most appropriate change. Healthy two-way persuasive approaches ensure that the best available options among the various parties are considered and agreed upon, leading to sustainable change.

Further Reflections on Methodology

Within the World Bank, development communication is conceived as the professional use of communication methods and tools to support operations mainly at the country level. Such work includes, among other things, building trust, facilitating mutual understanding, and sharing knowledge among stakeholders; assessing political risks and opportunities and broadening public access to information on reforms; strengthening clients' abilities to listen to their constituencies and to consult with them; and assisting in the design of effective strategies grounded in solid empirical research. The available body of evidence ascribes many failures in development interventions to faulty project design (Hornik 1988: Mefalopulos 2003), often due to inadequate involvement of relevant stakeholders in the analysis of the initial situation.

DevComm methodology is evolving to reflect not only the growing body of evidence in this field, but also, and especially, the lessons learned from the operational work carried out by its staff. The overall goal of DevComm methodology is to provide a consistent and systematic framework and related toolbox, to support and achieve social and behavioral change. Since the methods and tools used in development communication are too many to be discussed comprehensively here, this Sourcebook presents some among those most frequently used.

There are no universal formulas to address a situation successfully, but in most circumstances there are precise steps that, when followed professionally, provide the inputs needed for the strategic design of the communication intervention. Social marketing is not necessarily more effective than social mobilization; television is not always more persuasive than radio; and mobilization approaches are not always better than dissemination of information when a change in behaviors is sought. Deciding which approach or mix of approaches is best suited always depends upon a number of considerations, usually rooted in the findings of the communication-based assessment. The development communication professional, being familiar with the methodological framework and its practical applications, knows which approach, method, media mix, and techniques are the most appropriate according to the set objectives, the characteristics of the stakeholders/audiences, and the sociocultural environment.

The relevance of DevComm's work is rooted in the new emerging paradigm, utilizing communication to its fullest potential and broadening its scope and applications beyond the more renowned functions of information dissemination and persuasion. Regardless of the presence of a specific communication component, the analytical and participatory value-added of communication in assessing situations and in enhancing program design is increasingly recognized as crucial to strengthen the chances for success and sustainability in development projects. Success and sustainability cannot occur without active stakeholder involvement. The next pages illustrate the way communication approaches are conceived and applied in each of the four phases of the communication program.

3.1 Phase 1—Communication-Based Assessment

Communication-based assessment (CBA)[3] is a two-way research method that the Development Communication Division has developed in order to assess the situation, the political risks, and the best option to support and achieve change. It is the most crucial phase of the entire communication process. The success or failure of the overall initiative rests on the work and premises defined in this phase. Any unidentified gap or unaccounted risk can have negative effects further down the implementation line, jeopardizing the overall success of the initiative. Used at its best, the cross-cutting features of communication, using dialog and analysis, are uniquely capable of assessing a situation in its entirety, uncovering hot issues, usually in the political realm, and minimizing risks.

Communication-based assessment, in addition to the usual field research function of collecting useful information, explores technical issues to "connect the dots" with broader social issues and identifies the inputs to cement consensus around the development initiative. This allows communication to become the lens through which a bird's-eye view of the overall situation is gained, mapping priorities across various sectors and focusing the strategy where it is most needed. The importance of the cross-cutting nature of communication research is increasingly being recognized, as indicated also by the proposal included in the Declaration of the IX United Nations Roundtable on Communication for Development (FAO 2005: 10), which states, "Governments, donors, and development agencies should require the incorporation of a communication needs assessment in any development initiative."[4]

3.1.1 Understanding and Applying Communication-Based Assessment

The context, methods, and practices of development have changed over time. This shift is also reflected in the theory and practices of development communication. The most crucial part of the communication process is no longer exclusively on the channels, audiences, or messages, but also on the facilitating of two-way processes that engage stakeholders, ensure mutual understanding, assess the situation, and identify the best course of action for change.

When not included from the start, development communication's effectiveness is greatly reduced. It is difficult to quantify exactly how many projects' problems and failures would have been avoided in the last decades if dialogic methods had been employed properly from the beginning. It is evident, however, that by adopting the tools and practices of the two-way communication model from the beginning of the intervention, many of them could have been easily prevented (Mefalopulos 2003; Beltrán Salmón 2004).

Effective Dialog for Sustainable Change

Development is first and foremost about people; consequently, development communication should also aim, first and foremost, to ensure that the voices of people affected by a development initiative be heard, allowing them to share their knowledge and points of view. In most cases, dialog among stakeholders is key to the success of a project. Dissipating suspicions and misunderstandings is a great help, since failing to reconcile different perspectives has been a major cause of failures in development initiatives. The value of dialog leading to change can be seen in a visual image known as the Johari Window, shown in table 3.2.[5]

The Johari Window is a tool originally developed by Joseph Luft and Harry Ingham (hence the name) to better understand human interactions and communication. It also is used to map interaction leading to change at a broader level, highlighting the value of a participatory approach in communication (Anyaegbunam et al. 2004). The window illustrates the process that starts from common knowledge shared by both parties (that is, community and project) and aims to address the unknown by combining and applying knowledge exclusive to each group.

For simplicity's sake in this context, the term "They" refers to the various groups of external stakeholders (for example, Bank specialists, consultants, and so forth), while "We" refers to local stakeholders (for example, citizens, community groups, civil society organizations, and so forth). The first window describes the time and space where outside experts and other local stakeholder groups begin to interact, making sure that they understand each other. Window two is where local knowledge is disclosed and accepted. Next it is the turn of the outside experts to disclose their knowledge by exchanging notes with other stakeholders in window three. Finally, the last and more critical part of the process occurs in window four, the blind spot, representing the problem to address or the intended change.

Following this process reveals the importance, not only of carefully researching the issues, but also of including key stakeholders in the investigation. In a development initiative, the first three windows represent the problem-analysis phase, while

Table 3.2 The Johari Window

Window 1: OPEN KNOWLEDGE What We know and They know	Window 3: THEIR HIDDEN KNOWLEDGE What They know and We do not know
Window 2: OUR HIDDEN KNOWLEDGE What We know and They do not know	Window 4: THE BLIND SPOT What neither We nor They know

Source: Anyaegbunam et al. 2004.

the last is the problem-solving phase. This last window stands for the unknown, the problem, where all of the pieces of knowledge need to coalesce to define the best solution leading to meaningful and sustainable change. Thus, the Johari Window provides a model for engaging all parties in the search for the best option or knowledge leading to change. The strength of this and other similar approaches relies on a professional use of dialogic communication, and whenever adopted it produces significant results, as in the instance illustrated in box 3.1.

Achieving change is the ultimate goal of all development interventions. Even if the nature of "change" is still debated by different schools of thought (for example,

BOX 3.1 The Power of Participatory Communication for Social Change

Tostan is an international NGO based in Senegal, which has been working on the issue of female genital cutting, FGC—a tradition deeply entrenched in the social norms of many communities in that part of the world. Tostan was aware that a traditional communication-for-behavior-change approach would not have worked, due to the strong cultural system in which FGC was rooted, as well as the many social ramifications (for example, requested for marriages by most individuals in the communities). Hence, Tostan started its effort directed at eliminating, or greatly reducing, this harmful tradition with a nondirective and participatory use of communication. Tostan did not enter the communities trying to impose change, nor did it place blame or criticize their traditions; rather, it facilitated dialog, bringing in facts and making the community reflect upon some of the critical factors related to this issue.

To reach that point, however, Tostan had first to train and empower a number of facilitators on human rights and welfare issues, and then they would discuss such issues in the communities, again making sure that the communities would be the ones deciding when and what to change. Both traditional and modern forms of communication were used, but always based on a participatory mode. In 1997, 20 women of a small village in Senegal stood in front of a group of journalists and openly and formally announced that their community had abandoned the practice of FGC. Since then another 1,740 communities have followed the same path. Villages that made the changes and abandoned FGC become instrumental in influencing other villages to do the same, thus affecting the overall social network. Once this change starts to occur in some villages, changing this practice also appeals to the other communities' interests because marriages often occur among people of neighboring villages. Participatory communication thus is not only used to generate knowledge and reflect about change but also as a way to promote diffusion of innovations at a social level.

behavior change, social change, and so forth), nobody doubts the challenges implied. Since it is human nature to maintain the status quo and to be suspicious of any action requiring a modification of well-established beliefs, habits, or practices, inducing change is a difficult task. Sustainable change can be achieved only if people can see the need and the related benefits, and take an active part in that change. That is why a successful communication strategy must identify the appropriate approaches, techniques, and tools to engage stakeholders in the process leading to change.

The complexity of designing an effective strategy—with emphasis on effective—highlights the need for a professional application of theoretical principles and practical approaches in development communication. Some of the failures of projects and programs are not only due to the unprofessional or poor application of communication but are also due to the neglect of communication altogether, especially in projects dealing with straightforward issues needing simple, clear-cut technical solutions.

Another major source of problems affecting results of development initiatives often resides in insufficient common understanding of key issues. The Windows of Perceptions—WOPs—is another tool used in participatory rural communication appraisal (PRCA), not only to analyze the problem and its causes, but also to contrast and compare the perceptions of the problem and all related issues, such as needs, risks, and opportunities. WOPs originated from the realization that often development projects' failures and obstacles were not due to structural or technical causes, but to misinterpretations and differences in perceptions among different stakeholder groups about the problem itself and the intended change. In a number of cases, practitioners have successfully addressed these issues simply by including a step regarding WOPs in the planning sequence. This allowed the immediate identification of any gap or ambiguity that needed to be reconciled or clarified. The example in box 3.2 illustrates one of these cases.

Differences in perceptions and expectations can be a problem in all kinds of initiatives. Figure 3.3 presents a scenario[6] where software, designed by highly qualified computer experts, was not adopted as easily as expected by World Bank administrative staff, the intended users. The software was expected to improve work efficiency and effectiveness, thus making users' lives easier. Even though from a technical point of view the software was properly designed to improve work efficiency, the experts failed to fully understand and address users' less-technical mind-set and the software applications in everyday work. The result is illustrated in figure 3.3. The ISN (Information Solutions Network) column on the left represents the computer experts' intent and expectations, and the right column describes the World Bank administrative staff perceptions, which were significantly different from what the experts had expected.

Differences in perceptions are frequent but not the only cause of project failures. Another common cause that can damage results of well-intentioned projects is the

BOX 3.2 When Perceptions Diverge

In one development project, government officials identified an agricultural area in need of urgent assistance. Farmers were surviving through subsistence agriculture, that is, their harvest was consumed entirely for their survival. A donor was asked to fund a project to build a small dam that would serve the community. An irrigation project was designed to improve the living conditions of the community in the dry and remote rural area. The overall goal of the project was to increase food security and incomes.

The assumption was that with a regular supply of water throughout the year farmers could (1) exercise control over their crop production, thus ensuring enough food for each household on a regular basis, and (2) diversify their crop and adjust planting and growing schedules to meet market demands. The expected benefits, as envisioned by the project designers, were crop diversification leading to a richer diet; a decrease in malnutrition rates; income-generation through marketing more valuable crops (that is, tomatoes, carrots, and so forth); and finally, the overall benefit of making farmers more prosperous and confident in their abilities. With such positive expectations in mind, the dam was built after informing the local stakeholders about the construction but without consulting them or engaging them on the scope of the project.

After a couple of years, project management was worried about the large use and misuse of water but was confident about the success of the project. They considered charging a small fee to farmers for water use from the dam, originally provided free. With that, the situation, already tense, started to deteriorate dramatically. As a last resource, communication specialists were called in to help. A communication-based assessment, known as a participatory rural communication appraisal, was conducted to determine why farmers' participation was low and why many of them opposed the project.

The communication team, composed of local development workers and outside researchers, spent a couple of weeks in the community. They discovered that the perceptions of the community were the opposite of those envisioned by the project officers. Instead of feeling more confident and secure about food, the farmers felt trapped and less secure (see figure 1.1, presented in module 1, for a graphic illustration of this example). The main cause for these two divergent perceptions was found in the lack of communication with stakeholders before and during the project.

From the outset of the project, problems and solutions were perceived strictly from the point of view of "experts"; involving the local stakeholders in the process was not considered important. As a result, from the inception farmers were suspicious about the intentions of the project. When problems began to emerge, such as lack of proper training in new crop harvest, untimely availability of different seeds, lack of marketing knowledge, and so forth, project rejection grew stronger. By diversifying their crops, farmers decreased the production of necessary staple foods without gaining the expected benefits from crop diversification, and this increased their sense of insecurity.

Figure 3.3 Windows of Perceptions in a Software Innovation

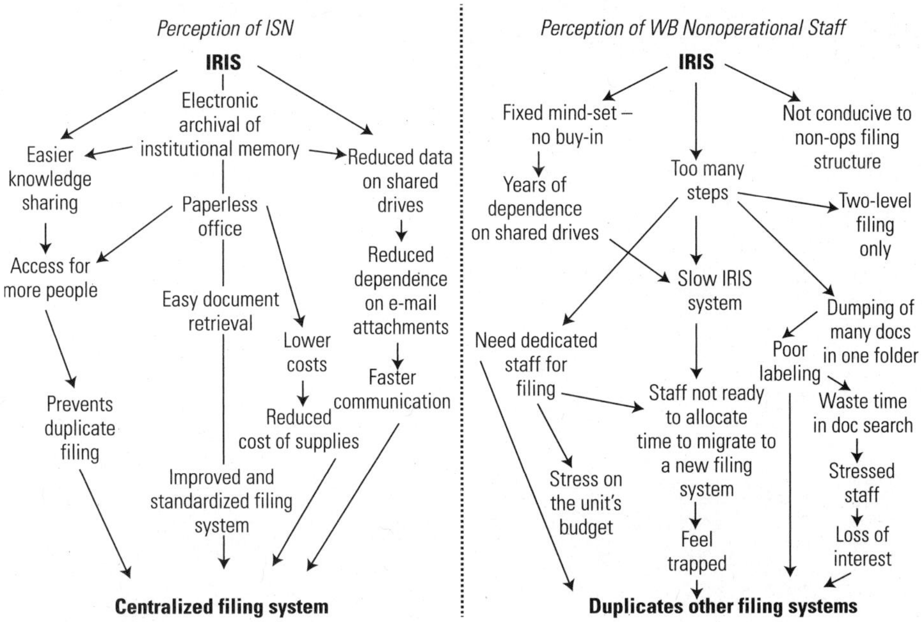

Source: Mefalopulos and Kamlongera 2004.

focus of the communication intervention on the wrong level of the awareness, knowledge, attitudes and behaviors (or practices) (AKAB) ladder (Anyaegbunam et al. 2004). For example, a development project may try to induce changes in attitude and behavior concerning personal hygiene, without realizing that people lack awareness of the issue as a problem. This highlights the peril that a well-intentioned project, based on a technically correct analysis of the situation and a "scientifically" appropriate solution, can still fail, as the example in box 3.3 illustrates.

Another powerful example, in its extreme simplicity, demonstrates the importance of listening before even thinking of communicating information, no matter how valuable and technically relevant. After years of costly research on how to improve agricultural productivity in a harsh region of Southern Africa, an agricultural project finally started its fieldwork, aimed at increasing crop productivity. Project extensionists had to train farmers and persuade them to adopt the proposed innovations in order to increase their crop production. The extensionists, however, soon encountered problems. They complained that local farmers were not only ignorant but also stubborn, because they refused to follow a number of procedures suggested to them as a way to improve their crop productivity.

One such procedure required farmers to plant their seeds in rows, while they had traditionally done it by broadcasting, throwing the seeds on the ground randomly. The project extensionists tried to persuade them that research showed a higher productivity rate when seeds were planted in rows. No matter how many times they explained, the farmers refused to adopt this and other new techniques.

3

BOX 3.3 Addressing the Correct Communication Entry Point or Level

A team of health experts conducted an investigation of the high rate of waterborne diseases in a region of Africa, some resulting in fatal illnesses, especially for children under five years of age. The specialists' research indicated that the situation was caused mostly by human waste contaminating the scarce water sources. The solution seemed obvious: build latrines—almost nonexistent in that region—to eliminate or greatly reduce the fecal problem. A major international organization was involved to fund and implement a project.

The multimillion-dollar initiative had a simple and direct approach. The project would provide training and supply all materials needed to build the latrines. At the same time, the plan intended to involve local people: the communities, on their side, would provide their time and labor to achieve the intended results. It would be a small price to pay for getting rid of a major health hazard, or so the experts thought!

A communication intervention aimed to inform people about the opportunity for training and materials to build latrines for free, in what was perceived by experts and project staff to be a major improvement in their lives. The communication campaign intended to persuade local villagers to build and use the latrines. The increased use of these latrines would greatly decrease the contamination of local water and subsequently reduce the rate of waterborne diseases as well.

Almost two years after the multimedia campaign began, a survey reported that only a tiny percentage of the concerned population joined the program and built a latrine. A communication assessment revealed the main reason: most local people did not associate the latrines with solving the waterborne disease problem. First, given the scarcely populated region, many locals were quite comfortable with not having a latrine and using "the bush." Secondly, most people were not aware of the causes of the illnesses, and therefore, they did not see any reason to undertake extra work and to change long-established behaviors.

The project strategy, well-intentioned and apparently correct in the application of the behavior change model, was a failure as far as the project and communication objectives were concerned. It assumed that people would adopt latrines regardless of other considerations. If a communication assessment had been carried out initially, it would have shown that audiences need to be aware of and knowledgeable about the issue, and their attitude should indicate a willingness to change, before a campaign is launched to change practices or behaviors. If awareness and willingness are not evident, the campaign needs to focus at those levels—raising awareness, providing knowledge, or changing attitudes—in a sequential order before addressing behavior change issues.

At that point, a communication team was called on to find effective ways to persuade farmers to adopt the innovations. As its first step, the team conducted an assessment of the situation and, as could be expected, found that there was a sound reason for the farmers' resistance. The area was infested with rodents and they were fond of the seeds. Farmers who planted in rows lost most of their seeds to rodents that were quick to figure out the pattern. Broadcasting their seeds was not due to ignorance but was a deliberate strategy that allowed farmers to save a significant amount of their crop from rodents. Incredible as it may seem, none of the project staff had thought of asking the farmers why they would not adopt this technique!

The Conspiracy of Silence

Instances such as the one illustrated above occur more often than one might think. In Western culture speaking out is a given, but in many other cultures, it is not. The art of listening and creating space for dialog is often more difficult than the art of talking and imparting knowledge. In many places, women might not talk in the presence of men; in others, youth will not talk in the presence of older members of the community. In many cases, villagers and other marginalized groups might adopt silence in the presence of external experts or might only respond to please them, rather than engaging in issues of substance. Ascroft (2006: 75), presenting further support to this argument, states, "There is an unintended conspiracy of courtesy on the part of local nationals, preventing crucial communication between them and alien experts from occurring freely."

These examples highlight the importance of having proper (that is, professionally applied) communication in all development interventions, regardless of the nature or sector of the interventions. When done at the early stages of the program or project cycle, a communication-based assessment can have a strong preventive function, eliminating or greatly reducing possible misunderstandings, potential conflicts, political risks, and other unforeseeable threats to success and sustainability.

When included halfway through a project, CBA is likely to be less effective than it would have been if adopted from the beginning, focusing on damage-control approaches or on supporting predetermined objectives not always properly designed or widely accepted by stakeholders. Proper timing of the communication inclusion affects overall effectiveness, both from the economic point of view (cutting unforeseen expenses for damage-control initiatives), and from the sustainability point of view (ownership and long-term commitment strengthened by involvement of relevant stakeholders in a project's objectives).

Applying Communication across Sectors

Communication-based assessment is not focused strictly on investigating communication issues. Rather, it uses communication techniques and tools to conduct empirical research on thematic issues of any nature: health, infrastructure, governance, climate change, rural development, education, and so forth. In this sense, it is quite different from the usual communication needs assessment, which investigates aspects related to communication issues only, such as media outlets and policies, institutional capacities, information, and communication networks.

Naturally, communication needs assessments are still important to investigate specific communication issues or as a subset of the broader communication-based assessment,[7] which usually also includes an analysis of the communication environment. An instance about a land reform project can help to further clarify the practical implications of the difference between a communication needs assessment and a communication-based assessment. If asked to implement a communication needs assessment, a specialist would investigate the communication environment (for example, media available, information systems, institutional capacities, audience profiling, and so forth) and the information needed to achieve the objectives of the project.

On the other hand, the CBA, before addressing communication issues, would use its methods and techniques to facilitate dialog with stakeholders and consider risks and opportunities in the political context. It would uncover crucial points such as different perceptions on land issues and how they rank in comparison with other issues. To better understand the entire situation, this approach would entail interviewing local officials, government representatives, farmers, and whoever else is related to the issue of relevance. It would require listening to different voices and linking their perceptions and knowledge back to project objectives. By assessing the situation in a cross-cutting manner, communication specialists help project managers to identify and properly arrange the various pieces of the puzzle, which include the communication-related ones as well as other technical and political issues related to project design.

For ultimate success, communication specialists must collaborate with sector specialists and key stakeholders. In addition to task team leaders on World Bank projects, DevComm staff seek the active cooperation of regional and local communication officers, who are familiar with issues of significance in that particular context, and with sector experts related to specific projects.

A CBA ensures that the cultural, economic and political risks in designing a project are minimized and that the development objectives are understood and shared among relevant stakeholders. Although this may appear to be a close duplicate of a social assessment and there might be some overlapping between the scope and analysis of the two approaches, the overlap is limited and the two assessments serve different purposes.

A CBA does probe social issues, but it also investigates other relevant political and technical issues, and it is of particular value in those thematic areas that cut across various sectors, such as governance or climate change. In addition, it investigates key issues related to communication and the networks used to gather and exchange information. Finally, a CBA addresses the overall project situation and can provide useful inputs for the overall design of the project as well as for the specific communication strategy.

3.1.2 Communication Applications in Operations

Communication-based assessment's main scope is to assess the political, social, cultural, and economic environment in which a development initiative is situated, exploring the best options for change. By engaging stakeholders and taking their voices, knowledge, and perceptions into account from the early stages of the project cycle, this approach strengthens the effectiveness and sustainability of the initiative. It is a valuable research method capable of probing all relevant issues, linking them, and ranking them in a comprehensive framework, regardless of their relationship to communication.

As a research approach using a substantial number of qualitative methods, communication-based assessment usually also includes or requires quantitative methods, such as baseline studies and surveys, to validate and quantify the extent of the initial findings. A survey investigates the perceptions and knowledge of particular audiences regarding specific issues, while a baseline study at the beginning of an intervention helps to measure the extent of the impact of that intervention after the completion of the project. In some cases, it can also help to further focus or refocus the nature of an intervention.

CBA can vary greatly in length depending on when it is performed and on the nature and characteristics of the project (size, sector, and so forth). When conducted in a relatively "quick and dirty" way, the investigation might be conducted in a few days or a few weeks. It is usually performed by DevComm staff, in some cases after an opinion survey, in other cases at the very beginning, with a follow-up survey or opinion poll done later to quantify the level of knowledge, attitudes, or behaviors related to specific issues identified in the investigation.

A relatively rapid CBA can provide valuable inputs for the design of a communication strategy, but in most instances, it leads to further investigations of key issues. In such cases, CBA provides a first snapshot of the situation and is instrumental in defining what areas and issues need to be further explored and probed through empirical research. Depending on the nature and extent of the project, the empirical research (that is, data collection and analysis) can take from a few weeks to a few months, especially when surveys and perceptions studies need to be designed and administered.

When DevComm performs a rapid version, the budget needed is relatively low. However, this is often only the first step in the more in-depth research needed to collect relevant data for the strategy design. For instance, in a proposed reform of the energy sector, CBA can help to identify key stakeholders and their opinions, assessing the risks, opportunities, and other issues surrounding the project. The findings then might require that a survey be carried out at a national level to gauge the nature and extent of the issues as perceived by various groups of stakeholders. Quantifying the perceptions and attitudes of stakeholders is necessary, not only to ensure a valid project design, but also to make key decisions regarding the best communication strategy to adopt. Table 3.3 summarizes the basic steps that illustrate the scope and outcomes of this approach.

In CBA the first part of the analysis usually focuses on the "why" of the situation. This is done through qualitative techniques such as interviews, focus groups, and rapid diagnostics. The second part is expected to probe deeper, addressing the "what" and "how much" of the circumstances, in order to triangulate the initial findings and to quantify them. Opinion polls and surveys are some of the tools fre-

Table 3.3 CBA Main Steps

Basic Steps	Activities	Outputs
1. Become acquainted with key issues	Review of relevant documentation about the project, its objectives, and the problem that it is trying to address	Identify knowledge gaps needed to be probed during the CBA
2. Identify, define, and engage key stakeholders (building trust)	Identify, engage in dialog, and explore stakeholders' perceptions on key issues	Relevant findings
3. Assess communication networks and capacities	Identify and analyze the communication and information systems of relevant stakeholders	Relevant findings
4. Probe problems, causes, risks, and opportunities	Explore the causes of the problems; assess political, technical, and economic risks and opportunities	Relevant findings
5. Assess and rank options and solutions	Analyze and discuss possible solutions to achieve the intended change	Relevant findings
6. Validate extent of the problem(s)	Use surveys or other quantitative techniques to validate and assess the extent of the problem on key issues for the relevant audiences or stakeholder groups	Relevant findings
7. Transform best options/solutions in objectives (and define impact indicators)	Synthesize all information and transform data into usable accounts to define or confirm proper (project and/or communication) objectives (and indicators to assess impact)	Define, validate, or refine project objectives and define communication objectives

Source: Author.

quently used to this end. The range of the tools, techniques, and methods used is wide: communication specialists select the most appropriate ones according to circumstances and objectives.

To conclude this part, it should be emphasized that communication-based assessment is not simply a tool, but a set of methods and tools to assess the development situation and to engage relevant stakeholders in key issues related to the intended change. It is instrumental in providing the inputs needed for the communication strategy design.

Communication-Based Assessment Toolbox

This section addresses a list of basic tools used frequently during the communication-based assessment. Some are particularly useful in the rapid version; others require a longer time for preparation and completion. This is not meant to be an exhaustive list. On the contrary, since there are a number of publications concentrating on such methods and tools, this toolbox simply intends to present some of the common ones and to illustrate the rationale for their use.

Interviews, focus group discussions, perception studies, surveys, and baseline studies are among the most common techniques used in the communication-based assessment. Interviews and discussions in focus groups, coupled with the review of secondary data, are usually the most useful tools for acquiring quick, firsthand knowledge of the situation. Surveys and other studies are done to verify perceptions and opinions or to refine the initial findings and to assess the extent of the change needed.

Interviews are qualitative tools to acquire knowledge or to probe specific issues, usually with one person at a time. This tool can be structured in different ways: free discussions around the topic of interest; in-depth discussions, usually with knowledgeable individuals; semistructured discussions with a predetermined list of questions for open-ended and closed-ended questions, providing answers that are easier to analyze, compare, and contrast. Semistructured interviews are used frequently, since they provide enough space for the respondent to answer freely and provide useful insights, while keeping a certain rigor and consistency to the issues addressed. In this technique, the main challenge is identifying the key persons to interview, those who have the most significant insights or knowledge about the issues of interest.

(*cont.*)

Communication-Based Assessment Toolbox (*cont.*)

Focus group discussions are another qualitative research tool derived from marketing. These are used to probe the knowledge, attitudes, and perceptions of specific groups of people around topics of interest. Focus group discussions are moderated by a facilitator and are usually composed of six to ten individuals who have some connection to issue being discussed. It is important for the group to be homogeneous or selected according to appropriate criteria, because the dynamics within the group help to portray the situation as perceived by a specific segment of the whole population. Depending on the topic and scope, the composition of the focus group can be based on criteria such as gender, age, socioeconomic status, religion, educational level, occupational status, or relation to the issue of relevance.

To implement the focus group discussions, the invited individuals sit in a circle for face-to-face contact. A note taker sits outside the circle. The facilitator asks a set of questions aimed to start and guide the discussion. His or her task is to keep an open space to encourage input from everybody, while making sure that the discussion is not derailed by issues of no relevance to the scope of the focus group. Focus groups have proved to be very successful tools in marketing and have been used successfully in a number of situations in development.

Baseline studies are surveys designed to probe perceptions, awareness, knowledge, attitudes, and behaviors of specific groups of stakeholders. They are usually carried out twice, the first time during the research phase to triangulate, validate, and measure the initial findings in a quantitative manner. For example, if the assessment indicates that many stakeholders are familiar with the causes of waterborne diseases, the baseline, among other things, will confirm that indication and provide a reliable estimate about the number of people who are familiar with the causes and those who are not. This kind of information is necessary for the design of a media campaign or other applications of the communication strategy. Baseline studies are then carried out a second time after the activities have been implemented in order to assess the impact obtained. By comparing and analyzing the pre- and post-discussion situation, baselines are able to evaluate the impact of the communication intervention accurately. Furthermore, baseline findings can refine the communication objectives and further refine the indicators needed to monitor the process.

Surveys are a research method often based on the administration of questionnaires to specific samples of people to explore or explain a given situation.

Questionnaires can be closed-ended, containing questions requiring a choice between the indicated answers (yes-no, like-dislike, and so forth), or open-ended, allowing the respondents to provide the answer in their own wording. Clearly, closed-ended answers are more limited in the potential insights provided, but they are also easier and less time-consuming to collect and analyze than open-ended ones. Design of surveys is a very sensitive task because the selection of questions and wording can lead to biased answers or overlook valuable insights. The role of the administrators of questionnaires is also crucial; they must be neutral in respect to the questions to eliminate any perception of bias in answers by the respondents.

Opinion polls are surveys to discover the opinions of selected, usually large, audiences.[8] This tool aims to identify, observe, and predict the patterns related to specific issues. Political polls, for instance, are intended to show which way the public is likely to cast their votes. Opinion polls are especially useful in positioning an institution, reform, or other issues in a broader context, helping to define the level of communication intervention needed.

Participatory Rural Communication Appraisal

Different from the other tools in this section, participatory rural communication appraisal, or PRCA, is not a specific tool or technique but rather a practical methodological approach that includes a set of methods and techniques to address a wide range of research situations, including those involving stakeholders with limited, or a lack of, literacy skills. Because a PRCA has a strong participatory connotation, it is particularly appropriate for community-driven development projects and other programs with a high emphasis on people's participation.

PRCA was first developed in Africa to fill a gap that emerged during the initial phase of a project meant to promote the use of participatory communication in the Southern Africa Development Community (SADC) region.[9] Research indicated that communication assessment methods were rather extractive (that is, collecting information from beneficiaries to be analyzed and used by external experts) and relied on the traditional vertical model of communication, allowing little space for people's participation. On the other hand, pure participatory approaches, such as participatory rural appraisal (PRA) and participatory action research (PAR), had strong horizontal connotations in their methods and techniques, but they did not have a specific focus on communication issues. PRCA fills that gap.

(*cont.*)

3

Communication-Based Assessment Toolbox (*cont.*)

Through PRCA, outside experts and people in the community can share their knowledge and make joint decisions concerning development issues. PRCA redefines communication as an interactive process that facilitates dialog; poses and refines problems; and assists in the design, planning, and implementation of development activities. It is especially useful in rural settings with grassroots communities, but its principles can be, and have been, adapted to a wide range of circumstances, including urban settings and interventions directed at higher-level decision makers. Often the most challenging part of a PRCA consists of starting up a dialog with stakeholders, especially if previous tensions are present, and gaining a mutual trust.

Because PRCA is placed within a clearly defined two-way communication model, its first step must be establishing a dialog among external (national and international experts) and internal (people who are affected and have a direct interest in the project) stakeholders. This process is best represented through the metaphorical image presented as the Johari Window. In PRCA, the starting point is always the knowledge shared by both parties (that is, community and project staff), which forms the basis of addressing the unknown by combining and applying knowledge exclusive to each group.

PRCA can be defined as an empowerment communication research approach, based on dialog. It involves people, especially rural people, in the decision-making process to design effective strategies to address their problems. Capacity building and individual empowerment are two of its major concerns, but these are attained while dealing with specific, practical issues addressed by communication. In PRCA, participation is subsumed or included within communication, which is not defined as the unbalanced vertical flow currently used in media and persuasion, but rather is closer to its original meaning, that of sharing.

PRCA has been conceived as a participatory communication research method that can be applied in two main types of situations: formulating new projects or improving and supporting the objectives of ongoing projects. Its findings are crucial in the design and planning of a strategy to address the identified needs, opportunities, problems, and solutions—or NOPS, as they are called in PRCA. NOPS provide the basis on which to build an effective communication strategy.

As mentioned previously, many projects introduce the communication component only when things are going poorly, thus greatly reducing its benefits. In such instances, communication is used as a diagnostic instrument, once the "illness" has already manifested itself, rather than a prescriptive one, preventing its appearance, as should ideally be the case. The following tools are some of those adopted most commonly in PRCA and similar approaches. They can be employed in a wide range of situations, but they are of greater use in rural and community-driven projects.

Typically PRCA starts wide, gradually narrowing or zooming in on the issues of interest. For the unfamiliar reader, this process is simplified by dividing it in four sequential phases, each using a set of PRCA techniques and tools for a specific purpose, namely, (1) to warm up, get to know each other and build trust among stakeholders; (2) to know the community better and to be acquainted with stakeholders' perceptions and their preferred information channels and communication resources; (3) to assess the situation (that is, needs, opportunities, problems, and solutions), prioritize problems, and address the main causes; and, finally, (4) to identify the best options and opportunities that can be addressed through communication.

The techniques and tools that can be used to achieve the above objectives are numerous. The following list highlights some of the most renowned tools.

Sketch map—local stakeholders drawing a map of their community. Maps can be general or focused on specific issues, depending on the situation. Generally they highlight social (schools, and so forth), cultural (churches, and so forth) and economic (crop fields, and so forth) resources available. The map helps break the ice by involving the community in an exercise in which all can participate, regardless of their skills and level of education.

Transect walk—a walk through the community of interest by the external researchers with a group of local stakeholders. Its purpose is to become familiar with the surroundings and to identify possible issues of interest, while breaking the ice.

Time lines—drawing a list of important past events in community life aimed at learning about the history and other key issues, which could be relevant to the problem. Often present conditions are rooted in the past, and this exercise helps to understand how they might evolve in the future.

Seasonal calendar—the seasonal activities of a community. Especially in rural settings, this exercise is important not only for general understanding but also to know when to plan activities requiring the involvement of the community (for example, when to call meetings), particularly when coupled with the daily activity profiles. These profiles trace the daily activities of community members and can, for instance, indicate what would be the best time to air a radio program.

(*cont.*)

Communication-Based Assessment Toolbox (*cont.*)

Problem/solution tree—an analytical exercise that relies on dialog to assess the main causes of the situation where change is sought. It can be rather complex, and the communication specialist must act as a facilitator, leaving enough space not to inhibit dialog but being careful to maintain the discussion within the intended boundaries. The participatory nature of this exercise can often provide unexpected results, proving very useful when problems are turned into solutions, setting the basis for the communication strategy.

Ranking—listing the main problems or issues of concern and then having the community weight them by assigning value to each. It can be done in an open-ended way to probe all sorts of problems or key issues, or it can be focused on specific issues (for example, health-issues ranking, wealth ranking, media, and so forth). Sometimes the first exercise is followed by pairwise ranking, meant to contrast and compare different issues.

Windows of perceptions—aim at uncovering and defining the perceptions of key stakeholder groups, mainly on problems, but can also be applied to needs, risks, and opportunities. It is often carried out through nondirective participatory communication tools (for example, dialog) facilitated by a development communication specialist.

Livelihood map—a map specifically directed at discovering the sources of livelihood in the community and how important each one is. This is very important when a project or program is expected to affect the income of a community.

Venn diagram—a type of mapping, involving listing, ranking, and connecting of key institutions and relevant sources of information for the community. It reveals the influential sources that stakeholders rely on, indicating the information flow among them. Linkage mapping is another tool that can be applied for a similar purpose.

Gender analysis—more than a specific exercise; it includes a number of techniques and tools aimed at finding out specific gender-related information (for example, through a daily calendar, activity profiles, and so forth). Each PRCA tool must be gender-sensitive and adapt according to the situation and cultural settings. For instance, in some settings women might not be allowed to talk or might feel intimidated talking in the presence of their men or to men from outside their family or community. PRCA researchers need to be aware of these issues and adjust accordingly.

3.2 Phase 2—Communication Strategy Design

The idiomatic expression "jumping the gun" (starting a race before the signal to begin) represents one of the most common flaws in the application of communication interventions; that is, a strategy design is created without analyzing the situation properly and understanding all of the crucial issues and perceptions of the various groups (Anyaegbunam et al. 2004). It is not a rare occurrence for communication specialists to be called in to assist projects whose objectives are blurred, controversial, or, more simply, poorly defined. Devising a communication strategy on those premises is a sure recipe for failure. The terms "strategy" and "strategic" are used frequently in the context of communication for development; however, this does not necessarily mean they are used appropriately.

The common understanding of the term "strategy," is "a plan or method for achieving specific objectives." Yet in order to achieve a goal or objective, certain requirements must be met. First of all, the objective must be not only specific but also feasible and clearly stated; secondly, the needed resources should be available. In sum, a strategy is about achieving specific, feasible, and clearly stated objectives, with the available resources, within an established timeline. Similarly, a communication strategy can be defined as a well-planned series of actions aimed at achieving specific objectives through the use of communication methods, techniques, and approaches (Mefalopulos and Kamlongera 2004).

This concept seems like common sense, and yet it is often neglected when communication experts are asked to design a strategy capable of addressing long-term problems with a quick fix in a short time. Not infrequently, managers demand a "miraculous" communication strategy, often without even seeing the need for a communication assessment. These kinds of requests occur too often and make it difficult for communication specialists to resist management pressure for quick action that is bound to fail or to produce only short-term results.

The definitions for "strategy" and "communication strategy" highlight that the starting point should lie in the objectives. When called in to provide support in an ongoing project through communication, the development communication specialist's first step should be to obtain a clear definition or validation of the project objectives. Once this is accomplished, the specialist can work on defining the communication objectives in support of the project.

Effective definition of the objectives is not always an easy task because proper identification and analysis of the main causes of a problem or situation are needed. This information defines the strategy objectives. To be effective, strategies should be based on sound research data, and in the new communication paradigm, research is not simply an extractive tool (that is, researchers "extracting" information to be elaborated on and used by outside experts), but part of a heuristic process engaging stakeholders in the investigative process.

Among its many definitions, communication entails making human interaction possible on a daily basis. This has somehow obscured the theoretical knowledge and specific skills needed to be a specialist in communication studies or, as Beltrán Salmón (2000) names it, a "communicologist." Being able to communicate well is not the same as being a professional communication specialist, or certainly not the same as being a development communication specialist. In addition to the theoretical and applicative knowledge in communication and related fields, development communication specialists should also be familiar with research methods and the foundations of planning and strategy design. Managers should rely on specialists with the proper skills for design of communication operational strategies.

It is not likely that an architect would be asked to provide the complete design of a building in a week, or that a sociologist would be asked to design and conduct a national survey on three days notice. The author of this book, however, has been asked more than once to perform communication miracles by designing "here-and-now" strategies in a few days, without sufficient background information or on the basis of fuzzy project objectives. Regardless of how strong the pressure is to deliver as soon as possible, the development communication specialist should not hesitate to stand firm about what is possible to achieve and what is not, according to the available information and the given time frame. It is usually feasible to make the case that it is in the project managers' interest to allow adequate time and resources to collect and interpret the information needed to shape the proper strategy and enhance the overall results.

Development communication specialists are not spin doctors or rainmakers—they should not be asked to perform their work in less than rigorous ways. When adopted in ongoing projects, development communication's effectiveness is heavily dependent on the project objectives. If those objectives are not well defined, if they are perceived differently by different groups of stakeholders, or if there are knowledge gaps in the way they are perceived, further research should be sought before defining the strategy design.

When communication is used to assess and probe the situation from the start, the strategy design will be proactive and more effective, since it can draw from a wide range of options based on the inputs of the wider stakeholders' engagement. On the other hand, when called to assist in an ongoing project, development communication specialists may find themselves facing a challenge different from what they expected. Sometimes they need to spend a considerable amount of time persuading the project management to get better data about the situation before operational work begins. In order to design an effective communication strategy, it is not enough to have a general idea about the solution. The key question to be addressed is not "what" is happening, but "why" it is happening.

3.2.1 Foundations of Communication Strategy Design

In discussing the basics of strategy design, the reader should keep in mind the broader role of communication, instrumental in assessing and linking various sectoral issues such as environment, governance, health, agriculture, or human rights, and in supporting overall project design. Communication-based assessment provides the basis for an effective strategy since its outputs (that is, definitions of the objectives) become the inputs needed to design the strategy leading to change.

Development is all about change. To be achieved effectively, that change must be agreed to by, and not imposed on, relevant stakeholders. Communication ensures sound foundations upon which to build the development initiative leading to change. Those foundations typically include an extensive knowledge of the stakeholders' sociocultural background, their positions on the issues of interest, an in-depth analysis of the causes of the situation to be changed, and most important, the definition in a clear and measurable manner of the objectives to be achieved. Once these elements are defined clearly, the planning process can begin, keeping in mind the categorization and rationale for adopting monologic and dialogic communication and the approaches related to each of the two modes, as mentioned previously and discussed extensively in modules 1 and 2.

Before entering into the various elements of the strategy, the communication specialist should look at the broader picture and decide which type of communication mix is needed. For instance, a communication strategy in support of a decentralization program might require (1) strengthening the internal communication of key institutions, (2) improving the image of the project or institution, and (3) engaging stakeholders in order to support change. In this case, the communication strategy will be multipronged, as it will have internal, corporate, and development communication strategic lines of intervention. In some cases, advocacy may also be required. Quite frequently, the communication strategy is drawn within a single type of communication.

When considering which communication approaches, media, or messages would be most effective to achieve the intended change, the development communication specialist must look back into the research findings. Mass dissemination of brochures and other literature on how to prevent the spread of a disease is of little use in areas with high illiteracy rates. A social marketing approach might be most effective in a health campaign, but it might not be so effective in a community-driven development project. Airing TV spots highlighting the effects and risks of drug or alcohol abuse in teens at parties might resonate well with parents, but these spots are likely to be less effective with teens, the primary audience. Factors such as these need to be considered and effectively included in the strategy mix, which combines professional knowledge with creative skills, making the design of a strategy an exercise in the art and science of communication.

Every design of a communication strategy is unique in content, methods, and media. The sequence to be followed when designing a strategy, however, tends to be consistent across the whole range of applications. The sequence described in this section intends to provide a basic frame of reference, especially useful for those who might need to manage the planning and monitoring of such a strategy.

Previous knowledge and experiences acquired in the field allow the use of this framework in a flexible and personalized manner. When designing a strategy, it is always important to be fully aware that the starting point is not the audience, nor is it the message. It is the problem or the desired change to be achieved with all its implications and related background information. That is why, in presenting the steps for designing an effective communication strategy, it is helpful to start with a presequence (see table 3.3), which could be used as a checklist to monitor the progress and effectiveness of the strategy.

The following example illustrates and clarifies some of the key issues involved in the logical organization of strategy design, which must always begin from a clearly defined objective. A major conservation project in one of the world's principal forests has been implementing a multifold strategy to maintain and protect certain areas of that forest. A communication specialist was called in to assist on a specific component, dealing with a major problem—the destruction of significant parts of the forest caused by farmers who burn their fields at the outskirts of the protected area. The project manager asked the specialist to devise a strategy to eliminate, or at least greatly reduce, this problem based on the data available. Table 3.4 shows the simplified analysis of the situation presented to the communication specialist.

The management of the project felt that the information above should be sufficient to initiate a communication intervention aimed at eliminating or reducing the destruction of the forest by these fires, but the communication specialist should know better. To design an effective strategy, a professional needs well-defined, specific, and appropriate objectives (that is, based on research), as well as in-depth

Table 3.4 Defining the Objective

Problem (as defined by management)	Main Causes of the Problem	Stakeholders' Perspective/AKAB	Solution/Change Needed/Objective
Deforestation caused by fires	Farmers using fires to clear their fields	Not sufficiently known	Persuade farmers to stop burning down the forest

Source: Author.

Note: AKAB stands for awareness, knowledge, attitudes, and behaviors (or practices) about the issue or issues of interest to the various stakeholders' groups. In the relevant literature, the "B" for behavior is often substituted by a "P" for practices.

knowledge associated with the causes of the problem. The farmers' backgrounds, systems of beliefs, perceptions, and knowledge of the specific issues are all variables that need to be known. Moreover, from the information synthesized in this table, it is not possible to know if those fires were set intentionally to burn beyond the farmers' fields, or if they were mostly the result of careless acts.

If reliable data regarding the main causes of the problem or of stakeholders' perceptions and knowledge are not available, the strategy is at risk of failing. In this situation, the communication specialist should not try to make an "enlightened guess"; rather, he or she should demand that a communication-based assessment be performed to fill the knowledge gaps. It is not enough to have identified the farmers as the main cause of the problem unless it is known why they are letting the fires burn the forest.

Without precise information, it is impossible to know which approach to apply (for example, social marketing, community mobilization, training and education, and so forth) and which level to address (that is, awareness, knowledge, attitude, or behavior). In order to identify and properly position the starting point for the communication intervention, it is vital to know the perceptions and positions of the farmers. A baseline study conducted to define and quantify farmers' awareness, knowledge, attitudes, and practices indicated that farmers did not have any specific intention to burn the forest. This could be attributed to a combination of two factors: their limited knowledge about fire control techniques when clearing their fields, and their lack of understanding of any problem or negative implications in letting the forest burn.

On the basis of those findings, the communication strategy was designed around two issues: a capacity-building program and an awareness-raising campaign. The first part was designed to provide technical training about fire control techniques to farmers of the area. The second part of the intervention was aimed at raising the awareness and knowledge of farmers and other relevant local stakeholders about the value and benefits of preserving the forest. If a proper communication-based assessment had been performed at the outset, the problem could have been defined more effectively as follows: "The destruction of the forest caused by fires set by local farmers when clearing their fields, which is due to their limited knowledge of fire-control techniques and to their lack of commitment to preserving the forest." The relative objective could have been promptly defined accordingly.

Defining Objectives: The Key Step

The statement above brings the process closer to devising an effective problem-solving strategy by identifying and assessing not only the problem but also, and especially, its causes, which are instrumental in defining the proper objectives. The definitions of objectives constitute the link between the communication-based assessment sequence (table 3.3) and the sequence for strategy design (table 3.5). Once the objectives have been defined and validated, the strategy can be delineated. To make strategy design easier, the objectives should be identified in a way that is specific, measurable, achievable, realistic, and timely (SMART).

A communication strategy meant to support an ongoing project should start by reviewing all relevant documentation of the project and then be followed by a communication-based assessment to identify sound and SMART objectives. If one could select one element of the strategy to be error-free (that is, technically sound, perceived as equally important by all stakeholders, socially and culturally appropriate, and so forth), that element should be the objectives.

Despite being the starting point, the sine qua non, as well as the completion point of any strategy, objectives are often the most overlooked factors in project design and the cause of most problems in a project. The overall communication strategy, therefore, should be devised and refined by constantly checking and revising each element of the design. Objectives are the core of the strategy, but each element is important and should be carefully considered because each is linked to the others and can affect the final outcome.

Most of the success of a communication strategy depends on the way the objectives are identified and formulated. The first step in table 3.5 includes the review of the focal problem (that is the root cause or causes of the main problem), as a way to double check and triangulate the validity and soundness of the objectives. The table highlights the thinking or logical sequence constituting the framework for designing a communication strategy. Each step is based on the previous one, and a column defining the implications of each step in a real-life situation is included. Some redundancy or overlapping of the steps is justified, not only to give the deserved emphasis to certain steps, but also to make it easier for the reader/learner to comprehend how this sequence is applied in practical situations.

As stated earlier, to make the strategy effective and easier to design, a communication objective should be as SMART as possible. This also helps focus the design to support the broader project or program objective (usually referred to as the management objective). The management objective is also the starting point of the Five Management Decisions (FMD), a tool devised by DevComm to help manage and monitor certain types of communication interventions. This tool is of particular use when applied in projects with a specific objective requiring a straightforward linear communication strategy. In the final section of this module there is a more detailed explanation of this tool.

3.2.2 Core Elements in Designing a Strategy

The type of method or approach to be used in designing a communication strategy depends largely on the complexity of the objectives. The example presented in table 3.5

Table 3.5 Main Steps of Communication Strategy Design

Basic Steps	Main Activities	Practical Example
1. Definition of SMART objectives (reviewing focal problem and its causes)	Solutions transformed into objectives in a feasible and measurable way	Reduction in the incidence of forest lost due to uncontrolled fires by 80% within next two years
2. Definition of primary stakeholders (1SHs) and secondary audiences and stakeholders (2SHs)	Define and probe main groups of interest or audiences, including those indirectly related to the issues	Local farmers (their cultural and socioeconomic context), their families, other local actors, NGOs, and governmental agencies
3. Definition of type/level of change	Define if change is related to awareness, knowledge, attitudes, behaviors, mobilization, collaboration, or mediation	For 1SHs: improve knowledge and skills of fire control techniques For 2SHs: raise awareness of consequence of fires
4. Define communication approaches or tactics	Select the most effective communication approaches (linear or interactive mode)	For 1SHs: capacity building, technical training For 2SHs: awareness-raising media campaign
5. Select channels or media	Select most appropriate media for 1SHs and 2SHs	For 1SHs: use preferred sites and venues to provide information For 2SHs: select appropriate media mix in that context
6. Design messages or content topics	Define key content/message and the most effective way to package them	For 1SHs: instructional design, key technical issues For 2SHs: messages for raising awareness and knowledge
7. Expected results once the strategy is carried out	Set goal for 1SHs: a change in behaviors or practices to reduce forest destruction Set goal for 2SHs: raising the awareness about the importance of conservation	1SHs: adopt more secure techniques to reduce incidence of uncontrolled fires 2SHs: become more aware of the importance or benefits of preserving the forest

Source: Author.

is straightforward, but in many other instances, the degree of complexity and difficulty is much greater, and the communication strategy needs to reflect that. For instance, a project supporting decentralization at a national level may require different types of communication (corporate, advocacy, and development communication), and the development communication modality might contain different approaches, such as awareness raising about the responsibilities and benefits of decentralization; behavior change of local administrators; community mobilization to ensure transparency and accountability; and, at a national level, a multimedia campaign to support the reform of the state. Such a multifaceted reality requires a complex strategy design.

In those cases where management objectives are straightforward (requiring unidimensional change in behavior) the use of the Five Communication Management Decisions template is an effective tool to manage and monitor the communication strategy (see toolbox at the end of this component). In any case, whatever tool or method is being used to design a strategy, there are certain elements that are always part of the design. The following pages present a basic illustration of these elements.

Audiences and Stakeholder Groups

Unlike other publications that refer exclusively to audiences, the Sourcebook prefers to use both terms, "audiences" and "stakeholders," since in many cases (for example, CBA, community mobilization, and so forth) the role of stakeholders should be a proactive one, and the term "audiences" would not reflect that connotation. Selecting the audiences to which the communication action should be directed usually is not difficult. Having an in-depth understanding of their cultural background, opinions, and other relevant information could be more difficult.

In order to select the most appropriate media and to design a message effectively, the communication specialist needs to know the norms, values of reference, actions, and aspirations of the audience. This can be achieved by adopting a high degree of empathy and doing proper research. Communicating the scientifically correct information is seldom enough to change audiences' attitudes and behaviors.

In the United States, a campaign to raise teenagers' awareness about the danger of smoking and to persuade them to quit had little effect, because the message (long-term health danger), even though scientifically correct and effectively packaged, would not resonate with teens. In the development context, a campaign to support a reform to fight corruption in the Philippines proved its value when messages meant to win the support of the government, the civil society, and the parliamentarians were designed and packaged in different media, keeping in mind the specific background and perspective of each audience (Campos and Syquia 2006).

Even in more interactive approaches, where the term "groups of stakeholders" is substituted for "audiences," it is important to be familiar with their backgrounds. To use a certain technique or visual aid, the communication specialist might need to know the educational background and cultural sensitivities of the stakeholders to make sure that the material used is appropriate to the context and not offensive to anybody. Stakeholders' and audiences' interests and priorities in the issue must be consistent with that of the project staff to avoid the common mistake of imparting knowledge that is technically sound but out of sync with people's perceptions.

Levels of Change

The communication objectives of approaches within the monologic mode imply a level of change that usually falls within one of the following categories: awareness, knowledge, attitudes, and behaviors (or practices) or AKAB. On the other hand, in the dialogic mode, change can be addressing broader issues at a social level, such as mobilization, collaboration, and (conflict) mediation or resolution.

In the first case the communication intervention will basically aim at raising awareness, increasing knowledge, changing the attitudes, and changing the behaviors (and/or adopting an innovation). This sequence, at times called the ladder of change, needs to be followed in order to induce change. The communication entry point is determined by the research, or CBA. If there is no awareness at all, the communication strategy will need to raise such awareness; it should then provide the knowledge about the issue and finally address specific attitudes and behaviors.

However, if the CBA reveals that relevant actors are aware of the problems and have the knowledge of how to change, the communication intervention could focus on the attitudes and behaviors right away. In any case one should not address specific behavior changes unless the previous steps have been addressed successfully or are already fulfilled. Trying to induce behavior change without the audience having the required knowledge or attitudes is likely to result in failure, as in the case illustrated in box 3.3.

Sometimes there is the need to address a change more on a social level, such as mobilizing communities to play an active part in the decentralization effort, having different groups of stakeholders collaborating on a common initiative, or mediating a conflict that has negative repercussions on the social development of the area. Such change is usually addressed by dialogic approaches. Inserting the required level of change in the strategy matrix helps to focus the intervention and ensure that the communication approaches and the evaluation indicators are in line with the objectives.

Basic Communication Approaches

It is not rare to find the terms "communication approach" and "communication strategy" used interchangeably. In the context of this publication, the term "approach" refers to a specific communication focus, or coherent set of tactical actions (for example, institutional strengthening, social marketing, community mobilization, edu-tainment, and so forth) aimed at achieving a certain objective. The term "strategy," however, denotes the overall design of the communication program, which might include one or more communication approaches and objectives. Where there is a straightforward objective to be achieved, e.g., in an immunization campaign, a communication approach can sometimes define the overall strategy. A strategy, however, is usually more complex and articulated than a single approach. The following list illustrates some of the most common approaches.

Social marketing is an approach rooted in the principles of marketing applied to social issues. It has been widely used, especially to promote health practices, such as immunization campaigns, sanitation, and others.

Advocacy is mainly applied to promote a specific issue or agenda, generally at a national level. It is often directed at changing policies or supporting policy-making changes, either addressing policy makers directly or winning the support of the public opinion.

Information dissemination and *campaigns* refer to the targeted dissemination of information to fill specific knowledge gaps. This approach relies heavily on diffusion models through media campaigns, which can be applied in a number of circumstances, either for broader national audiences or for populations in specific areas. Different from the past, where they tended to rely heavily on a single specific medium, campaigns nowadays take advantage of a mix of different media.

Information, education, and communication (IEC) refers to a broader set of tactical approaches aimed at disseminating information and educating large audiences. It is based on the linear transmission model where information is disseminated through a number of media.

Education and training is an approach applied in programs requiring instructional design, usually based on an interactive modality, often at an interpersonal level. Educational approaches are generally aimed at increasing knowledge and comprehension, while training approaches are usually focused on improving professional skills.

Institutional strengthening is directed at strengthening the internal capacities of an institution (for example, through training) and eventually also at positioning and improving its image with external audiences.

Community mobilization is an approach that implies a systematic effort to involve the community to take active part in the resolution of specific issues related to their well-being. Sometimes it can require the formation of groups designated to participate in the decision-making process and to follow up on specific issues (for example, monitoring the activities indicated by a project work plan).

Nondirective participatory communication occurs when two-way communication is used not only to assess the situation but also to jointly define objectives and design strategy. It is based on dialog that seeks consensus on social change considered meaningful and relevant by all local stakeholders. The added term "nondirective" emphasizes the genuine use of participation from the beginning of the process and its being open to various outcomes.

The list of approaches presented above is not exhaustive, and in some cases, there is significant overlap among them. As discussed in module 2, approaches belonging to the monologic mode are closely linked to diffusion models, while those belonging to the dialogic mode rely on the horizontal model used in participatory communication. What is important to understand is that each approach serves a different purpose. Selecting the most appropriate one will shape subsequent steps, such as message design, media selections, and other crucial elements of a communication strategy. Although it is not within the scope of the Sourcebook to discuss message design in depth, its basic principles and features are presented below.

Basics of Message Design

In development, message design should be first and foremost about listening in order to understand and ensure that messages convey what is relevant and needed by stakeholders in a given situation (Mody 1991). The design of appropriate and effective messages refers to the packaging of information deemed important to induce a desired voluntary change in specific audiences. Even if messages are determined and designed in advance, there are instances where relevant content is presented and discussed in an open form through discussion themes (Anyaegbunam et al. 2004). Discussion themes, even if open-ended, allow participants to reveal their knowledge and to discuss key issues openly, thus raising awareness and generating knowledge on specific issues.

In the message design component, the many options can include (1) the content design for messages to persuade individuals to change, (2) the design of materials to stimulate open-ended discussions between different groups of stakeholders, (3) the design of messages to promote or advocate specific issues, such as public reforms, and (4) the instructional design of training courses to build capacity in specific skills and techniques. What these diverse messages have in common is that, to be effective, their content should be formed through an effective design, based on relevant content that is identified, probed, and validated during the communication-based assessment phase.

In general, the type of message design adopted depends on the objectives and the communication approaches selected for the development initiative. Whatever the message, it is necessary to have an in-depth understanding of the intended audiences and all the relevant background data. An effective message design cannot be delegated solely to experts of the specific sector (engineer, medical specialist, or economist, for example) but needs to be shaped by the professional skills of communication experts. Information is not equal to communication: presenting a certain amount of information in a technically correct format does not guarantee that audiences will "buy" the message, or even understand it. As Joseph Stiglitz stated at the recent World Congress on Communication for Development (WCCD),[10] "information is part of communication and not vice versa."

The current conception of communication for development has led to a broadening of the way message design can be conceived and adopted. Bella Mody (1991) was one of the first development communication scholars and practitioners to argue that participatory message design is more effective than the traditional "expert-driven" type of approach. More recently, Anyaegbunam, Mefalopulos, and Moetsabi (2004) highlighted how message design can be considered also in a dialogic mode. In this sense, it is referred to as "discussion theme" and regards open-ended content aimed at stimulating dialog among various groups of stakeholders (see figure 3.4). This approach is particularly valuable when addressing sensitive issues on which the audience's knowledge and inputs are considered particularly beneficial.

Generating and sharing knowledge can also occur in other ways. Whereby words are usually associated with messages and exchanges of meaning, in certain cultures the absence of words can also carry a meaning, and the communication specialist must be aware of this in order to avoid unexpected situations and misunderstand-

Figure 3.4 Using Communication Materials to Facilitate Dialog

Source: Author.

Note: This photograph was taken in a rural community of Southern Africa. It shows a group of women using a flipchart while engaging in dialog and probing key issues related to the welfare of their community.

ings. The indigenous population of Izozog, in Bolivia, for instance, attributes a great value to silence, as a way to manifest their opposition to an issue. As indicated by Mefalopulos (1999): "If words gain the consensus, silence can express the dissent."

Other ways to express messages and exchange information are through visual aids or "codes," as they are called in the "Training for Transformation" methodology derived from Freire's work. These visual aids are effectively used for generating discussion and empowering marginalized sectors of society. A code can be defined as "a concrete presentation of a familiar problem, about which the group present has strong feeling" (Hope and Timmel 1984: 75). For instance, a picture code of a woman who discovers a condom in her husband's trousers has been used successfully in rural communities of Southern Africa to initiate discussions about AIDS and probing needed changes in behaviors, without referring to a specific top-down message. Health promoters used the picture to ask questions and to stimulate the womens' responses in a double-sided effort: to raise the awareness on this issue and to look for possible solutions or strategies to deal with the problem of AIDS.

Clearly the most common conception of message design is one in which the message is transmitted through one or a mix of media channels to inform and persuade audiences. Even though the message is usually transmitted through linear models of communication (that is, from one or a few sources to multiple receivers), to be effective the message should be defined and packaged with the information collected during the two-way communication model of the first phase—always keeping in mind the audience's background. From the identification of themes to the treatment of content, the creative part of this process requires professional skills and imagination linked to the communication specialist's knowledge, experience, and understanding of the contextual situation.

When designing a message, it is helpful to think about both the *content of the message,* the information to be included in the message, and the *take-away message,* the main message or idea for the audience to retain, which usually is not the whole package of information received. With this duality in mind, it is easier to avoid the common mistake of assuming that a message received is a message understood and retained by the audience. Effective messages are those that have the information packaged in a clear and easily understandable manner, contain the right appeal to get the audience's attention, and fill the gap between what the audience knows and what they need to know. Messages get "decoded" or interpreted in different ways by individuals, and they can also be reinterpreted or negotiated through interpersonal communication among individuals. It is imperative that messages be pretested with a relevant sample of the intended audiences before starting the production of communication materials.

In order to ensure the effectiveness of the desired outputs, when defining or supervising the design of messages, the following basic factors, derived mostly from those presented by Mody (1991) in her book *Designing Messages for Development Communication*, should be kept in mind.

Sociocultural sensitivity—Content and presentation should be appropriate for the cultural environment. In a number of cases, cultural issues, not content, were the main cause of a campaign failure. In one case, a campaign was encouraging women to vaccinate their children so they could have healthier and longer lives. But the color of the campaign posters was white, which in that particular culture symbolizes death and mourning. It is not difficult to see why the posters were not so effective.

Language appropriateness—This theme overlaps with cultural sensitivity, but it deserves special attention because it is often neglected. Many North American teens are not likely to identify themselves with two peers shown in a TV commercial meeting, shaking hands, and greeting each other by saying, "Hello, how do you do?" But if they touch fists, hug, and say, "Hey yo' wha'sup," the scene is more likely to catch teens' attention. To be effective, it is not so important that messages be grammatically correct or expressed in a scientifically appropriate manner but that they convey the take-away message in a way that relates to audiences' way of life and understanding.

Political compatibility—The degree of free expression and transparency varies significantly among countries. Communication specialists seldom operate in ideal circumstances. Hence, they should always weigh the effectiveness of messages—especially when used for campaigns at a national level—with the political situation of the country and the boundaries of what is appropriate. While development communication specialists should never bend to political pressures for "massaging the messages" or allow interference aimed at derailing the nature of the development intervention or stakeholders' best interests, professionals should be able as much as possible to avoid confrontations that could be detrimental to the achievement of the agreed-upon objectives.

Economic compatibility—Any innovation or reform needs to be implemented within a larger setting. A message can be effective if it considers how such an innovation would fit into the broader framework. For instance, in an energy sector reform, a message promoting an increase in fees by emphasizing the increased effectiveness and quality provided by electricity services would not have much impact if most users cannot afford to pay for that service.

Psychological appropriateness—It is imperative that each message resonates with its specific audience. Each message should have a specific appeal that catches audiences' attention. Appeals can be diverse in approach and nature. They can be rational—highlighting safety, economic effectiveness, health, and other similar issues, or emotional—appealing to ambition, attraction, fear, embarrassment, romance, or a sense of belonging. One of the classic examples is that of a major antitobacco campaign directed at teens, which emphasized the health risks connected to smoking—

people who smoke would get sick more often and could die younger. The problem with the message was that teens are not typically concerned about getting sick or dying. The campaign started to have an impact when the messages changed based on research and emphasized how teens who smoke have an unpleasant taste when they kiss. That indeed proved to be a major concern for teens, and the message managed to help decrease smoking among teens.

Expected achievements—Prior to message design, intentions should be clear. It is crucial to know the level being addressed in the AKAB scale. Is awareness being raised or knowledge increased on a certain topic? Are the messages aimed to influence public attitude toward a certain reform or to change behavior regarding habits that could improve audiences' living conditions? Whatever the case, the message, its content, and its appeal should be addressed to the targeted level. For instance, if designing a campaign to promote hand washing for health reasons in rural areas, it is crucial to know if people have easy access to water and if they are aware of the benefits of washing their hands, in order to address the right level of change (that is, awareness, knowledge, attitude, and/or behavior).

Communication Channels and Media

Often this topic is simply referred to as media. The term "channels," however, carries a connotation broader than the technological one of electronic media. Hence, both terms are being included in the Sourcebook. Communication channels and media can range from electronic media, such as video, radio, and the Internet, to traditional channels, such as popular theater, drums, and storytelling, and pass through the whole range of printed products, such as newspapers, leaflets, brochures, posters, and flip charts. Sometimes opinion leaders or individuals having a significant influence or credibility in the community can become effective channels in a communication program.

Which specific channel or media mix to use depends on a number of factors: objectives of the communication intervention (for example, awareness raising, advocacy, mobilization), characteristics of the audiences (such as literacy rates, preferred information sources), the social environment (available media, cultural context), and available resources, among others. Without necessarily mastering all the specific aspects involved in the production and use of each medium or channel, the communication specialist should always be aware of the strengths and weaknesses of each.

While television is known for its high appeal for entertainment and awareness raising on specific issues, it is not equally effective in changing audience attitudes and behaviors, unless used in conjunction with other channels. Often, radio is the preferred medium in rural settings, but, except in the case of the many community radios that use it in a more participatory way for development-oriented purposes, it has similar limitations to television. Printed materials can be of value when most of the population can read and write, which is not always the case in project settings. Traditional forms of communication, such as storytelling or popular theater, even if reaching more limited numbers of individuals, can be rather effective in discussing sensitive issues and gradually inducing change in the attitudes and behaviors of the audience.

Whatever channel is selected, it is important to have a sound rationale for the selection. Using a communication mix is often crucial. In many instances, multimedia campaigns have been demonstrated to be more effective than one-medium campaigns in achieving intended results (Coldevin 2003). New information technologies, such as the Internet, provide a wider range of options whose potential is yet to be fully explored and taken into account. Once all the elements of the strategy have been discussed, assessed, and defined, the path is clear for implementation of the message design activities.

Communication Strategy Design Toolbox

The communication strategy design phase is the most creative one, and, because of that, it is not possible to define a one-size-fits-all formula for it. Nevertheless, there are some methods and steps that help in designing and managing an effective communication strategy. A method frequently used by DevComm is known as the Five Communication Management Decisions. This is a template to help in managing and monitoring communication strategies, especially those in need of straightforward, linear communication interventions.

However, the Five Management Decisions is not the only tool. In projects and programs requiring a more complex and multifaceted communication intervention, other planning methods, such as logical framework analysis, also known as logframe,[11] or the objective-oriented project planning, also known as ZOPP,[12] might be more effective.

The situation analysis framework, known also as SAF, is another method used effectively to enhance project design through participatory communication strategies, especially in rural development projects.[13] It provides useful guidelines on how to develop and organize a participatory research-based communication strategy, and it can be used effectively for complex and multi-level communication interventions.

At the end of the next component (Implementing the Communication Program) there is a map synthesizing the various steps presented so far in this module of the Sourcebook. The map provides basic guidelines on how to design a communication strategy and can also be used in more complex situations. This process has been applied effectively also in a number of experiential workshops aimed at designing strategy.

The Five Management Decisions

This Five Management Decisions (FMD) template is of particular value in managing and monitoring initiatives with straightforward objectives requiring clearly defined behavior changes in the monologic/diffusion mode. The FMD presented in the template on the following page has been changed slightly from its original form, developed by Cabañero-Verzosa, in order to highlight the link between management objective and communication objective. Also, in the last column, it refers specifically to indicators, rather than to the evaluation process.

FMD helps to inform the design of communication programs and to simplify the planning process by highlighting the key factors to be addressed and taken into account to achieve the desired behavior change. Its simplicity, however, while an asset in dealing with certain projects, can become a constraint if used in projects with broad and complex objectives addressing a broader level of social change or in projects that require the parallel adoption of different types of communication interventions (such as advocacy, internal, corporate, and development communication).

For example, if the management objective of the project is that of reducing the air pollution of a major city, the communication objective could be aimed at inducing behavior changes in the heating consumption and driving habits of citizens (assuming that they are the main sources of pollution). In this case the FMD template could be a useful tool to monitor and manage the strategy because it defines some of the needed key elements (that is, audiences, behaviors, messages, channels, and evaluation indicators).

However, in a project whose objective is to promote the decentralization of services and goods in a certain country, the FMD template might not be an adequate approach, since the strategy design would require a diversified approach with a number of different audiences, approaches, messages, and lines of action. Such a strategy can be articulated effectively by following a series of steps such as those highlighted in figure 3.5.

As evident from its design, the Five Management Decisions template rests on the management objective.[14] In reality, these objectives are not always a given as a starting point. On the contrary, often the most difficult issue lies in the identification and/or proper definition of the management objective, without which the whole template becomes ineffective. It is crucial, therefore, to have a well-defined and realistic management objective to guide strategy and to determine project success.

(*cont.*)

Communication Strategy Design Toolbox (*cont.*)

Once the management objective is properly defined, usually through empirical research, the communication objectives supporting the broader management objective can be defined. In some cases the two coincide, but more frequently they are separate, with the communication objective supporting the management one. With the objectives clearly identified and defined, the Five Management Decisions can become a valuable management tool, especially when the project objective is a public communication program and/or a straightforward behavior change of specific audiences. The template is used as a tool to strengthen the understanding of the main elements forming a communication strategy. It addresses five basic communication concepts, closely resembling the Lasswell (1948) five question model presented in module 2: WHO, says WHAT, in WHICH channel, to WHOM, with what EFFECT.

The Five Management Decisions template helps to organize the information needed to define and monitor a communication strategy, asking the following questions: (1) Which audiences need to be reached? (2) What behavior changes are required or need to be avoided? (3) Which messages will induce the desired behavior? (4) Which among the available channels are most effective for the audience of interest? (5) How will the communication process be monitored and evaluated? These five questions are instrumental in ensuring that communication activities are relevant and supportive of the project objectives.

The Five Management Decisions Template

Management Objective (and communication objective)				
Audience	Behavior	Messages	Channels	Evaluation Indicators

Source: Cecilia Cabañero-Verzosa 2002.

3.3 Phase 3—Implementing the Communication Program

This phase encompasses the activities necessary to implement the work plan (for example, design of communication materials, training of relevant staff, and so forth) and to produce and distribute media and information products. This part of the process is the most resource-intensive in both human and financial terms, but it is not necessarily the most crucial phase. If the work in the previous two phases was done properly, the implementation is the most straightforward phase, needing only the professional application of tasks and competencies identified to ensure the achievement of the objectives. Usually this is done through an action plan, which can be considered a map indicating what needs to be done, by whom, when, and at what cost.

The activities presented in table 3.6 provide a model of reference to define a basic sequence of special value for instructional purposes. The actions in this phase, however, can vary greatly and depend mostly on the strategy design. Starting from

Table 3.6 The Communication Action Plan

Activities	Explanation	Example
1. Objective(s) (SMART)	Review and confirm objectives (possibly SMART)	Vaccinate 70% of the children under five in area X
2. Audiences/ stakeholders	Who are the audiences or groups being addressed (primary, secondary, etc.)?	Primary: mothers Secondary: sons/daughters (students) and fathers
3. Activities (and approaches)	What are the activities needed (media production, message design, etc.)?	Information campaigns (audiovisual and printed materials), field visits, meetings
4. Resources needed (human and material)	Experts in audiovisual design and production (experts in training, related materials, etc.)	Design information campaign, pretest and produce materials; provide training to health promoters
5. Party responsible (action promoter)	The source/initiator responsible for the action	Field officers of the Ministry of Environment
6. Time frame	The sequence and time needed for each activity	6 months to design the campaign, 2 months for training, 6 months to implement, 8 months for field visits and meetings
7. Expected outputs (outcome indicators)	What is expected by the communication initiative?	70% of children under five being vaccinated

Source: Author.

3

the set objectives, typically an action plan details intended audiences, selected activities, inputs needed, expected outputs, and the time frame for each activity. Table 3.7 illustrates a way of drafting such an action plan—one way among many possible ways. It intends to provide a scheme of reference, which can and should be modified according to the situation. To make the process clearer, the last column relates the various steps to actual practice.

The communication objectives (possibly expressed in SMART form) constitute the "North Star" of the strategy when drafting the action plan, thus shaping the activities to be implemented. The action plan should state clearly who is responsible for each activity and what is the expected outcome once the activities are implemented. In other words, the action plan is a way to organize and enhance the management and implementation of decisions taken in the design of the strategy. Table 3.7 provides a simple and linear presentation of an action plan, but complex projects and programs would need more articulated and multifaceted action plans.

One should not assume that for each objective there is a single corresponding action: for a specific objective, there might be five activities, two expected results, and a great and diversified number of resources needed. This network of activities should be implemented under the direct supervision of a communication specialist (for example, video producer, campaign expert, or trainer) who verifies that the communication outputs are directly and effectively linked with the objectives.

In the example in table 3.7, the communication objectives and communication outputs coincide, but this is not always the case. The objective of a training workshop, for example, could be to provide the skills to extensionists for a new cropping method. The expected results, however, could be that the extensionists are successful in promoting the new methods among farmers. Outputs and outcomes are not the same things. Evaluation should focus also on the outcome of an intervention—and not only on the outputs, as is often done.

Before the implementation of the planned activities can begin, there are usually a number of preparatory actions to be carried out. These can be divided broadly into two types: production of materials and training of relevant personnel. According to the needs identified in the research and defined in the strategy, it might be necessary to produce posters, brochures, radio programs, and other kinds of audiovisuals. It is not within the scope of this publication to address the production aspects of such materials. What is important is that each medium has certain characteristics that should be considered when project leaders decide what, how, and when to use it, and they should make sure they hire specialists with the proper production competencies.

3.3.1 Pretesting Communication Materials

Most important, communication specialists should always pretest the materials being produced, no matter how well done they are and how carefully they are revised by other experts. Pretesting should be conducted with pilot groups and representatives of the intended populations before reaching the stage of mass production. It is astonishing to find out how many messages have failed to reach their intended audiences simply because no pretesting was done, and the assumptions of experts were proved inadequate by real experience.

Bella Mody (1991) told about one of the most famous of these cases. Villagers failed to respond in the expected way to the dangers of malaria presented to them in a film on the subject. For dramatization purposes in the film, mosquitoes were depicted as much larger than they are in reality. As a result, the villagers did not recognize them as a threat, and they assumed that there was nothing to worry about since there were no such big insects in their area!

3.3.2 Putting the Pieces Together: Drawing Up an Action Plan

The other parts of the process leading to an action plan have been described in previous sections. By combining the three main tables of each phase (table 3.3 on communication-based assessment, table 3.5 on communication strategy design, and table 3.7 on a communication action plan), the reader has an overall view of the entire process needed to design and implement a communication program. Figure 3.5 combines the steps of each table of the first three phases into a sequence leading to sustainable change. The figure is derived from years of experience designing and applying development communication projects and development programs in the field and it can be used as a road map for the overall process of the communication strategy, its inputs, activities, and expected outcomes.[15]

In the map in figure 3.5, each specific step relates and interacts with other steps, usually the ones above and below. The information presented in this part of the Sourcebook aims to make clearer the overall sequence of a communication program from the research phase to the strategy design and the relative action plan. Practitioners can use the sequence in the map as a basic checklist to guide the implementation of strategic activities in operations, as also illustrated in narrative form in box 3.4.

Figure 3.5 The Communication Program Design and Implementation Process

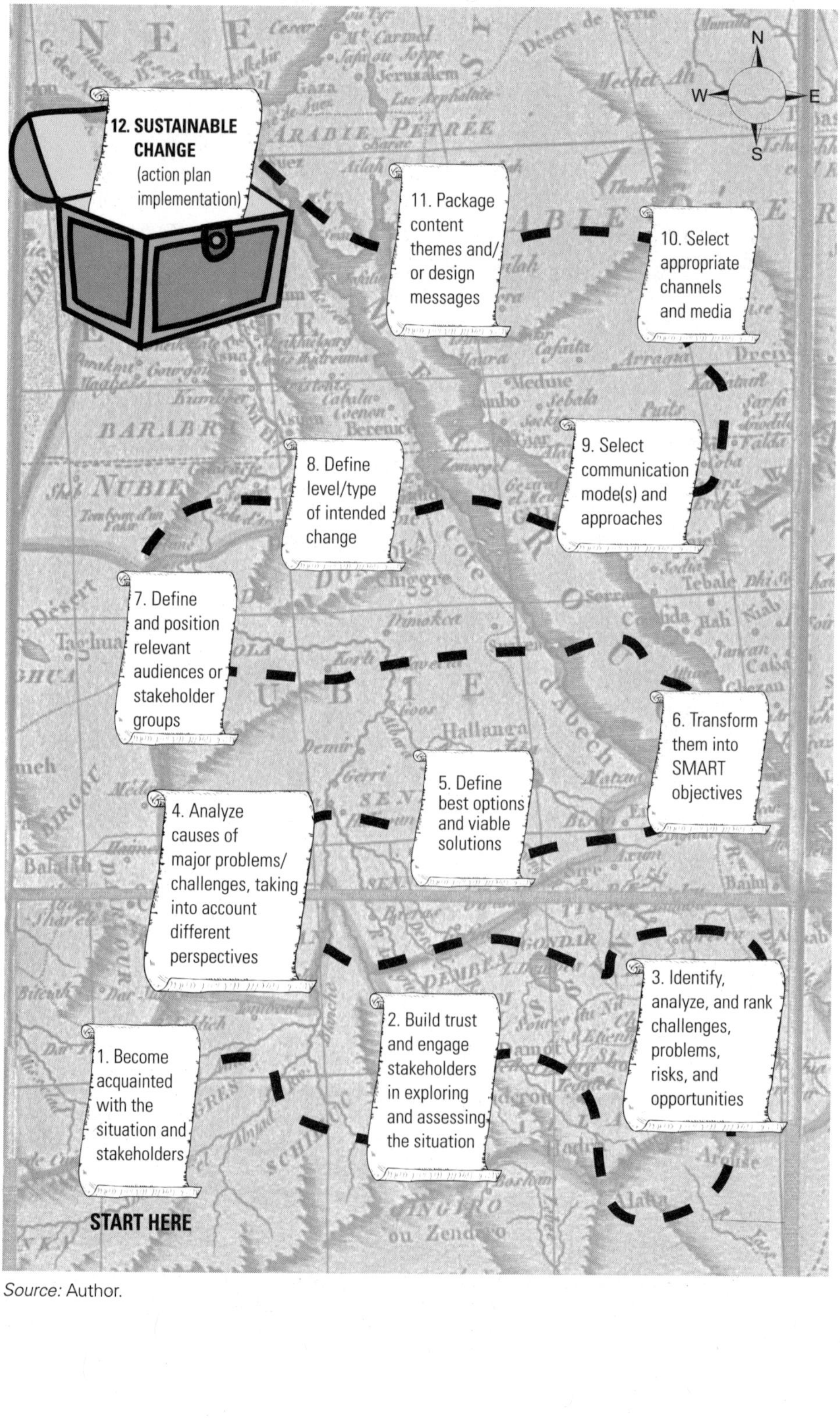

Source: Author.

BOX 3.4 A Communication Road Map to Change

Figure 3.5 illustrates the process that is usually adopted to design the strategy and the implementation of a communication program. The presentation of the road map, step by step, is carried out here in narrative form. The context within which a strategy is defined needs to be considered as well. The starting point is always about getting acquainted with the situation, but if communication is included at a beginning of a broad process (such as Poverty Reduction Strategies) it will have a broader range of action than if it had been included in a program whose main objectives had been already defined.

In all cases step 1 requires reviewing available documentation and conducting interviews with individuals of relevance. Step 2 is where the genuine field research begins by engaging stakeholders in order to build trust and mutual understanding. The investigation usually begins in a broader manner, gradually zooming in on key issues in the next steps. In step 3, communication is used to uncover risks and opportunities while probing stakeholders' knowledge and perceptions about the main problem(s). In step 4 a communication specialist is expected to identify the main causes of the problem(s) that need to be solved. Looking at the causes is often more important than accurately defining the main problem, because to be successful the solutions devised need to address the root causes of a problem, rather than the problem itself. Step 5 is where viable options and solutions are assessed and identified. These are then ranked in terms of best choices.

Step 6 is critical because, based on all relevant data from the previous steps, it aims to transform the top solutions identified into SMART objectives, that is, objectives that are specific, measurable, attainable, realistic, and timely. This step marks the end of the research phase (or CBA) and the beginning of the strategy design phase. Step 7 requires the definition of primary and secondary audiences of the communication strategy, taking into account their background, knowledge, opinions, and ways of life and other relevant information collected in the CBA.

In step 8 the communication specialist defines the level of change that is targeted by the communication strategy. As stated earlier, it is very important to make absolutely clear the type of change that communication is expected to achieve. It can be knowledge, behavior, or empowerment, among others. Whatever it is, it should be defined clearly at this point, as each type requires different communication approaches. Step 9 is concerned with the selection of the communication approaches, which are naturally linked with the type of change defined in the previous step. Social marketing, information dissemination, and community mobilization are some of the most frequent approaches.

Once the approaches have been defined, in step 10 the communication specialist can proceed to select the right media and channels for the intended objective(s). Once again, this decision is taken reviewing all the information collected during the research phase. A similar approach is

BOX 3.4 A Communication Road Map to Change (continued)

required for step 11 about message design. To be effective, messages must be developed having in mind the audiences' needs and ways of thinking. In other words, the design of the message, no matter how creative, should be derived from local stakeholders' world view, not from that of the specialist.

Finally, step 12 indicates the end of the journey. While each step can be different according to the situation and the objective of the initiative, the overall process remains the same most of the time. The main tip to remember is to make sure to analyze the issues properly and not to assume that the best technical solution guarantees the highest rate of success. Quite often sustainable change is about social ownership and local knowledge, rather than externally imposed solutions, no matter how technically valid.

Communication Toolbox for Implementation

Operational managers for projects and programs usually oversee most implementation activities. With information and recommendations from the development communication process, the managers can work directly with the various specialists, such as radio and video producers, training specialists, and graphic designers. DevComm staff consult with many of these specialists in the research and design phases of the process, even if they are not usually involved in the implementation stage of communication activities. A professional development communication specialist should know the characteristics and potentials of each medium and the criteria for its best utilization, but he or she is not necessarily the person involved, for example, in the production of a radio show or in the printing of posters.

The tools used in this phase relate mostly to the specific media selected (for example, print, radio, video), and on the training needed to carry out the successful implementation of the activities. Considering the wide range of applications in the production of communication materials and media and the vast amount of publications available on this subject, a reader can easily access any of those publications dealing with any of the different media of interest, such as radio, video, print, or the Web.

3.4 Phase 4—Communication for Monitoring and Evaluation

Evaluation can be defined as the process of determining whether, and to what extent, a certain intervention has produced the intended result (Babbie 2002). Evaluation is considered one of the most important components of development initiatives, but because numerous structural and practical factors (disbursement procedures, timing of project cycle, and so forth), whose explanation is beyond the scope of this Sourcebook, evaluation of development efforts remains a challenging and, at times, controversial issue. The challenge is even more pronounced in the evaluation of the impact of communication interventions whose results are visible over a longer period of time.

Evaluation in the social setting is also referred to as evaluation research, or program evaluation. Having the word "research" associated with "evaluation" emphasizes that it is an investigative task to be defined and planned from the very beginning, rather than at the end of the intervention. Its purpose is to evaluate the impact of specific interventions, in our case, communication interventions in the development context. Evaluation is needed to assess if the intervention produced the intended result and to what degree.

Evaluation is usually divided into formative evaluation, also referred to as monitoring, and summative evaluation. The first, formative evaluation or monitoring, assesses the work in progress, checking that the design and implementation of the activities remain in line with the objectives and relative planning. The other type, summative, is concerned with measuring the final impact of the intervention, and it is referred to in a number of ways in the literature, such as summative, research evaluation, program evaluations, or, more simply, evaluation. In the Sourcebook, the two different types are referred to as monitoring in the first case and evaluation in the second.

3.4.1 Key Issues in Monitoring and Evaluation

Evaluation is a crucial aspect of development communication interventions, a field still being challenged to demonstrate its value-added with hard data. Measuring and evaluating the impact of social interventions is never simple and, in the case of development communication, becomes more difficult and complex, mostly because of the broader functions of communication. The issue can be expressed with a straightforward question: Are the concepts and practices of the new development communication paradigm making a difference? Development communication specialists and project managers who have used it in the past would answer positively, as was indicated in a survey of policy makers in 2006 (Fraser, Restrepo-Estrada, Mazzei

2007), but many others, less familiar with its applications, remain dubious and demand hard evidence of the impact of communication in development initiatives.

This skepticism can be understood, especially if the issue is framed within the scientific-positivist paradigm, which requires precise and quantifiable measurements. Things, however, are more complex than that. To address the cause of past failures, communication needs to engage stakeholders from the start, building mutual trust, reducing potential conflicts and misunderstandings, and providing inputs for project design based on a wider consensus. In other words, when used properly, development communication would prevent most problems before they arise.

The main challenge is how to accurately measure such preventive function. So far, there does not seem to be a "scientific" and widely acknowledged way to measure the effectiveness or the impact of inputs derived through a dialogic approach in the design of a strategy, especially when such inputs are preventing problems that might appear at a later stage. However, an insightful peer-reviewed study of scientific journals dealing with this issue has indicated that there is "compelling evidence of positive contributions of communication toward programmatic goals" (Inagaki 2007: 43).

Cost of Noncommunication

The impact of communication becomes more apparent when reviewing the significant body of evidence about the cost of noncommunication, indicating how much time and money have been wasted because of problems that could have been avoided if communication approaches had been applied from the beginning of the initiative. One example is provided by Hydro-Quebec, a leading Canadian firm in the energy sector. The firm has estimated that the cost of inadequate communication with indigenous peoples regarding their hydropower scheme in North Quebec led to controversies that caused project delays of more than 20 years. The company's cost estimate for these delays is US$278 million.[16] Currently Hydro-Quebec and indigenous people in Canada have developed a working partnership that allows a dialog aimed at addressing issues from both perspectives and that has eliminated most of the past problems and conflicts.

Dialog as an explorative tool is often instrumental in building trust and consensus, ensuring that objectives are properly defined and understood by relevant stakeholders, often preventing problems and conflicts before they arise. It is extremely difficult, if not impossible, to assess the benefits of something that has not and may not occur. In some instances, this can be done by approximation, as in the case of preventive medicine. Even in that case, however, the detailed and exhaustive health records kept in many of the richer countries allow the use of statistics to carry out accurate cost-benefit analyses over long periods of time, which by comparison provide reliable projections and estimates on the advantages of preventive medicine.

In the case of communication for development, the challenge of precise measurement can be even harder to address successfully, since it is often dealing with what might be considered intangible results (that is, empowerment, risk mitigation, prevention of conflicts, consensus building, and so forth). However, intangible outcomes are often as important as tangible ones. Passing a reform is a tangible outcome that can be measured once the reform has been passed, but if there is not enough consensus to support the reform in a democracy, it is unlikely that the reform will pass. Obtaining the needed consensus might be considered an intangible result, but without that consensus, no tangible output will be achieved.

That different outputs, tangible and intangible, might require different types of measurements but should not lead to discrimination in favor of one over the other. Both dimensions are equally valid and relevant. Past experience has shown that without proper understanding and agreement (that is, communication), projects are likely to fail. Quantifying the costs of such failures would be possible by doing a comparative cost analysis of the resources and time wasted because of the lack of proper communication, but this task is beyond the scope of this publication.

Why Assess Program Impact?

The reasons for conducting evaluations are numerous: to monitor the process and take corrective actions where possible; to learn from past mistakes and make future interventions more effective; to ensure the accountability of the resources dedicated to the initiative; and, most importantly, to be able to assess, demonstrate, and quantify the effectiveness of the intervention. In 2005, the World Bank, in collaboration with other partners, sponsored an e-forum on measuring the impact of communication for development. The subsequent report (World Bank and DFID 2006) debated the many challenges to be faced in evaluating development programs. It confirmed the following reasons for evaluating the impact of communication:

- Assessing the role of a particular project or process in contributing to a development project or social change
- Gaining advocacy with decision makers
- Refining and fine-tuning the process of implementation
- Learning from past mistakes, what has worked and not worked
- Ensuring a positive process for the community and the stakeholders
- Ensuring good management and accountability to donors and decision makers
- Making continued funding possible
- Improving research and evaluation methods and approaches

Nobody questions the importance of evaluating development initiatives. However, there is a lively debate about how evaluations should be designed and carried out, and in some cases, even about whom and what should be evaluated. These questions are linked to the rationale for evaluating. The main rationale guiding evaluation is often shaped by the way the broader context of development is conceived and understood.

If development is seen primarily in economic terms, it is clear that the main focus in evaluating results would be to assess improvements in the economic domain. But if development is conceived in terms of people's choices and empowerment, the rationale for the evaluation design would have to consider assessing stakeholders' active participation in the decision making process. Whatever the case, evaluation must be included in a rigorous manner from the beginning in order to monitor the progress and to guarantee the needed transparency and accountability of development results.

What and How to Measure?

When dealing with evaluation of development communication initiatives, things get more complicated because of the nature of communication and the longer time span under which change becomes visible. To better understand the multifaceted nature of evaluation in communication, the reader should be familiar with the two main perspectives on development communication discussed in the previous modules: diffusion/monologic and participation/dialogic. The different purposes, functions, and conceptions of communication clearly affect the variables and indicators related to what should be measured.

As background, it is worthwhile to present some of the basic evaluation concepts and principles. Evaluation is always concerned with measuring change in its various forms: behavior, social, and structural. If the goal of development is to improve people's quality of life, evaluation will need to assess if such an improvement took place. The crucial point in this respect is to define what is meant by quality of life and what are the best indicators to measure it.

Indicators are units of measurement, used to assess change. They help provide the rigor needed to evaluate the results in a reliable manner. For instance, an indicator of success in a campaign aimed at persuading parents to vaccinate children against polio would be the number of children being vaccinated and could be stated as an objective: 90 percent of children in a certain area being vaccinated. It is evident that to be able to assess change, indicators need to de defined and measured at the beginning and then compared with another set of measurements done at the end of the initiative.

Indicators can be of quantitative or qualitative nature. When the aim is to gain community support toward decentralization, the indicators could still have a quantitative connotation and be focused, for instance, on the knowledge level; that is, how much do citizens know about decentralization and about what is required to achieve it. To address the qualitative dimension involving the realm of attitudes and practices, the indicator could be defined as people's engagement in decentralization activities, which needs to be identified and clearly operationalized[17] (for example, participation in meetings, review of local public budgets, and engagement with authorities if necessary).

Clearly, the evaluation system is always linked to the objectives of a project or program. The ways in which objectives are defined and operationalized determine which indicators should be considered for evaluating the final results. As stated by Mazzei and Scuppa (2006), communication objectives are either about changing specific knowledge, attitudes, and behaviors or practices in individuals and groups of individuals, or they are about improving the degree of mutual understanding, social and cultural exchange, or the cooperation among different groups of stakeholders, engaging them in the development initiative.

Some of the above elements, such as awareness, knowledge, attitudes, and behaviors, are not too difficult to measure. Usually it is enough to do a baseline at the beginning and then one at the end to have an accurate idea of the level of change that took place in the populations of interest. Current evaluation methods are capable of providing such measurements in an accurate way, as indicated by the well-documented body of evidence on this subject.

The situation gets much more challenging when other intangible and less easily quantifiable dimensions become part of evaluation: mutual understanding, stakeholders' participation, empowerment, risk mitigation, conflict resolution, and problem solving.[18] In many such instances, the issue is not just how to measure them, but what exactly to measure. What are the indicators that are capable of assessing if and what empowerment has occurred, or those indicating that conflicts have been reduced or prevented? What indicators might assess project sustainability that has been strengthened by opening up a dialog and building trust from the beginning, resulting in a better design of the initiative? In sum, when addressing the issue of what to measure, it is important to be aware of the project objectives and of the communication functions.

3.4.2 Basics of Evaluation Design

This section presents a basic introduction to key elements in monitoring and evaluation systems needed when managing the evaluation of a project or program. More on this topic can be found in other in-depth sources, such as the handbook by Kuzek and Rist (2004), titled "Ten Steps to a Results-Based Monitoring and Evaluation System."

For the purpose of this Sourcebook,[19] it is enough to offer a basic explanation of the various types of evaluation design. It is important to know which design would fit better in different situations. Traditionally, research in evaluation design has been divided primarily into three broad categories, each of which contains a number of different specific designs clustered around a core set of principles.

Experimental designs usually require the study of two population samples, selected through rigorous randomization methods. The first, the treatment group, is subjected to the intervention, while the second, the control group, is not. Hence, the difference in the specific issue being studied should measure the impact of the intervention, assuming that all other variables are considered. Accounting for all variables in a social setting is a nearly impossible task, which is why this research design is effective in tightly controlled laboratory situations but has proved to be not as effective in less controllable social environments.

Quasi-experimental designs differ from experimental designs primarily in their lack of random assignments to the treatment and control groups. Control groups can be chosen in ways that are less rigorous and demanding, thus reducing the costs. On the other hand, this also reduces the reliability and accuracy of the measurements and increases the problem of the selection bias.[20]

Qualitative research designs, sometimes referred to as nonexperimental designs, are less structured and pay more attention to qualitative issues than quantitative ones. They are particularly valuable in identifying and assessing issues not easily measurable, such as participation, empowerment, or accountability. They are also valuable in providing insights that can later be triangulated and assessed more precisely by quantitative methods. Qualitative methods appear to be most useful in understanding and interpreting a situation, while quantitative methods appear to be better in measuring the extent of that situation. According to Babbie (2002: 353), "the most effective evaluation research is one that combines qualitative and quantitative components."

On a more practical note, the following points are important when designing the evaluation of communication interventions. While conducting the initial communication-based assessment, communication professionals should identify the key indicators from the start to assess the impact of communication in the overall process. Both the identified objectives and related indicators should be triangulated and refined through qualitative methods such as interviews, focus groups, or observation.

Second, if they are called in after the project has already started, communication professionals should assess and triangulate the extent of the needed change, validating or, if necessary, modifying the set objectives. Even if it is not the best option, this can be done halfway through the project, usually through quantitative methods, such as surveys or baseline studies, whose findings can also help to refine the objectives of the intervention.

Third, when assessing the impact at the end of the communication intervention, often through a post-baseline survey, it is important to consider and to assess if and how external variables have influenced the outcome. For example, a campaign for flu prevention could have poor results because of a sudden shortage of available vaccines, and not because of flaws in the communication strategy. Similarly, a health campaign aimed at convincing people to eat more vegetables could have wide success because the price of vegetables in the market suddenly dropped during that time period. Such variables need to be taken into account to accurately assess the role of the communication campaign vis-à-vis external factors, such as a decrease in market price.

3.4.3 Measuring Results: Beyond the Quantitative versus Qualitative Debate

Traditionally, evaluation methods have been divided into two broad camps: quantitative and qualitative. The first follows the scientific method rooted in the positivist tradition, heavily biased in favor of quantitative analysis as a means to measure the results of the intervention accurately and "scientifically." The qualitative perspective, instead, challenges the quantitative by arguing that human nature is too complex and unpredictable to be measured in strict quantitative terms. In this sense, it is grounded in a different epistemological perspective based on an approach that highly values the social construction of reality. According to this perspective, social change needs to be measured from the stakeholders' perceptions and points of view rather than from numbers related to project outputs, which are often incapable of accounting for the richness and complexity of social dimensions such as empowerment, freedom, and even happiness.

The two perspectives are not mutually exclusive, nor should they be considered antagonistic. Usually quantitative methods are more appropriate in diffusion modes, providing valid and reliable measurements through objective and scientific methods, including surveys, polls, and other statistical comparative measurements. On the other hand, qualitative methods rely mostly on observation techniques and interviews, which appear to be most effective in capturing the complexity of human nature as viewed in participation.

Currently, the long-standing methodological debate of quantitative versus qualitative approaches is losing relevance, and there is an increasing acknowledgment of the value in a more integrated approach. The a priori contraposition between the two perspectives is being replaced by a case-by-case approach, which adopts and, in many cases, combines the methods more appropriately according to the objectives of the intervention. Baseline studies, presented in the first component of this module, combine qualitative and quantitative elements to provide an accurate representation of the perceptions, awareness, knowledge, attitudes, and behaviors of stakeholder groups.

Key Issues in Evaluating the Impact of Diffusion Approaches

In the diffusion perspective, or monologic mode as presented in module 2, the linear diffusion model is the main reference. The objective in general is to use information effectively to change behaviors along the AKAB ladder (awareness, knowledge, attitudes, and behaviors). This presupposes a linear progression leading to change, from being aware and becoming knowledgeable about the issue of interest, to acquiring the right attitude and finally being able to change behavior and sustain that change over time. To reach the last step of the ladder and change behaviors, all the other steps must have been climbed. There is no use trying to change a certain behavior if the audience does not have a supportive attitude or the related knowledge needed to induce the change.

Even if some authors have revisited the linear dimension of this model, diffusion of innovation still remains largely within the one-way mode of communication. Haider et al. (2005) are among those highlighting the usefulness of diffusion for behavior change, especially in health projects. However, they also acknowledge the main critical issues associated with diffusion of innovation, namely that it tends to blame individuals for rejecting new behaviors, neglecting wider social considerations, and that it has a pro-innovation bias, assuming that all members of a community should accept an innovation regardless of their needs and perceived benefits.

This is why behavior change should be associated with broader social considerations. Furthermore, even when used in the monologic/diffusion mode a communication intervention is not always geared to changing behavior. Depending on project objectives and the baseline findings, communication could be intended only to increase awareness or knowledge on a specific issue (for example, campaigns aimed at increasing public awareness about the indiscriminate killing of whales, dissemination of information about project activities, or about the upcoming elections), or it could be the first step of a longer process aimed at changing specific behaviors (for example, a campaign aimed at eliminating unsafe sexual practices to prevent the spread of AIDS).

Naturally, evaluation should focus on the specific objective of the communication intervention. If it were to raise awareness or provide knowledge about certain issues, the measurements and related indicators should be about changes in those two dimensions, and not on how the increased awareness or knowledge has changed individuals' attitudes or behaviors. If, instead, the intervention is expected to achieve changes in certain behaviors, as in a campaign on AIDS prevention, the evaluation should measure changes in those behaviors, even if, to be effective, the awareness and knowledge dimensions should also be taken into account.

There is a vast literature documenting the impact of communication interventions, not only in increasing knowledge and changing behaviors, but also in promoting "new wants" in audiences or consumers, an area watched with suspicion by some. Many of the approaches related to the diffusion model in the development context have looked with interest to communication principles and the successful appeals used in commercial television. Social marketing and edu-tainment are two such approaches used frequently in development communication. Even though the findings do not always indicate a high degree of effectiveness of such interventions, there is no doubt that in some cases they have obtained significant results.

The effects of the impact of diffusion approaches are usually felt after the implementation phase, which is different from the participation approach that can affect the process from the very beginning. This makes evaluating the impact of diffusion intervention easier, since there can be a pre-assessment of the situation and then a post-assessment, which is often carried out through baseline studies. The difference between pre-assessment and post-assessment should account for the impact of communication, provided that all other variables influencing the results have been identified and taken into account.

Key Issues in Evaluating the Impact of Participatory Approaches

Assessing the impact of communication interventions in the participatory theoretical framework, or in the dialogic mode, presents a higher degree of complexity. Results are not simply measurable by changes in the AKAB dimensions. The explorative scope of the dialogic mode implies a measurement of trust, mutual understanding, empowerment, and consensus building, among other factors.

Measuring these dimensions appears to be an almost insurmountable challenge, because it seems very difficult to measure scientifically complex human and social dimensions. Difficulty occurs when attempting to operationalize (that is, providing indicators to measure) concepts such as mutual understanding, trust, or empowerment—or to assess the impact of stakeholders' participation in preventing problems before they arise. Due to these kinds of challenges in quantifying its impact, the key role of two-way communication is not always fully understood.

Most international development institutions are governed by economists, and quantitative, verifiable data fit better into their methodological frame of reference and mind set. In this context, the intangible results of communication must be quantified to gauge their full value. However, practitioners need not accept that intangible results are less significant than tangible ones. The assumption that quantitatively measurable results are more relevant than intangible ones is being challenged increasingly, as it was in an e-forum on this subject organized by the World Bank, DFID, and FAO, with the participation of scholars and practitioners from many countries (World Bank and DFID 2006: 22):"There is a school of thought among communication specialists that does not believe communication practitioners should bow to the demands of the economists and administrators who demand details of impact and cost and cost/benefit ratios before they decide to provide funding for communication."

Results of the communication intervention should always be documented and presented as valuable evidence, regardless of whether they are concrete and quantifiable (as an increase in knowledge or a change in behavior) whether they relate to intangible results (as in establishing trust where there was suspicion, or averting a conflict). Communication specialists should not be timid in pointing out intangible results, even if they are not supported by statistical analysis or scientifically quantifiable data. As stated in the joint World Bank and DFID publication (2006: 17), "Hard data cannot truly capture the complexity of the human dimension and social processes. The development context is dynamic and unpredictable, with unanticipated events and variables that are difficult to quantify. Human behavior change may not always follow a logical progression from knowledge to an issue, through a change of attitude to a resulting change in behavior."

Participatory evaluation approaches are increasingly challenging the assumptions of past approaches. They do not blindly accept that evaluation's predominant scope and indicators should be set solely by technical experts. Rather, those factors should be decided by or with the very people who are supposed to benefit by the initiative. In development, proponents of participatory evaluation argue that decisions concerning who, why, and what to evaluate should be decided by local stakeholders. They also dispute that quantitative measurements can accurately represent the social reality in an objective way, as Patton (1990) stated: "Numbers do not protect against bias, they merely disguise it." Even if the structure and practices of the current development context are hardly compatible with participatory evaluation, this perspective is gaining increasing attention, and communication specialists should be familiar with its principles.

3.4.4 Assessing the Evidence about Development Communication Results

Acknowledging the challenges and complexities in measuring the results of two-way communication does not mean it is impossible. On the contrary, there is a rich body of evidence about the impact of communication interventions, and the piece by Mitchell and Gorove in module 4 deals with this issue in more detail. The purpose of this section, however, is not to provide an exhaustive exposition on the available evidence on the impact of communication for development, but to highlight what kind of evidence should be sought for different types of communication interventions.

The relevant literature contains many results that can be ascribed, or at least partially attributed, to development communication interventions, but that evidence does not always meet the standards required by the scientific paradigm of "hard sciences." The validity of such standards is debatable, and it has been debated in development circles. In an online forum on the impact of communication for development, hosted by the World Bank in 2005, one of the participants wondered why the pressure for proving the value of communication should fall so strongly on communication specialists, while economists and political scientists do not seem to be under the same type of pressure—even though for years they have been primarily responsible for shaping development practices that, to a significant extent, have failed to deliver expected results.

Assessing the Impact of Different Types of Communication

When operating in the monologic mode (diffusion or transmission model), evaluation should be focused on the main types of change expected in such cases: raising awareness, attaining knowledge, and changing attitudes or behaviors and practices. Measuring the impact of communication in diffusion approaches (for example, media campaigns, social marketing, advocacy, and so forth) is not particularly complicated and, when they are planned properly, evaluation results are consistent and reliable. Well-documented and successful instances of campaigns aimed at raising awareness or informing specific audiences about key issues or initiatives have used both media and interpersonal methods to help people voluntarily change attitudes and behaviors to bring about intended change. The power of this kind of communication is further confirmed by the huge amount of money spent for advertisements, political communication campaigns, and advocacy initiatives.

If communication approaches belonging to the diffusion family can be assessed in a relatively straightforward manner (for example, a baseline study at the beginning and after the intervention), those related to the participatory or dialogic family present a higher degree of complexity. Initiatives based on dialog are much more complex and challenging to assess. First, their immediate ouput is not usually predetermined, or, if so, it provides only a broad indication of what should be achieved (for example, an assessment of stakeholders' perceptions and knowledge on a certain issue or the identification of risks and opportunities). Second, the scope of the participatory mode is key to proper design and implementation, and although it does not provide any direct and visible results, without its use many initiatives would be destined to fail.

A mechanical analogy applies: if somebody claims that the most important element of a car's engine is the oil, such an assertion can be difficult to sustain just by looking at the mechanical parts of the engine. The engine oil is not part of the hardware of the engine and is not visible in a running engine, but try to start a road trip with no oil in the engine and see how far you will go! In this sense, two-way communication is the oil of development initiatives.

The immediate objective of dialog is not a change in the AKAB ladder—at least not at the beginning. The objective is to ensure that all relevant voices are heard and used to generate new knowledge, strengthen the project design, and enhance the overall results. Can this be measured? Perhaps in certain cases; nonetheless, what is quite evident to observation should be accepted even if it cannot be measured in a "scientific" way.

A dialogic approach adds value by giving voice and often dignity to the poorest and most marginalized segments of society. This value can hardly be measured in an exact manner, but who can argue that it is not happening or that it is not important just because it cannot be quantified in exact terms? Many failures of the past have been ascribed to the lack of involvement of the so-called "beneficiaries." Do we need to quantify exactly which percentage of those failures should be ascribed to lack of participation in order to take corrective action?

These considerations should be self-evident to development managers and practitioners, and the available data surely reinforce this point. Even if such data were not available, the value-added of such approaches would be hard to dispute. Perhaps it would be wiser to accept that not everything related to human nature can be accurately evaluated. Some aspects of the human dimension are too complex and unpredictable to be assessed by rigid methods that reduce everything to quantifiable entities. Trust, mutual understanding, and empowerment are some of those dimensions that so far have eluded researchers' scientific measurement.

Hence, the emphasis should be on "impressionistic" methods of accounting for stakeholders' perceptions and opinions about initiatives and their degree of involvement whenever measuring the impact of the dialogic mode of communication. This does not automatically guarantee project or program success. However, it is an indication that many practical and potential obstacles and risks were addressed from the beginning and that they were removed or minimized. It also means that a broader consensus was sought among stakeholders, who are more likely to perceive the ownership of the initiative, thus strengthening its long-term sustainability.

As more projects are opting for integrated approaches including both modes, that is, monologic/diffusion and dialogic/participation (Morris 2003), evaluation needs to account for the value and impact of both. For example, Inagaki (2007) cites how the Soul City project in South Africa and an entertainment-education project in Nepal activated community mobilization through the use of mass media. Evaluations of this kind need to be further refined, but evidence at hand is already indicating the value of such integrated approaches.

Conclusions

In sum, the available body of evidence confirms that communication can be effective not only when adopted to induce change in awareness, knowledge, attitudes, and behaviors, but also as a tool to build trust, share knowledge, and explore options enhancing the overall results and sustainability of development initiatives, especially when one-way and two-way communication methods and media are combined in the same strategy. Evaluation needs to reflect the different scope and functions of communication approaches in order to account for their impact. Even if media are always in high demand, there is evidence (Inagaki 2007) indicating that, quite surprisingly, interpersonal communication constitutes the core communication modality used both in diffusion and in participatory approaches. In diffusion it is used in conjunction with vertical communication flows. Interpersonal communication is expected to reinforce and amplify messages transmitted in the media channels to family and peers. On the other hand, in dialogic/participatory approaches, interpersonal communication has primarily a generative function, as Inagaki states. It is used to explore options, allowing stakeholders to identify common problems and needs and build broader consensus toward change.

In view of how many projects have failed because of the neglect of factors that could have been easily anticipated if proper communication research had been used, this section highlights how to assess the impact and value of communication also through its absence. These factors include building flaws into project design, avoiding opposition of stakeholders, and strengthening stakeholder support. The literature on this subject indicates that the rate of failure of development projects is significant. A number of studies suggest that many development project failures could have been avoided if relevant stakeholders had been involved in the definition of problems and in the solutions—that is, if authentic communication had taken place.

The timing of evaluation design is an important and often neglected aspect in the communication program cycle. Evaluation design for communication interventions cannot be devised effectively once the project has commenced, since, in general, impact is assessed through comparative measurements of the change before and after the intervention. To be accurate and meaningful, evaluations should be conceived, prepared, and budgeted during the research phase, and proper indicators should be set out and measured.

Once this practice has become the norm, it will be much easier to have a systematic assessment of the communication impact in development initiatives. In order to avoid repeating the mistakes of the past, communication must exploit also its full dialogic and analytical potential. It should be included from the beginning of development initiatives, regardless of whether the initiative's nature is related or not to communication issues. Once these propositions are applied professionally and systematically, the value-added of development communication will become increasingly evident through the evaluation of all types of development initiatives.

Communication Toolbox for Monitoring and Evaluation

Similar to the previous component concerning implementation, this component does not contain specific tools and techniques to evaluate the impact of communication in development initiatives. The reasons for this are twofold. First of all they would require a treatment of significant depth and length to be properly dealt with, and there are already many publications dealing specifically

(cont.)

Communication Toolbox for Monitoring and Evaluation (*cont.*)

with this topic, including some from the World Bank. Second, some of the key tools used to evaluate the impact of the intervention, such as baselines or surveys, are similar to, if not the same as, those used during the first phase of the communication program (that is, the research phase or CBA), and they are discussed in the toolbox of the CBA component.

Evaluation methods are usually divided into quantitative and qualitative categories, and in addition to those presented in the toolbox of the first component, some have also been touched upon in section 3.4.2, Basics of Evaluation Design, of this component. It is important to stress that evaluation is carried out through indicators that need to be identified as soon as possible, so that measurements can be taken at the beginning and at the end of an intervention to compare them and assess the degree of change. Such indicators can be a combination of qualitative and quantitative ones.

Methods such as interviews, surveys, and baseline studies are frequently used for both ex ante and ex post evaluations. The comparative approach accounts for a higher degree of consistency and reliability in the assessment of the communication impact. In conclusion, it is essential to think about monitoring and evaluation indicators from day one, because taking measurements at the end of a project only is equivalent to measuring a distance when you have only the mileage at the arrival point, but not that of the journey's start.

Summary of Main Points in Module 3

- The main mandate of the Development Communication Division (DevComm) is to mainstream and incorporate communication into operations to enhance overall results and sustainability of projects and programs.
- DevComm's work entails three basic lines of services: (1) communication in operations, which is the main one, (2) opinion polls and research, and (3) knowledge and learning. All of them are closely linked with the operational work of the World Bank.
- A four-phase methodological process guides communication programs as they are applied in operations; that is, research or CBA, strategy design, implementation, and monitoring and evaluation.
- The first phase, about research, is the most important. DevComm uses a flexible set of methods and techniques, known as the communication-based assessment, or CBA, to engage stakeholders in the analysis of key issues, in the assessment of risks and opportunities, and in the definition of priorities facilitating behavior and social change.
- CBA differs significantly from the widely used communication needs assessment, or CNA. The latter is concerned exclusively with communication-centric issues (that is, media, messages, information systems, communication capacities, and so forth), while CBA uses communication to investigate all issues that might be relevant, regardless of the sector and regardless if they are directly linked to communication aspects.
- The second phase contains the key elements needed to design a communication strategy. They are also presented in the form of a table that shows the sequence of the steps required to develop an effective communication strategy.
- Implementation is the third phase. Even though DevComm staff are not usually directly involved in this phase, they can assist in drafting action plans to manage and monitor communication activities.
- The last phase is monitoring and evaluation. Even if in order to assess the impact of an initiative, evaluation is carried out at the end of an initiative, it is necessary that relevant indicators and related measurements be defined and carried out also at the beginning of the intervention. Measuring the difference between the starting and the ending points is often the only way to measure the impact of communication.
- Accurately measuring the impact of communication is not always easy. However in most cases it is possible to assess its impact, using qualitative or quantitative methods or a combination of both. Clearly, the measurement instruments vary according to the scope of the communication initiative and to what has to be evaluated.

Notes

1. Such a budget line can be relatively inexpensive, especially if capacities at country offices are strengthened. DevComm estimates that a typical CBA of a two-week period would cost about US$30,000. The cost would depend on the country where the work takes place and the scope and extent of the initiative.
2. Module 2 gives more detail on the theoretical underpinnings of development communication theories.
3. According to the situation, CBA can be considered either as a quick and dirty investigative tool, capable of providing sufficient insights to draft a course of action, or as part of a bigger empirical research effort, providing the inputs for validating, refining, or identifying further research areas.
4. The usual term "communication-needs assessment" is now being replaced with "communication-based assessment" to emphasize that, at the initial stage, communication is used to assess the overall situation, not only communication issues.
5. This is an adaptation of the Johari Window as presented in Anyaegbunam et al. 2004.
6. The example is taken from one of DevComm training programs.
7. For a more detailed discussion on the differences and similarities between communication needs assessment and communication-based assessments, see box 1.3 in module 1.
8. Surveys and opinion polls can overlap significantly, but in this context they are treated separately. The term "survey" indicates a wider scope, including knowledge, attitudes, and behaviors as well as other issues, while polls are intended to investigate opinions and attitudes on specific issues often on a global or national level.
9. PRCA was originally developed in 1995 by a team of FAO communication experts in conjunction with SADC experts working on a project that led to the establishment of the SADC Center of Communication for Development, in Harare, Zimbabwe.
10. The first WCCD took place in Rome, Italy, October 25–27, 2006.
11. The logical framework analysis approach is a method widely used by development organizations to plan, design, implement, and evaluate projects.
12. Objective-oriented project planning is a method to plan and manage projects based on a participatory approach.
13. The situation analysis framework is a planning method combining the logical framework analysis approach with elements of participatory communication. It was developed in Zimbabwe in the 1990s (Anyaegbunam et al. 2004).
14. The management objective is equivalent to a program or project objective.
15. The monitoring and evaluation phase is left out of this map; however, relevant indicators can be included from the beginning and checked in key steps, while the overall impact of the communication initiative can be evaluated at the end, once all planned activities have been implemented.
16. Presentation by John Paul Murdoch, Legal Counsel, Cree Nation, Hydro-Quebec, World Bank Energy Week 2005.

17. Operationalization is the process by which a specific concept is "broken down" in steps or operations in order to measure it.
18. Recently, there have been calls to evaluate even more subjective dimensions of the human sphere, such as happiness, as part of the shift to a more exhaustive conception of human development.
19. DevComm is rarely involved in the evaluation phase of projects, even though during the communication-based assessment its specialists usually assist in identifying relevant indicators for monitoring and evaluation.
20. This refers to the biases that one might incur when selecting the population samples. To be valid and reliable, samples should be as representative as possible, and when selected individuals need to participate in the initiative, as required.

References

Anyaegbunam, C., P. Mefalopulos, and T. Moetsabi. 2004. *Participatory Rural Communication Appraisal: Starting with the People* (2nd ed.). Rome: FAO and SADC.

Ascroft, J. 2006. "A Conspiracy of Courtesy." In *Communication for Social Change Anthology,* ed. A. Gumucio-Dagron and T. Tufte, 71–75. United States: Communication for Social Change Consortium, Inc.

Aycrigg, M. 1998. "Participation and the World Bank: Success, Constraints, and Responses." Social Development Paper 29. World Bank, Washington, DC.

Babbie, E. 2002. *The Basics of Social Research* (2nd ed.). Belmont, CA: Wadsworth/Thomson Learning.

Beltrán Salmón, L. R. 2000. *Investigación sobre Comunicación en Latinoamérica.* La Paz, Bolivia: Plural Editores.

Cabañero-Verzosa, Cecilia. 2002. "Determinants of Behavioral Intention in Developing Country Organizations." Unpublished doctoral dissertation, Department of Communication, University of Maryland at College Park.

Campos, J. E., and J. L. Syquia. 2006. *Managing the Politics of Reform.* Washington, DC: World Bank.

Coldevin, G. 2003. *Participatory Communication: A Key to Rural Learning Systems.* Rome, Italy: Food and Agriculture Organization of the United Nations.

FAO (Food and Agriculture Organization of the United Nations). 2005. *Communication for Development Roundtable Report: Focus on Sustainable Development.* Rome: FAO.

Fraser, C., S. Restrepo-Estrada, and L. Mazzei. 2007. "What Do They Think? Policy Makers and the Role of Commmunication for Development." In *Glocal Times* 7, http://www.glocaltimes.k3.mah.se/viewarticle.aspx?articleID=106&issueID=10.

Haider, M., R. Pal, and S. Al-Shoura. 2005. "Diffusion of Innovation and FOMENT: A Synergistic Theoretical Framework in Health Communication." In *Global Public Health Communication,* ed. M. Haider. Sudburt, MA: Jones and Bartlett Publishers.

Hope, A., and S. Timmel. 1984. *Training for Transformation: A Handbook for Community Workers,* vol. 1. Gweru, Zimbabwe: Mambo Press.

Hornik, R. C. 1988. *Development Communication: Information, Agriculture, and Nutrition in the Third World.* Lanham, MD: University Press of America.

Inagaki, N. 2007. "Communicating the Impact of Communication for Development: Recent Trends in Empirical Research." Working Paper No. 120, World Bank, Washington, DC.

Kuhn, T. S. 1970. *The Structure of Scientific Revolutions.* (2nd ed.). Chicago: University of Chicago Press.

Kuzek, J. Z., and R. C. Rist. 2004. *Ten Steps to a Results-Based Monitoring and Evaluation System.* Washington, DC: World Bank.

Lasswell, H. 1948. "The Structure and Function of Communication in Society." In *The Communication of Ideas,* ed. L. Bryson, 37–51. New York: Harper.

Mazzei, L., and G. Scuppa. 2006. "The Role of Communication in Large Infrastructure.: The Bumbuna Hydroelectric Project in Post-Conflict Sierra Leone." Working Paper No. 84, World Bank, Washington, DC.

Mefalopulos, A. 1999. *La Participación entre bastidores: La comunicación y la toma de decisiones entre los Guaraníes del Izozog, Bolivia.* Rome: FAO.

Mefalopulos, P. 2003. "Theory and Practice of Participatory Communication: The Case of the FAO Project 'Communication for Development in Southern Africa'." PhD diss., University of Texas.

Mefalopulos, P., and Kamlongera, C. 2004. *Participatory Communication Strategy Design* (2nd ed.). Rome: FAO and SADC.

Mody, B. 1991. *Designing Messages for Development Communication: An Audience Participation-Based Approach.* New Delhi, India: Sage Publications.

Morris, N. 2003. "A Comparative Analysis of the Diffusion and Participatory Models in Development Communication." In *Communication Theory* 13: 225–48. Blackwell Publishing.

Patton, M. 1990. *Qualitative Evaluation Research Methods.* Beverly Hills, CA: Sage Publications.

———. 2004. *Communication for Development in Latin America: A Forty-Year Appraisal.* Southbound. http://www.southbound.com.my/communication/cul-ch.htm.

World Bank. 2002. *Public Communication Projects for Privatization Projects.* Washington, DC: World Bank.

World Bank and DFID (Department for International Development). 2006. *Listening and Learning: Measuring the Impact of Communication for Development.* London: DFID.

Yum, J. O. 1989. "The Communication Network Paradigm and Intercultural Communication." In *Rethinking Communication,* ed. B. Dervin, L. Grossberg, B. J. O'Keefe, and E. Wartella, 486–96. Newbury Park, CA: Sage Publications.

MODULE 4

Development Communication Services and Operations at the World Bank

It has been remarked that almost every tragedy represents a failure in communication. In most cases, we may surmise, the failure is due not so much to what has NOT been said, as to what HAS been said; said, and misunderstood.
(Ashley Montagu)

This module addresses those who want to know more about the way development communication is positioned and applied at the World Bank. It presents in a detailed manner the services offered by the World Bank's Development Communication Division (DevComm). Project managers who incorporate communication or who are considering its use in the development process, communication practitioners, and students of communication will find the detailed accounts of World Bank procedures and practice helpful in their work in the growing and invaluable field of development communication. The second part of this module contains a number of articles by different authors dealing with various applications and aspects of this field.

Contents

Part II: The World of Practice: Some Experiences

Introduction: Development Communication Services and Experiences at the World Bank

In the previous modules of the Sourcebook, readers have been introduced to development communication theories and practices, especially in reference to World Bank operations. This fourth and last module of the Sourcebook illustrates the work of the Development Communication Division (DevComm) in more depth before presenting a series of articles addressing specific issues related to this field.

As part of the External Affairs Vice Presidency (EXT) of the World Bank, DevComm works in all regions and most sectors of operations within the World Bank and with its client countries and development partners. Its main goal is to enhance the design and the impact of operations through the professional use of development communication. To fully understand the value of DevComm's work, it is important to keep in mind how its scope and functions differ from and complement those of the other types of communication presented in modules 1 and 3 (that is, corporate, internal, or advocacy).

In the past, communication has focused mostly on the corporate side, disseminating information and using media for one-way communication to support development projects and programs. The inclusion of communication as an integral part of operations is relatively new, both in concept and in the provision of services. The emerging realization that communication, when applied at the outset of an initiative, can play a crucial role in assessing risks and facilitating the constructive participation of stakeholders has made it inevitable.

This evolution is reflected also within the World Bank. When it was established in 1998, DevComm had a manager and four staff; today it has more than 20 staff and a large group of skilled consultants with the capacity for working and delivering programs in a wide variety of languages and different environments. Such cultural richness is a key feature in development communication, whose results often depend on ensuring mutual understanding among different positions and perceptions. The following are DevComm's main goals:

- Strategically integrate communication components into operations to mitigate nonfinancial risks and maximize development outcomes[1]
- Explore and assess stakeholders' motivations and perceptions toward reforms and other development initiatives, using two-way communication approaches, public opinion surveys, and other empirical research methods
- Strengthen development communication capacities among clients and Bank staff to enhance results
- Build global partnerships in development communication

These objectives are reflected in the services DevComm provides to regions, sectors, specific operations, and client countries within the World Bank framework and with external partners. In the beginning, such services were restricted to a handful of projects in a few countries. Within a few years, the demand for these services grew steadily, and an inventory taken in 2004 indicated that DevComm was working on 93 projects in a wide range of different sectors, as indicated in figure 4.1. Another snapshot taken two years later revealed that DevComm was now involved in 126 projects.

Figure 4.1 DevComm Portfolio in FY04 and FY06

DevComm Portfolio by Sectors—June FY06 [total = 126 projects]

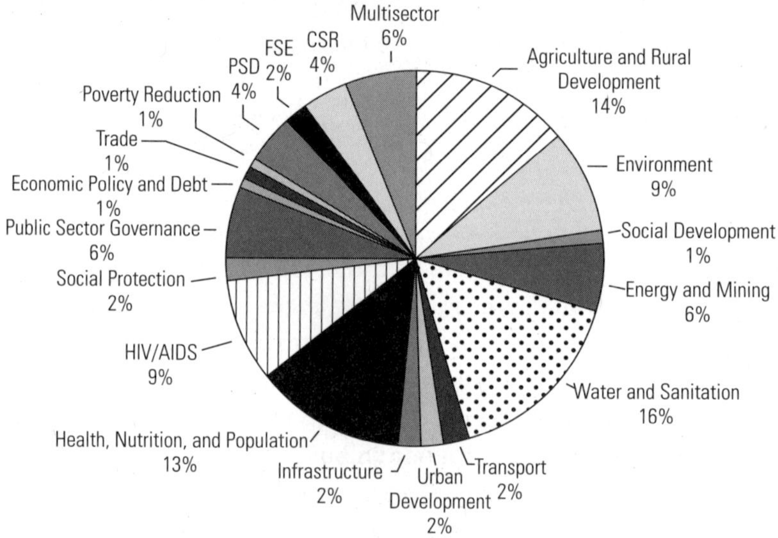

DevComm Portfolio by Sectors—October FY04 [total = 93 projects]

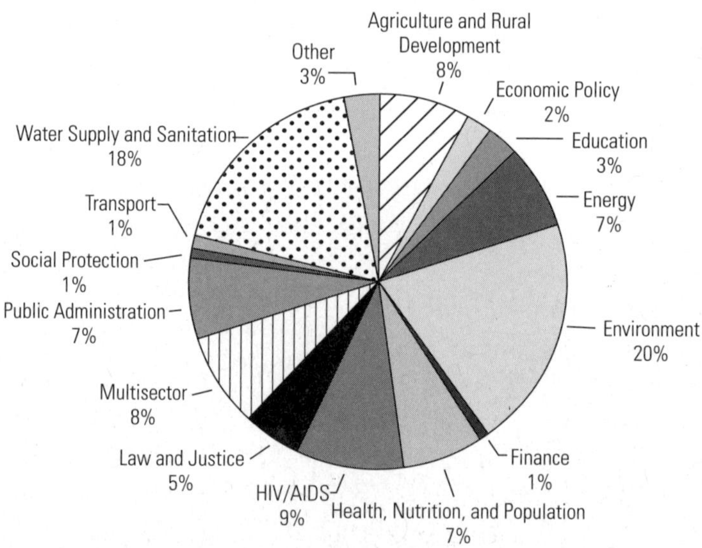

Source: DevComm statistics.

Note: PSD = Private Sector Development, FSE = Financial Sector Development, CSR = Corporate Social Responsibility.

Part I: DevComm Scope and Service Lines

4.1 The Development Communication Division Scope and Service Lines

M. Bruni, P. Mitchell, P. Mefalopulos, M. Faria, and D. Chung

DevComm is involved in activities covering a wide range of Bank operations, including specific projects, reform programs, and economic and sector work. Ideally, to be most effective, DevComm should start its assistance at the beginning of the project cycle, integrating its work with the project task team from the project identification phase. In reality, its involvement is often included after a project has already started implementing its activities. As illustrated in previous modules, a typical communication program can be divided into four main phases: (1) research or communication-based assessment, (2) communication strategy design, (3) program implementation, and (4) monitoring and evaluation.

DevComm Work in World Bank Operations

The application of development communication tools starts with operations at the country level, DevComm's intervention in the core strategic documents—the Country Assistance Strategy (CAS)[2] and Poverty Reduction Strategy Paper (PRSP).[3] The interventions at this level include instruments such as the client surveys and country portfolio reviews (CPR). DevComm also provides communication services during the implementation of these strategies.

In fact, DevComm inputs are vital to the adoption of participation and consultation processes leading to the formulation of documents and implementation of planned activities. The Bank's procedures on Country Assistance Strategies highlight the importance of consultations to help increase the Bank's understanding of country conditions and to promote public acceptance.

DevComm also carries out country portfolio reviews,[4] exercises that assess key issues, challenges, constraints, and opportunities faced by the various individual projects, and identifies countrywide social and political risks that can be addressed and mitigated through communication. These reviews often lead to changes in project design and work program agreements on communication. Country portfolio reviews are often conducted in coordination with World Bank External Affairs officers, a practice that helps to develop more integrated communication strategies and programs.

In addition to this work, DevComm also intervenes in ongoing projects at different stages of the project cycle when called upon. These types of intervention can be focused on a number of different issues and challenges faced by specific projects. Among them, the most common involve the use of communication to assess risks and opportunities, effectively inform key audiences about specific issues, strengthen institutional capacities, address conflict situations, promote reforms, devise damage-control approaches, or define overall strategies to enhance project design and activities.

To address the many challenges within development initiatives and to integrate communication in World Bank operations effectively, DevComm activities embrace sound opinion research, knowledge management, training, and building of strategic alliances and partnerships. DevComm work is organized into three service lines, illustrated in the following pages.

4.1.1 DevComm Service Lines

DevComm bases its functions on a demand-driven model with service lines devoted to World Bank priorities: (1) communication in operations, (2) public opinion research, and (3) knowledge and learning.

Communication in Operations concerns the application of communication approaches and methods for behavior and social change in development projects, reform programs, and economic and sector work in support of World Bank initiatives. DevComm is actively involved in more than 100 projects a year in various sectors and areas, such as environment, infrastructure, public sector governance, health, and social development.

The Public Opinion Research Unit conducts analysis on a global, regional, sectoral, and project level. This research creates valuable knowledge about perceptions on relevant issues, provides strategic guidance for development initiatives, and improves operational outcomes. About 30 polls per year are designed, delivered, and integrated into the World Bank strategic planning.

The Knowledge and Learning Unit activities help Bank staff, governments, and local partners build capacities in communication, strengthening knowledge and skills in communication-related aspects. DevComm Knowledge and Learning Unit has a menu of core courses and also develops and delivers training programs customized to clients needs for specific projects and programs.

The following pages deal with each of these services in a detailed way. These services are not self-contained; instead, many of the activities in a line of service may overlap with those of another.

Service Line #1: Communication in Operations

Operations is the main service line of DevComm and includes all interventions in Bank-financed projects and programs. At the core of this work is research—that is, investigative and analytical activities, usually based on two-way communication approaches to engage key stakeholders and to assess significant issues. DevComm is engaged in a wide range of activities related to operations. Its line of work encompasses political risk assessment and research studies; the strategic application of communication approaches and methods for behavior change in development projects and reform programs; and the application of two-way communication to facilitate stakeholders' participation and to support community-driven development, economic, and sector work.

Because of the increasing relevance of development communication, DevComm has received a number of trust-fund donations from donor countries to augment its capacity, to focus on specific areas of work, and to effectively address the growing demand for its services. Two of these funds led to the establishment of thematic units within the division. The Communication for Sustainable Development in Operations (DevComm-SDO) Unit was the first in the division to be supported by a trust-fund donation. This unit was established in 2001, and it was consolidated in 2002 with a contribution from the Italian Ministry of Foreign Affairs. The other major trust-fund donation was made by the United Kingdom Department for International Development (DFID), which is the original donor to the Communication for Governance and Accountability Program (CommGAP). CommGap was launched in 2006, and it is currently funded through what has become a multidonor trust fund of several million dollars.

In addition to these two units, another important area of thematic work in DevComm, closely related to the work in operations, is partnership building. These areas are discussed in greater detail in the following pages.

Communication for Governance and Accountability Program (CommGAP)

The Communication for Governance and Accountability Program (CommGAP) seeks to promote good and accountable governance through the use of innovative communication approaches and techniques that strengthen the public sphere. CommGAP has three interrelated core program areas:

- *Research and advocacy.* CommGAP, through a series of dialogs and consultations, brings together leading thinkers and practitioners from around the world—in communication, the allied social sciences, and international development—to discuss, debate, identify, and fill existing gaps in current theory and practice. CommGAP organized two multidisciplinary learning dialogs in 2007: "Governance Reform Under Real World Conditions: A Dialogue on Communication Challenges," and "Generating Genuine Demand with Social Accountability Mechanisms." Relevant research from these fields has been brought to bear on finding solutions to real-world governance challenges.

- *Training and capacity building.* On the basis of the research agenda mentioned above, CommGAP is developing an innovative training and capacity-building program for reformers in development organizations and client countries. This training program is designed to equip reformers with communication-based solutions for challenges such as securing political will; gaining the support of public sector middle managers; addressing powerful vested interests and indifferent, or even hostile, public opinion; and stimulating citizen demand for good governance and accountability.
- *Support to operations.* CommGAP tests and refines innovative communication approaches in selected development projects and programs, ranging from communication support for the World Bank's first stand-alone governance project (Cambodia's Demand for Good Governance Project), to comprehensive communication support to the post-conflict states of Sierra Leone and Liberia, and to the strengthening of the institutions of accountability and demand-side governance in Bangladesh and Mozambique.

Through this work CommGAP seeks to fill two gaps in the design and implementation of governance reform. One gap is at the process level, the other is at the structural level. At the process level, although there is increasing awareness that for reform programs to succeed, reform managers must confront challenges concerning stakeholders, vested interests, coalition building, and either hostile or indifferent public opinion, these issues are put in a black box and described as "political economy issues." CommGAP seeks to illuminate this black box and provide a way to deal with difficult issues in order to make governance initiatives more successful and sustainable.

At the structural level, there is insufficient appreciation that the democratic public sphere is an essential part of how to secure good governance and accountability and, therefore, should be a part of how governance programs are designed. Although some of the constitutive elements of the democratic public sphere are now part of the governance agenda, a framework that ties everything together and takes advantage of the mutually reinforcing nature of the different elements of a democratic public sphere is entirely missing. CommGAP seeks to heighten understanding of the importance of the public sphere in supporting good governance, both by influencing the policy debate and by improving practice in the field.

Communication for Sustainable Development in Operations Unit (DevComm-SDO)

The Communication for Sustainable Development in Operations Unit (DevComm-SDO) was created in 2001 with a mandate to mainstream development communication into development projects and programs. Later, a contribution from the Ministry of Foreign Affairs of Italy made it possible for the unit to grow and bring in added expertise. The unit, in addition to promoting the policies and practices of sustainable development communication in operations, also focused its activities on knowledge management, partnership building, corporate social responsibility, and multistakeholders' dialog, and in leveraging funds for global environmental protection.

Over the last seven years, the scope and extent of the communication interventions led or advised by the DevComm-SDO unit expanded considerably to meet the rising demand from World Bank task team leaders. With the recognition of the fundamental role of communication in the sectors of infrastructure, tourism, water supply, and sanitation, among others, the scope of the unit's work has gone beyond its initial focus on sustainable development, namely, in environment, climate change, biodiversity, conservation, agriculture, and rural development. As a result, since 2003–04, DevComm-SDO has been involved in a number of different sectors—from sustainable tourism to public sector reforms, and from corporate social responsibility[5] to human development projects. While most of its activities are in Latin America, Africa, and Eastern Europe, DevComm-SDO has assisted more than 200 projects in over 50 countries in most regions since its creation.

DevComm-SDO has also been working steadily to leverage additional financing that complements its activities, both at the operational and the knowledge management level. One such example of additional financing was a contribution from the European Commission for the activities aimed at establishing a better environment for corporate social responsibility in Central and Eastern European (CEE) countries. Over the years this Unit has developed research and literature on a number of topics, from corporate social responsibility to communication for sustainable development, and from communication in infrastructure to participatory communication.

In line with the work carried out at the division level, DevComm-SDO staff assess perceptions, attitudes, knowledge, and behaviors of various stakeholders vis-à-vis the proposed project, and on the basis of that assessment, they advise project teams on how to develop and structure a communication program that addresses the challenges and obstacles the project faces and builds on the opportunities for success. DevComm-SDO also provides advice and guidance on the procurement of communication activities and services, whenever needed. Its lines of activities, in addition to providing technical assistance in development projects throughout the world, also lead to establishing and enhancing partnerships and alliances with key players in the organization of international conferences, learning events, and knowledge products.

In partnership with FAO and the Communication Initiative,[6] and in collaboration with other institutions, both internal and external to the World Bank, DevComm-SDO was instrumental in proposing, organizing, and carrying out the first

World Congress on Communication for Development, which took place at FAO headquarters in Rome, on October 25–27, 2006. This event constituted a major benchmark in the field that attracted a highly inclusive and diversified public and was particularly successful in bringing together, for the first time, three key audiences that seldom interact: practitioners, academicians, and policy- and decision makers.

The preparatory work leading up to the Congress was a challenging and innovative effort by itself. Not only did it foster an interagency effort seldom seen for such events, but it also included in the organizational structure different types of organizations (for example, academia, NGOs, UN agencies, donors) that, for the first time, were able not only to interact but also to provide inputs that refined the scope and structure of this event. However imperfect, such an open and participatory approach in the organization of an event of this magnitude had not been witnessed before, either at the Bank, or outside.

More than 900 participants from a variety of different organizations and institutions were present for this three-day event. They included representatives from donor countries, bilateral organizations, United Nations agencies, nongovernmental organizations of different sizes and scopes; representatives of a number of governments, especially from developing countries; and many practitioners from all over the world. This wealth of diversified perspectives stimulated a rich and unique exchange among the participants on many of the main principles and challenges that shape this field. The Congress concluded by embracing the Rome Consensus (see the appendix), a document that broadly defines the scope and boundaries of this interdisciplinary field and helps provide a common ground for facilitating the creation of partnerships and inter-institutional collaborations.

Partnership Building

Within the World Bank framework, specific units of the External Affairs Vice Presidency, such as EXT Europe and United Nations Affairs New York, are responsible for political relations with the UN and European donors. Even if not defined by a specific unit, this area of work also has a high priority in DevComm, which is responsible for partnering with UN agencies, bilateral donors, think tanks, foundations, academia, and other international financial institutions to enhance the use of communication to promote effectiveness in development programs and projects. In all cases, these partnerships are made possible by the credibility DevComm has acquired over the years with its work, both at the operational level and as a knowledge center.

DevComm represents the World Bank on different kinds of bodies and inter-institutional meetings, from the operational ones—that is, those forming strategic alliances and partnerships to enhance the work at project level—to the policy- and decision-making ones. United Nations Roundtables on Communication for Development and OECD-Development Assistance Committee (DAC7) meetings are an example of such collaborations. DevComm also provides substantive inputs into various international forums, such as the recent London School of Economics Forum, "Media Development in Africa"; the German Agency for Technical Cooperation (GTZ)-sponsored forum on "Media and Crisis Countries"; the 5th International Public Relations Forum; and the interagency forum on Communication for Avian Flu.

Among the activities dedicated to partnership building, DevComm has leveraged resources for joint programs from approximately 19 donors over the years. It also provided technical assistance to help promote or strengthen development communication units and programs within various institutions, such as the African Development Bank (AfDB), Inter-American Development Bank (IADB), United Kingdom Department for International Development (DFID), the Swedish International Development Cooperation Agency (SIDA), and the French Development Agency (AfFD). This area of responsibility also involves working with these organizations to produce global public goods in communication that everyone can use, thus harmonizing work across the development community.

Service Line #2: Public Opinion Research

This unit oversees the design, management, and development of polls at a global level as well as opinion research initiatives across the Bank. Its work focuses on external constituents—clients and other stakeholders—whose views and perceptions often influence opinion about the Bank and its work. DevComm oversees survey efforts with beneficiaries as well, in order to assess and identify the risks associated with specific projects. Polling efforts ensure that operational and organizational strategies are based on sound foundations and resonate with critical audiences. In addition, the surveys are designed to identify overall risks and opportunities objectively and independently for the institution or the development initiative among constituents.

DevComm manages the client survey program at the World Bank. These surveys measure the views of the Bank held by key stakeholders in various countries and in specific areas of Bank work. While it is not mandatory, the institution encourages country teams to conduct these objective and independent opinion assessments while preparing their country assistance strategies and, consequently, in the preparation of specific projects as well.

The surveys are tailored to the needs of the country. The program allows for country teams to track views (and specific indicators) over time. Country teams use the findings to inform their communication and engagement strategies and to guide the way they do business in countries. In particular, the surveys provide insight into how well aligned the Bank's priorities are with a country's development priorities.

This may influence the Bank's communication approach (for example, linking the Bank's work more effectively with the stakeholders' priorities) or the focus of the Bank's work. Since 2002, client surveys have been conducted in more than 60 countries and have involved at least 8,000 respondents.

Service Line #3: Knowledge and Learning

In 2002, DevComm developed a learning program for the External Affairs Vice Presidency, conducting courses on communication to support lending operations and knowledge products for Bank managers and for staff of developing client countries. DevComm represents External Affairs on the World Bank's Learning Board. Its activities have grown steadily from its inception, and in 2007 DevComm delivered more than 50 training events to more than 2,500 participants.

The main goal of this service line is to equip Bank staff and country clients with the knowledge and skills in communication and client engagement needed for effective development programs. The Knowledge and Learning Unit helps Bank staff, governments, and other local partners enhance their capacity to implement and sustain communication activities. The unit works with various Bank departments, especially the World Bank Institute, to offer training—face-to-face, distance learning, and blended course—on different types of communication for development.

DevComm integrates formal learning and informal knowledge-sharing activities and reaches a comprehensive set of participants from among Bank operational staff, communication specialists, and developing country partners from governments and NGOs. This unit aims to sustain learning interventions through linkages with DevComm's technical assistance activities. The basic set of core courses for World Bank staff includes Art & Science of Strategic Communication (I and II), Managing Political Risk, Stakeholders' Consultations, Communicating Effectively for Results, Strategic Communication, Client Engagement and Communication, Crisis Communication, Media Training, and Research for Strategic Communication: Survey Techniques and Tools.

Moreover, the Knowledge and Learning Unit offers distance-learning courses and operational customized workshops that are designed according to the specific needs of programs and projects, drawing from available knowledge and experiences. Services are delivered to Bank communication and operational staff and to client government operational and communication staff. Programs are also delivered to partner development organizations to strengthen their capacities to design, implement, and evaluate development communication interventions and to disseminate knowledge products based on the experience gathered throughout the project cycle.

In addition to training courses and learning programs, this unit is also engaged in collecting, systematizing, and sharing knowledge products built on experience with project interventions and technical assistance. Such products are then published in print as stand-alone publications in the World Bank Working Paper Series and online through the DevComm Web site. The scope of these publications is to provide valuable insights to practitioners and decision makers and further promote the value-added of development communication approaches with policy- and decision makers.

4.1.2 DevComm at Work: Key Issues, Strengths, and Challenges in Operations

Rather than supporting operations through information dissemination, as is the case for other types of communication (that is, corporate, advocacy, and internal), the core of DevComm's work is an integral part of operations. This distinction is a significant one, since development communication activities are key elements in assessing and mitigating risks, exploring opportunities and solutions, defining objectives, and shaping the project design. Particularly when used for maximum effectiveness from the inception of projects and programs, development communication adds value at each phase and enhances sustainable results in operations.

Initiation of Project Work

Given their cross-cutting and interdisciplinary nature, development communication activities work best when designed and performed through teamwork in coordination with other Bank staff involved in the projects and other stakeholders. In this context, the term "stakeholders" should be taken in its broadest sense, indicating relevant World Bank colleagues, government officials, representatives of civil society, and the range of other individuals involved.

At an operational level, DevComm specialists carry out their work in close collaboration with project team leaders. DevCommers' first contact should be with colleagues from the World Bank's External Affairs Vice Presidency (EXT) engaged in relevant work, especially those based in client countries. EXT's main goal is to increase understanding and support for the World Bank Group's mission and work, but one of its strategic lines is to enhance development effectiveness in operations through the use of communication.

External Affairs communication officers in regions and countries are involved in a number of different activities, mostly related to advocacy and corporate communication. However, their in-depth knowledge of the sociopolitical context and of related key actors make their inputs very valuable for communication-based assessments or for other development communication activities at country level. For maximum effectiveness, there should be an active collaboration among DevComm experts, country communication officers, and sectoral specialists (that is, economists and other experts in different fields such as infrastructure, environment, rural development, and so forth) related to the project.

DevComm and the Communication Program Cycle

To enhance projects' effectiveness, DevComm's modus operandi emphasizes both the dialogic and analytical functions of communication as well as monologic approaches. DevComm's methodology is based on a communication program cycle divided into four main phases, as shown in figure 4.2.

Research or communication-based assessment (CBA) is the initial phase of any intervention and generates the inputs for designing the project communication strategy. It is carried out through several methods and techniques that either can be implemented in their entirety by DevComm specialists or, more often, be partly outsourced. These activities include, among others, the stakeholders' analysis, sociopolitical risk assessment, consultative schemes for dialog, and qualitative and quantitative opinion and perceptions surveys.

The communication-based assessment identifies key clusters of stakeholders; gains an understanding into social, cultural, and political nuances and roadblocks affecting the initiative; identifies the position and behavior of stakeholders; and generates valuable inputs needed to define or validate priorities and to design effective messages. The assessment determines which strategies are needed to build consensus, and the ways to communicate effectively with relevant audiences. The CBA also helps to assess communication capacities, both inside and outside the involved institutions, including the broader media sector, which is often crucial to support development initiatives. Building on the CBA, DevComm works with World Bank operational task teams and government counterparts to prepare communication strategies. The following are some specific contributions of CBA to operations:

Figure 4.2 Basic Phases of a Communication Program

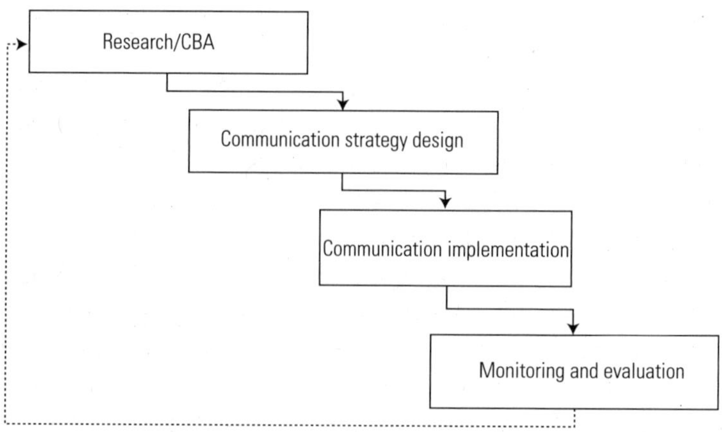

Source: Author.

Note: CBA = Communication-based assessment.

- Probing key issues, problems, and opportunities
- Identifying audiences' or stakeholders' perceptions and positions
- Assessing and mitigating social and political risks
- Identifying "champions" for the initiative
- Giving an understanding of decision-making mechanisms
- Providing inputs for project design
- Providing inputs for effective communication strategy
- Defining or aligning development objectives

Throughout project preparation, qualitative and quantitative opinion surveys are designed and carried out to refine the program logic and to create the baseline for the monitoring and evaluation framework (M&E). A set of instruments is generally applied at this stage; among the most common are interviews and focus groups used to do the initial probing of key issues. Afterwards, quantitative research instruments are used to validate and assess the extent of the initial findings.

As discussed in other parts of the Sourcebook, when the communication-based assessment is not properly performed in a timely manner, the risks of misunderstandings, conflicts, and problems increase exponentially. In the Yacireta hydroelectric project, for example, communication was not considered a key component, and it took three decades to acknowledge the seriousness of this negligence. In 2004, a review by the World Bank Inspection Panel[8] signaled the absence of a communication strategy as one of the major shortcomings of the project—a shortcoming that led to major delays and misunderstandings with local stakeholders.

Responding to this message from the panel, the Yacireta project management requested the inclusion of communication, and a communication-based assessment was conducted. Unfortunately, it was three decades too late, and communication could only suggest minor adjustments to improve a seriously compromised situation. Most of the problems and conflicts were firmly entrenched in the historical structure of the project and in the related sociocultural environment. If CBA had been conducted at the beginning of the project, the assessment would have found and addressed critical issues, and most, if not all, shortcomings in the project design and implementation might have been avoided.

Communication strategy design, the next step in the development communication process, is based on the research findings. In this phase, DevComm staff advise—in dialog with the client country counterparts and the task team—on the design of the communication program strategy. When the DevComm specialist participates in the project preparation as part of the project team, issues of relevance (even those outside the communication domain) that might otherwise be neglected are often uncovered and addressed, thus contributing to the enhancement of the project's quality and sustainability. The design of a strategy, no matter how complex, usually results in an action plan containing key elements for implementing the activities (see module 3).

Communication program implementation begins when the project or the client government starts the activities needed to achieve the set objectives. In the early stages of this phase, DevComm can assist with capacity building to strengthen the ownership of the communication processes and to fortify prospects for sustainability. Activities carried out in this phase with DevComm assistance can include training programs, audiovisual production, or implementation of campaigns for behavior and social change.

Monitoring and evaluation concludes the project cycle. This phase allows specialists and managers to understand the reach of the communication program and to determine if the expected outcomes have been achieved. Indicators for monitoring the activities and evaluating the final impact should be identified and set from the very beginning (that is, during the CBA). The instruments used to carry out evaluations are similar to the ones used in initial research—baseline study, surveys, and interviews—since they usually measure the same variables or the difference between the situation before and after the intervention took place. The importance of carrying out such baseline studies at the start of the initiative is illustrated in the example in box 4.1

Without the initial baseline, the data to evaluate the communication impact in the example above would not have been available, and it would have been impossible to assess how communication affected the overall project. Each phase of the project can be enhanced by communication, and the specific impact of communication can also be assessed for each of those phases, even if not always in an accurate manner. Figure 4.3 illustrates how the communication program relates, supports, and interacts with the project cycle—always keeping in mind that, in some cases, different situations might require different modalities of intervention. Different communication functions and the outputs expected from each communication phase, which are also helpful in defining evaluation indicators, are linked to specific phases of the project cycle, helping to visualize the interaction between the two.

Figure 4.3 also indicates that much of the experience gathered throughout the communication program cycle is condensed in knowledge products. These are of crucial importance in the dissemination of both instances of successes and failures and in being able to learn from them. Learning from past experiences greatly helps to improve future projects' assessment and design, steadily enhancing results in the long term.

This presentation of the structure and modus operandi of DevComm highlights the link between the concepts and principles of development communication and the daily practices of projects and programs supported by the World Bank. Practical communication applications can be different in scope and activities, but they should always be based on a consistent methodological framework that starts with CBA.

The next part of the module presents a number of cases and experiences related to DevComm's work. Some of the articles illustrate how development communica-

BOX 4.1 Evaluating the Performance of Communication in Public Sector Reforms

The monitoring and evaluation of a communication component measures both the outputs and outcomes, and more generally, is designed to evaluate the performance of a component. Between 2004 and 2006, Nicaragua carried out a complex communication program as part of the public sector reforms program supported by the World Bank. The program integrated different communication perspectives and tools in an effort to establish a two-way communication system between citizens and government. The communication program promoted the participation of local public administrations in decision-making and monitoring processes for national investments, the enhancement of public sector transparency, and the building of a consensus around the reforms.

The communication program's initial baseline measured 110 indicators, both on program performance (that is, the number of newsletters issued) and on program "impact" on perceptions and attitudes (that is, people's expectations of a better personal economic situation in the future). The monitoring and evaluation system allowed the government to track the program's performance, to readjust the planning of activities on a regular basis, and to evaluate what the program produced.

The communication program established a public sector communication network in 17 institutions, achieving a coherent visual image and training 47 communication specialists from ministries and national agencies. Departmental Development Committees (CDD/R) were established in 14 departments and 2 autonomous regions; annual negotiations roundtables were organized as a place for dialog between CDD/R and the national government, allowing the local public administrations to prioritize an increasing percentage of the public investment budget (5 percent in 2004, 15 percent in 2005, 25 percent in 2006). From May 2005 to August 2006, people's perception of corruption by government officials decreased by 7.2 percent, and public opinion expectations for a better personal economic situation in the future increased by 7.6 percent.

Source: Bruni, M. Forthcoming. "Participation, Transparency, and Consensus Building in Support of Public Sector Reform: The Case of Nicaragua." In *Governance Reform under Real-World Conditions: Citizens, Stakeholders, and Voice,* ed. S. Odugbemi and T. Jacobson.

tion is used for cross-sectoral purposes (for example, Poverty Reduction Strategy Papers) or with specific media (for example, community radio).[9] Others discuss the relevance of communication in specific areas of development in which that role is not always widely acknowledged, such as disabilities. The challenges faced in build-

Figure 4.3 Links between Communication Program and Project Cycle

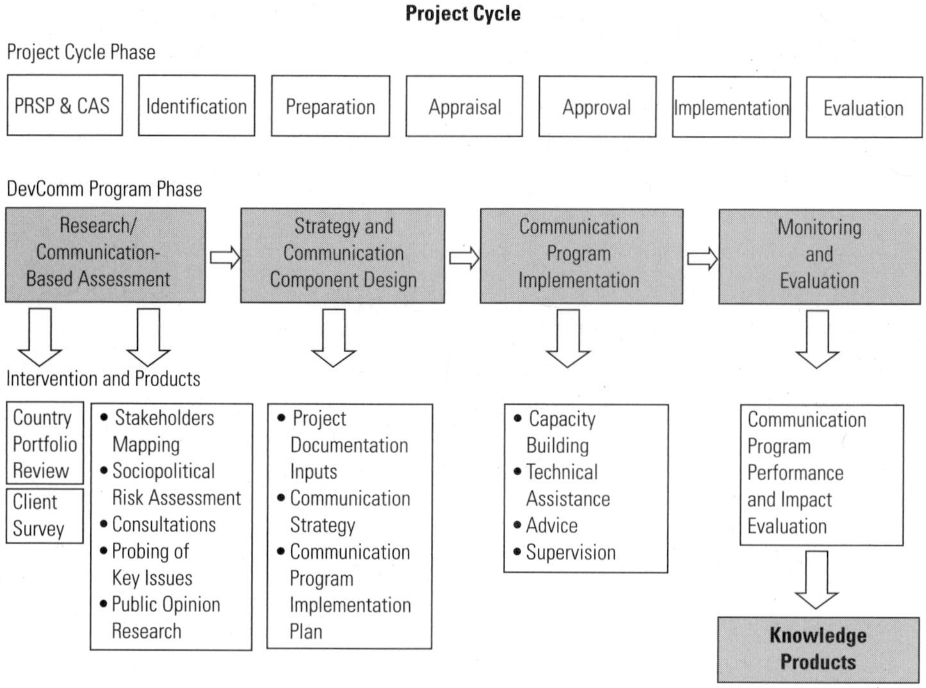

Source: Michele Bruni and Paolo Mefalopulos.

ing communication capacities in multilateral institutions are also discussed. Finally, this module concludes with an article on the impact of development communication—a major challenge that must be addressed in order to scale up and mainstream this interdisciplinary field in development policies and practices.

The articles presented in the following pages do not intend to represent the entire work in development communication; rather, they provide useful insights into some of the key aspects related to this field. The interdisciplinary and cross-cutting nature of development communication allows its use in virtually all situations. Its absence, on the other hand, significantly elevates the risks of misunderstandings and problems that could jeopardize the overall success of an initiative. If a common thread is to be found through all of these different pieces, it is the importance of using two-way communication in a professional, analytical, and systematic way at the onset of development initiatives. Everyone seems to agree on this, but too few decision makers seem willing to put it into practice at the project or program level.

Notes

1. A major factor in this respect would be the incorporation of a communication-based assessment (CBA) at the onset of all relevant development initiatives. This method investigates issues while promoting the active participation of key stakeholders.
2. Country Assistance Strategy is a kind of business plan that the Bank adopts to identify and assess key priority areas and activities. It is prepared about every four years for each country in which the World Bank has an assistance program.
3. Poverty Reduction Strategy Papers are prepared by member countries through a participatory process, usually every three years, and describe the macroeconomic and structural situation of the country, prioritizing areas in need of assistance.
4. Country Portfolio Reviews are a required periodic exercise carried out jointly by World Bank and the member country. Its main purpose is to strengthen the country portfolio and impact of operations.
5. DevComm-SDO took a leading role in corporate social responsibility; it was actively involved in conferences related to this topic and a number of publications that can be found on the World Bank DevComm Web site. See http://go.worldbank.org/BXYX66PE10.
6. The Communication Initiative (CI) network is an online space for sharing the knowledge and experiences in communication and media for economic and social development and change.
7. It is the Development Assistance Committee (DAC) of the Organisation for Economic Co-operation and Development (OECD) that deals with issues related to cooperation with developing countries.
8. The Inspection Panel was established by the executive directors of the International Bank for Reconstruction and Development (IBRD) and the International Development Association (IDA) on September 22, 1993. Its primary purpose is to address the concerns of the people who may be affected by Bank projects and to ensure that the Bank adheres to its operational policies and procedures during design, preparation, and implementation phases of projects.
9. Most of the work on community radio in the World Bank is not carried out by DevComm; nonetheless, significant experiences of other communication experts in the Bank are included here, given their importance to the field of development communication.

Part II: The World of Practice: Some Experiences

4.2. Development Communication to Fight Poverty through Poverty Reduction Strategy Papers

*Masud Mozammel**

Introduction: How It All Began

In the late 1990s, the major global development actors led by the World Bank and the International Monetary Fund (IMF) developed a new approach to fight global poverty and to build a new kind of relationship with low-income countries. In December 1999, the Board of the World Bank and IMF formally introduced this approach, centered on the development and implementation of poverty reduction strategies or PRSs, which "was in many ways novel."[1] These strategies were to be "country-driven," prepared by the countries themselves, with strong focus on inclusion, "predicated on [the] broad-based participatory process of formulation, implementation, and outcome-based progress monitoring."[2]

The development and implementation of the PRS document, popularly known as the Poverty Reduction Strategy Paper or PRSP, is also to be "partnership oriented," taking into account the participation and engagement of all key stakeholders—governmental and nongovernmental development partners, both local and international, ensuring "effective ownership, participation, and accountability."[3]

In the couple of years following the introduction of the Poverty Reduction Strategy Papers, country experience showed a strong need for a strategic and comprehensive communication intervention to ensure the effective participation of various stakeholders through genuine inclusion. Participation in the formulation of PRSPs "tended to be 'broad' rather than 'deep' with a wide range of stakeholders engaged, but only to a limited extent."[4] The communication intervention was needed not only to ensure a two-way flow of information among the stakeholders and to provide the PRSP organizers with tools to communicate with, listen to, and engage all stakeholders, but more important, to create a public space for an informed and inclusive national dialog to face the challenges of fighting poverty.

As the need for systematic communication interventions grew stronger, many countries started applying these methods and tools in the Poverty Reduction Strat-

- The author is a senior communication officer in the Development Communication Division, External Affairs Vice Presidency of the World Bank.

egy Paper process. Communication, however, was mostly used to disseminate information about the PRSP through publications, seminars, and workshops. The focus was limited primarily to information sharing; it did not address the more difficult task of facilitating the genuine and meaningful engagement of stakeholders. The assumption could not be made that "an information-rich environment would ensure the effective participation of stakeholders and establish ownership of the effort."[5] If the sociopolitical, historical, cultural, and economic dimensions of a given country are not taken into account, information flow alone cannot solve the priority problems.

Development Communication in Poverty Reduction Strategy Papers: An Evolution

Communication in Poverty Reduction Strategy Papers addresses issues beyond the standard information interventions in development projects or programs, such as health, education, environment, or agriculture. The more typical approaches, such as social marketing, public relations, media campaigns, or public education, do not apply. Largely based on a two-way model, communication interventions for PRSPs involve a set of disparate actors and factors.[6]

The actors crucial to the process are a diverse set to engage—from governments' line ministries to top government offices of the president or prime minister, from civil society to donors, or from academia to the private sector. Most important for communication interventions in the PRS process, a whole set of critical factors, unusual for a typical communication program, becomes a bigger challenge. These factors range from politics to bureaucracy and from economics to sociology. They involve parliaments and technocrats and deal with issues beyond the standard format of democratic governance.

As the Poverty Reduction Strategy Paper experience grew older, communication and information challenges supporting its core principles[7] became more complicated and went beyond the goal of achieving the relatively straightforward objectives of putting together a campaign, building awareness through public education, or holding a consultation. The evolution of communication approaches in PRSPs can be broadly divided into two phases of the PRS process: the formulation stage and the implementation stage.

Communication in the Formulation of Poverty Reduction Strategies

Workshops and seminars on a country's major development issues and activities on building awareness about the PRS process as part of the "consultations" for a Poverty Reduction Strategy Paper became popular in a number of countries. They were regarded as communication interventions to promote and ensure the participatory character of the process. As time went by and more PRSPs were formulated, there was an increased awareness that it was essential to move beyond the consultation-centered communication approach.

The first major review of poverty reduction strategies in 2002 clearly states, "The challenge for most countries is to move away from ad hoc consultations to more institutionalized forms of dialog."[8] The review also indicates concern on "whether governments are limiting participation to information sharing and consultation, and whether civil society can extend its role in the decision-making process beyond targeted poverty reduction programs to the macroeconomic policy and the structural reform agenda, especially trade liberalization and privatization."[9]

The demand for a strategic application of communication methods and tools aimed to create an environment where informed dialog and debate would result in better policy making for poverty reduction. In addition, these two-way communication approaches would establish ownership of the process, promote accountability in governance, build momentum, and manage expectations. The following are some of the major topics that many countries regarded as key objectives for communication programs in the poverty reduction strategy process:

- Establish a two-way communication process to share knowledge and information about poverty and development issues through open and inclusive dialog
- Design and implement a systematic communication program with specific timelines, responsibilities, and resources to build ownership, create momentum, and manage expectations
- Strengthen internal communication with various stakeholder groups, such as parliamentarians, government apparatus, civil society, trade unions, academicians and researchers, community organizations, development partners, and so forth
- Institutionalize and build capacity in the country to develop, implement, and manage PRSP communication activities
- Create a knowledge base on PRSP-related information and experiences on national, regional, and international levels

Since it involves a wide range of issues related to culture, language, behavior, socioeconomic and political dynamics, psychological patterns, existing communication channels, and networks in the given country, the design of a communication strategy for Poverty Reduction Strategy Papers varies from country to country. In 2002 the World Bank's *PRSP Sourcebook* included a chapter on "Strategic Communication in PRSP," which offered practical guidance on developing and implementing communication programs in the context of poverty reduction strategies. It includes case examples where communication interventions were used for information sharing and dissemination in formulation of PRSPs. It also elaborates a set of

Table 4.1 Steps in Developing a Communication Plan for PRSPs

Objective	Set Objectives for Short, Medium, and Long Term
Research	Data collection
Activities	Define activities for information sharing and dissemination Set goals for each activity Define timing, budget, and responsibility
Audience	Select audience groups; understand their interests, advantages, and disadvantages Analyze audience status, education, and position
Messages	Develop group-specific messages
Networks	Identify existing networks Understand dynamics of the networks
Channels	Assess the existing channels at national, regional, and local levels Identify the accessibility
Feedback	Incorporate feedback to the PRSP
Costing	Establish existing and required capacity for human and financial resources

Source: "Strategic Communication in PRSP." In *PRSP Sourcebook,* Washington, DC: World Bank.

essential elements to consider when developing a communication action plan as part of a PRSP communication program.[10]

Communication in the Implementation of Poverty Reduction Strategies

In the early days of poverty reduction strategy planning, information interventions to build ownership of national poverty reduction plans through effective engagement of stakeholders became more challenging than envisioned. The major difficulties were not with technical challenges for the design and implementation of Poverty Reduction Strategy Papers or similar approaches but with sociopolitical and structural issues. Political environments and structural dynamics under which governments operate are critical factors for building ownership of and participation in the poverty reduction process. These complex factors are not always carefully considered.

The necessary capacity to participate effectively is another major issue to be considered in the Poverty Reduction Strategy Paper process. While in many countries this has not emerged as a major challenge, in general it is a vital issue to be addressed. The following are major sociopolitical and structural issues arising in the PRS implementation stage that relate to communication interventions:

- Access to information and true freedom of media and expression
- Tension between ministry of finance or other government departments and the department(s) in charge of the PRSP or similar poverty reduction plans (such as

the ministry of economy; planning commission; offices of the president, prime minister, or the vice president)
- Tension among civil society organizations and frustration within them
- Unclear role of groups created during the PRSP preparation phases to ensure ownership and participation of key stakeholders, including groups, known as participation councils, or working groups, that play the role of advisory team, oversight group, and technical working group to plan communication and participation strategies, and their implementation and coordination among other key thematic teams, such as sectoral teams, macroeconomy teams, and so forth
- Lack of a clearly defined role for and engagement of the elected representatives, including the parliamentarians
- Using PRSPs as a promotional tool for the ruling political parties, as "champion," without enough emphasis on the real focus of creating an open and inclusive dialog on poverty issues and translating that into policy actions

From "Dissemination and Publicity Strategy" to "Communication Program"

The Ghana poverty reduction strategy experience highlights the evolution in communication, from a dissemination and public relations tool to a more integrated and sophisticated element of the strategy.

Communication Interventions in the First Ghana Poverty Reduction Strategy in 2003

The preparation for the formulation of the first Ghana poverty reduction strategy (GPRS) began in early 2000 and focused on the consultation and dissemination aspects of its communication activities. The "formal consultations for the GPRS" identified and involved several groups, including community groups, media, trade union congress, professional bodies, and student unions, NGOs in service delivery and religious bodies, members of parliament, representatives of political parties, sector ministers and their deputies, development partners, a parliamentary select committee, and so forth.[11]

Raising awareness was deemed to be the central role of communication, a goal clearly stated under its dissemination and publicity strategy: "Government wishes as many Ghanaians as possible, especially the poor, to be aware of the content of the final GPRS document and how they can benefit from it or use it in their development efforts," read the introductory sentence of the section on the strategy reasoning. Its objective was "to create a national understanding of the GPRS for effective participation of communities, groups, or individuals in influencing decisions on development policies and expenditures."[12]

One of the key challenges for successful strategic communication interventions in the poverty reduction strategy process was to influence policy decisions. It took a few more years, however, to start focusing on the concepts and strategic use of communication tools and techniques to attain the goal of influencing policy decisions. This, in fact, would be one of the major contributions of communication interventions in poverty reduction efforts. In Ghana, this shift in focus from "dissemination and publicity" to the deeper and more challenging role of communication and information interventions became clear in the second generation of its GPRS document prepared in 2005.

Communication Interventions in the Second Ghana Poverty Reduction Strategy in 2005

The Ghana Poverty Reduction Strategy (GPRS II) also involved a consultation process. This time the goals were widened, based on a set of "strategic objectives" to "inform the public on the Government's Growth and Poverty Reduction Agenda; highlight the new policy areas of GPRS II for stakeholders; solicit their views on its priorities; and promote ownership of GPRS II by all Ghanaians."[13]

The section in the GPRS II document titled "The GPRS Communication Program" focuses on the implementation of a "communication strategy to deepen ownership and to ensure effective implementation, monitoring, and evaluation of the strategy." Apart from dissemination and awareness-raising objectives, the program also focuses on "forging and strengthening of strategic partnerships with state and nonstate actors for effective coordination of the dissemination of GPRS II and its Annual Progress Reports, management of expectations and feedback for the policy review process, and deepening of the development communication program and process to foster the necessary attitudinal change in support of growth and poverty reduction."[14]

Identifying the lack of a coherent communication strategy as "one of the major limitations of GPRS I," GPRS II, in the subsection "Enhancing Development Communication," under the section "Political Governance," emphasizes that "strategies to strengthen the critical role of the media in enhancing development communication will be promoted."[15] It also lists development communication as a focus area and mentions government's commitment "to enhance access to public information and [an] enabling environment for media," a policy issue that is linked to the "effective implementation of public information law" in the country.[16]

Contribution of Communication to Fight Poverty through PRSPs

The role of communication in Poverty Reduction Strategy Papers does not only promote the system and culture of information sharing within government machinery and between government and nongovernment entities (CSOs, media, network, associations, and so forth). Ensuring information flows is also critical for successful implementation of PRSPs or similar development plans to fight poverty and for achievement of economic growth and development. The systemic and transparent planning of policies and strategies such as PRSPs is one part of this effort.

The processes of resource allocation through various approaches to budgeting and through the systems monitoring the implementation of such policies and strategies are also critical parts of ensuring the successful implementation of poverty and growth strategies. In fact, a well-designed poverty reduction strategy monitoring system can be a key factor in ensuring a realistic and transparent policy-making process. A PRS monitoring system involves a wide range of activities, including information sharing and feedback to the policy process. It also entails a set of government and nongovernment actors to undertake those activities and requires institutional arrangements to ensure better monitoring vis-à-vis country policy planning. This whole process demands multidimensional information and communication flows. "Unless the interface is established, a vicious circle spins, wherein adequate information is not available for decision making, and decision-making processes do not demand adequate information."[17]

The PRS monitoring system, seemingly focused on technicalities of traditional notions of monitoring and evaluation systems, is really looking at some much deeper challenges of fighting poverty. It focuses on a set of goals that go beyond the quantitative dimension of information exchange and relies on human interactions. Such interactions are clearly more complex and difficult to evaluate than information, but they are necessary to address transparency and public accountability successfully.

Poverty Reduction Strategy Papers: Communication and Beyond

In its early stages, the major reasons for using communication tools and techniques in PRSPs focused on attaining the core PRSP principles, including the challenge of promoting country ownership, results orientation, or partnership through engaging various stakeholders at different levels. As the PRSPs grow older, the issues of information and communication go deeper into the overall approach to government policy planning, resource allocation, and monitoring of the implementation of national development plans and strategies. These have different labels but are generally focused on fighting poverty and achieving economic growth and development in a number of countries across the globe.

From a communication point of view, the process of integrating communication in PRSPs actually demands the free flow of information among stakeholders to establish accountability and transparency in policy planning, resource allocation, and other sectors that run a government system. The experience recognizes the role of communication and shows the value of—slow but eventual—integration of human cultural and social factors into information processes that plan and implement national development policies and strategies such as the poverty reduction strategies.

Notes

1. World Bank and IMF, *2005 Review of the Poverty Reduction Strategy Approach: Balancing Accountabilities and Scaling Up Results* (Washington, DC: World Bank, 2005), 1.
2. Jeni Klugman, "Overview." In *PRSP Sourcebook* (World Bank, Washington, DC, 2002). http://povlibrary.worldbank.org/files/5301_overview.pdf.
3. Masud Mozammel and Barbara Zatlokal, "Strategic Communication in PRSP." In *PRSP Sourcebook* (World Bank,Washington, DC, Oct. 2002), 3. http://povlibrary.worldbank.org/files/12981_comm0916.pdf.
4. World Bank/International Monetary Fund, *Poverty Reduction Strategy Papers—Progress in Implementation* (World Bank/IMF, Sept. 2004), 3. http://siteresources.worldbank.org/INTPRS1/Resources/prsp_progress_2004.pdf
5. Masud Mozammel and Sina Odugbemi, *With the Support of Multitudes: Using Strategic Communication to Fight Poverty through PRSPs* (Washington, DC: World Bank, 2005), 12.
6. Note that DevComm basically adopts the same communication process when called to work in country assistance strategies interventions.
7. The five core principles of PRSPs are (1) country-driven and -owned, predicated on broad-based participatory processes for formulation, implementation, and outcome-based progress monitoring; (2) results-oriented, focusing on outcomes that would benefit the poor; (3) comprehensive in scope, recognizing the multidimensional nature of the causes of poverty and measures to attack it; (4) partnership-oriented, providing a basis for the active and coordinated participation of development partners; and (5) based on a medium- and long-term perspective for poverty reduction, recognizing that sustained poverty reduction cannot be achieved overnight. See Klugman, "Overview," p. 3.
8. IMF and World Bank, *Review of the Poverty Reduction Strategy Paper Approach—Main Findings and Issues for Discussion*; SM/02/53 and IDA/SecM2002-0086 (Washington, DC: World Bank, 2002), 9.
9. Ibid, 9.
10. Mozammel and Zatlokal, "Strategic Communication in PRSP."
11. Republic of Ghana, *Ghana Poverty Reduction Strategy 2003–2005: An Agenda for Growth and Prosperity*, vol. 1, *Analysis and Policy Statement* (Accra: Republic of Ghana, Feb. 2003), 5–12.
12. Ibid, 10.
13. Republic of Ghana, National Development Planning Commission, *Growth and Poverty Reduction Strategy (GPRS II) (2006–2009)* (Accra: Ghana NDPC, Nov. 2005), 11.
14. Ibid, 12.
15. Ibid, 64–65.
16. ibid, 143.
17. World Bank, *Beyond the Numbers: Understanding the Institutions for Monitoring Poverty Reduction Strategies* (Washington, DC: World Bank, 2006), 2.

4.3. Community Radio: Supporting Local Voices through the Airwaves

*Loty Salazar and Craig Hammer**

Introduction

The community broadcasting environment, like the larger media and communication environment, is subject to both rapid and continuous change. There are significant disparities among countries concerning the pace of this change, to say nothing of the state of community radio development from community to community. Accordingly, this paper does not offer a "one-size-fits-all" approach to community radio. Rather, it provides some of the lessons derived from research examining good practices, using practical observation of community broadcasts, and analyzing case studies. Community broadcasting refers to both radio and television, but for the purposes of this publication, the focus is on community radio, and, therefore, the terms are used interchangeably.

What Is Community Radio?

Bolivia and Colombia in the 1940s had early examples of community radio. Others were underground transmissions by community-based movements and groups supporting efforts to air important issues and cultural information in languages the communities could understand.[1] They sought to create momentary alternatives to government and commercial broadcasts. Experiments with community broadcasting have since been conducted around the world with mixed results. Some stations have vanished, while others have become firmly established and have flourished.

The phrase "community radio" is widely used, but every individual community radio station is unique. Each is inextricably linked to the particular community that developed it and is tailored to the culture, concerns, history, and current events of the community it serves. Even so, it is possible to identify and distill certain good practices to which successful community radio stations adhere. In particular, successful

* Loty Salazar is a communication and information officer in the East Asia and Pacific Region, the World Bank. Craig Hammer is coordinator of the CEERD Program, the World Bank Institute. The views expressed are those of the authors and do not necessarily represent those of the World Bank Group or its Board of Directors. All errors are our own.

community radio stations feature the following three characteristics: they have community ownership, and orientation, they are nonprofit, and they are independent.

Community Ownership and Orientation

The community radio station is owned, managed, and accountable to a community. The "community" can be either based on geography or interests, as defined by the group itself, describing a homogeneous group of people or a diverse group within a locality. Communities can be large (as when a culturally or ethnically homogeneous group, or interest group, covers several local districts) or small, such as a village; and they can be in a large city or remote rural area. Different and dissenting opinions from within the community must be allowed to have a voice. There are many ways that a station may be "owned by" a community (for example, through NGOs, farmer groups, cooperatives, and grassroots organizations that elect the management of the station). The means that the community has to hold the station accountable to it are crucial to its success and sustainability. The operation of a community radio station should adhere to practices that promote community participation in its programming and operations. This includes relying on volunteers from the community to produce and present on-air programs and community news; to mobilize resources, and to operate and manage the station; to empower the listening audience to request topics to be discussed on the air; to hold regular community feedback to improve programming; and to involve youth in operating and managing the station.

Not-for-Profit

The community radio station is not run for profit, but it does mobilize resources to pay for operational costs. Indeed, fundraising may be encouraged where sufficient safeguards exist to protect the independence of the station from outside manipulation and where surplus monies are reinvested in the station and the community. The station's fund-raising practices and financial records need to be available to the general public. Governance structures designed to promote transparency, such as an independent, elected board of community trustees, can help to ensure that the station remains responsive to community needs and wishes, particularly when outside money is involved.

Independence

Good practice among community broadcasters demonstrates that stations should be nonpartisan and nonsectarian and should be oriented to support the social development of the community they serve. No branch of local or central government, no political party or political group, should directly or indirectly control the community radio station; where this is clearly articulated at the establishment of the station, experience shows that community stations strongly resist cooptation. Community radio stations are service-oriented, and to be so, should maintain editorial independence—over and above legitimate restrictions that are applied to all broadcast media—to protect and sustain the expectations and input of the community they serve. Good practice demonstrates that government agencies may pay community radio stations for air time for their public service announcements (the practice in South Africa is a good example). Similarly, community radio stations should not be subject to any undue influence from donors, commercial interests, and advertisers. All relationships between the community radio station and outside entities must be governed by clear mutual agreements to defend the nonpartisan, community-run nature of the station, within the limits of the station's charter and applicable laws.

The Importance of Community Radio

Despite the growing popularity of television and the advent of newer information and communication technologies (ICTs), such as the Internet and mobile telephony, in various countries across disparate regions, even in challenging regulatory environments, community radio remains a useful channel to enhance civic engagement in poor and marginalized communities. Community broadcasting can help social groups articulate priority issues, even if they live in remote communities or face linguistic, ethnic, and literacy barriers. It can also help build sustained capacities, institutions, and practices.

Community radio can additionally magnify the impacts of development initiatives by involving and engaging the local listening audience to solve problems. It can also build capacity and self-confidence by providing listeners with access to needed information from on-air experts, such as health advice from doctors or nurses for treating illnesses or region-specific farming techniques from an agricultural professional. Community radio also gives listeners access to sensitive subjects that might not otherwise be addressed by the community or in individual households, such as how to protect against sexually transmitted diseases, information about alcohol or drug abuse, and how to confront violence against women and children. Programs that address these and other subjects may encourage families and community members to discuss them. Experience shows that informed discussion can significantly affect individual and group behavior and improve the ability of community members to raise problems, analyze them, and work together to solve them.

Programming

Community radio stations typically adopt program formats that promote community participation and enable an open exchange of information and opinions in local languages. This includes call-in and write-in question-and-answer programs, weekly thematic and cultural programs, music and entertainment, discussions of local issues, community reporting, broadcasts of local government meetings, and development-oriented programs on a wide range of topics. Community radio programs perform public services for their constituencies, elicit listeners' views and concerns, enable community members to comment on wrongdoing, facilitate dialogs with local government officials over the air, and encourage continuing discussions of issues among themselves. This and similar kinds of broadcasting may also mitigate feelings of isolation, from which many impoverished communities suffer.

Even very basic community radio stations are capable of delivering quality educational and development-oriented programs to diverse audiences. Measurable economic improvements can result from the access to key information that community radio stations offer.

Technical Requirements

Community radio stations can be efficient mechanisms for disseminating information because they are relatively inexpensive, have broad coverage (depending on the transmitter and topography), can be powered on or off the grid using conventional and alternative energy resources such as solar power, and are accessible to the illiterate. Limited resources typically mean that many community broadcasting stations in developing countries operate with a basic ensemble of recording, mixing, and transmission equipment. Some of these technologies can be constructed by community members themselves. Donors wishing to support community radios should opt for solutions that are simple and appropriate to the local context, using equipment that can be repaired within the country and preferably within the locality.

Mobile telephony enables listeners to participate in community radio programs by calling in questions and comments. Internet access is scarce, particularly in rural areas, but where it is available to stations, its impact can be maximized among communities since broadcasters may download online material to be incorporated into their broadcasts. Community broadcasters may even upload digital recordings of the station's programming, to be accessed by listeners around the world.

Regulatory Environment

Many developing countries have an ambiguous regulatory framework for broadcasting that does not recognize community broadcasting as a distinct subsector. Without this differentiation, prevailing licensing fees that are set for commercial broadcasters also pertain to poor community broadcasters and present a high barrier to entry. Further, experience shows that when a portion of the radio-frequency spectrum is not allocated for community nonprofit uses, frequencies are typically auctioned to all broadcasters—both commercial and nonprofit stations—at one time, which results in the crowding out of nonprofit community radio.

Good practice demonstrates that the legal and regulatory frameworks for broadcasting recognize and differentiate between public service, private commercial, and nonprofit community broadcasting. This good practice, used by the United States, the United Kingdom, France, Australia, and South Africa, and in large measure by Mali, Colombia, and other countries, includes (1) government allocation of an appropriate portion (usually about 15–20 percent) of the radio-frequency spectrum to community uses; (2) the institution of a separate and simplified process of licensing for community stations, which is managed in a transparent manner and with minimal administrative burdens; and (3) the establishment of low, affordable fees for community radio licenses. Indeed, instances of good practice are emerging in the broadcasting policies and regulatory regimes that are under development in a growing number of developing countries, including Liberia, Ghana, Nepal, India, and elsewhere. These and other features of good practice in the legal and regulatory framework are discussed, with country examples, in the World Bank book, *Broadcasting, Voice and Accountability: A Public Interest Approach to Policy, Law and Regulation* (2008).[2] However, in some cases governments have set rigid parameters for community broadcasters, such as instituting low limits on transmission power, which limits the number of listeners. For example, while good practice demonstrates that community radios should transmit at between 100 watts to 1 kilowatt (depending on the topography and geographical reach of the community to be served), in Chile the law limits the transmission power of all community radio to a single watt, which is only enough power to broadcast to listeners within several hundred meters of each station.

Even so, community radio is slowly gaining recognition as an important part of a diverse and pluralistic media landscape, recognized in regional charters such as the African Charter on Broadcasting, and in national law and regulation. Indeed, some experts remark on the correlation between the existence of a robust media industry inclusive of community broadcasting in developing countries and levels of political, economic, and social development in those countries.

Funding and Sustainability

Funding is a complex issue for community radio stations. The World Association of Community Radio Broadcasters (AMARC) maintains that a significant feature of community radio is that community members must act for themselves, rather than rely too heavily on outside assistance. Experience suggests that three forms of sustainability are important to community radio stations: social, institutional, and financial. *Social sustainability* is arguably the most important: good practice demonstrates that community members who donate their own time to organize and support the station are more likely to develop a sustainable station than communities with lower levels of volunteer involvement. Most community broadcasters depend heavily on volunteers to support the creation of interactive programs, raise funds, provide expertise on issues important to the community, and otherwise remain actively involved in sustaining the station. The involvement and commitment of the community includes contributions in cash and kind to sustain station operations.

The *institutional sustainability* of community radio depends on the management skills of directors and core staff, and the basic skills of volunteers. These skills can be strengthened with training and advice from expert practitioners, who have developed sustainable community broadcasting stations elsewhere in the country or region, and can share their experiences with fledgling station personnel. Community broadcasting training manuals are also widely available online.[3] Training and support may also be available from national community radio networks, where they are available.[4]

The *financial sustainability* of a community radio station is also contingent on the director's management skills, chiefly, mobilizing resources and encouraging community groups, grassroots organizations, and local businesses to provide ongoing financial support. This funding may take many forms, including regular donations from community-based societies; fees charged by the station for individual announcements; fees paid by government agencies for air time used for public service announcements and programs; sponsorship of programs by community members or groups; and even the establishment of separate microenterprises that are affiliated with the station, such as a restaurant or market stall, which generate revenue to subsidize the station. Community radio stations also accept commercial advertisements from local businesses, if the purpose of the business and the nature of the advertisement is consistent with the values of the station.

The diversity of funding sources is important, because it contributes to the independence of the community station. Few community radio stations are fully self-sustaining, however. In some countries, such as France and the United Kingdom, certain government tariffs—either taxes on revenues of commercial advertisers, or license fees for use of TV or radio receivers—generate resources that are pooled into a fund for broadcasting diversity, to help support the operating costs of community broadcasters who conform to certain stated criteria.

Good practices and experience demonstrate that the regulatory framework for community broadcasting should allow for flexibility by community broadcasters to raise funds to support the stations' operations and development. This should allow for economic support from within the community itself, and for other forms of support, such as that from international development agencies, advertising, private or commercial sponsorship, government payment for air time, and the potential for sustained forms of public funding that may be levied from within the broadcasting sector.

Strengths and Constraints

A realistic assessment of community radio reveals inherent strengths and constraints. An examination of these can be useful for development practitioners as they develop projects and assess progress. Community radio has a number of strengths, including the following:

- The continuous exchange of information can help highlight issues important to the community to reduce social risks, encourage community action to respond to changing circumstances, and equip the community to demand good governance and accountability.
- Public policy can be influenced because political officials typically respond to informed voters and well-covered issues, particularly since community broadcasting is a useful tool to facilitate public scrutiny of government action.
- The self-confidence of the community served may be enhanced, such as from the practice of articulating their views and discussing important local issues, and the impact of hearing their own and neighbors' voices on the air, speaking in the local language.
- Community members can be encouraged to directly engage government officials, and involve the broader listening audience in the exchange, for example, to seek improvements in service delivery.
- Impoverished community members may be encouraged to mobilize expert advice on issues important to them, and to embark on follow-up discussions over the air and among the community at large.

Often there are also a number of constraints, among them:

- Government regimes or powerful political party members may be concerned that freedom of expression—a key feature of effective community broadcasting—will threaten local or national government authority, particularly if that government significantly restricts access to information.
- Funding and technical support are critically important to the sustainability of community radio stations and may be difficult to ensure while simultaneously trying to preserve the independence of the station.
- Local news can at times be marginalized in favor of larger, national news because of time and/or resource constraints whereby community broadcasters will just focus on general issues.
- The legal recognition of a community broadcaster by a government can subject

a station to unreasonable constraints. Some governments are overly protective of commercial media and thus impose restrictive licensing requirements on the community sector, which threaten the stations' viability.

Personnel shortages and turnover of skilled staff and volunteers present a challenge: skilled staff and volunteers will tend to migrate to better-paying jobs in the commercial sector, so that continuing outreach and iterative training of volunteers is an ongoing cost. Although these are arguably manageable challenges, support programs for community radio development should take them into account from the outset.

World Bank and Community Radio

The World Bank has long recognized that a free, independent, and pluralistic media is crucial to effective development. It continues to support training for journalists, acknowledges the importance of independent print media, and is increasingly addressing access to information issues, while pressing for better regulatory frameworks. Since the late 1990s, the World Bank has broadened its development focus to include broadcast media development, including community broadcasting, particularly community radio. This support has been compounded by the institution's growing governance and transparency agenda, and by decentralization efforts that call for increased community participation and oversight, and stronger capacity, performance, and service delivery of local and provincial governments.

By 2002, the Bank had increased support to community radio by stressing its contribution to participatory approaches, both fostering two-way communications and helping to amplify the voice of the poor and disadvantaged. Bank investments, particularly in community-driven development (CDD) projects, aimed to include support to community radio development and local civic engagement in countries such as Ghana, Indonesia, Kenya, Mongolia, Nigeria, Sri Lanka, and Timor-Leste.

Community Radio in Bank Operations

Typically, CDD projects have been vehicles for several small grants to local communities to support economic activities, community infrastructure, and other community-level initiatives. CDD projects have supported the participatory development and capacity strengthening of community radio stations, under the communications component of each project. The intent has been to move beyond communicating particular messages by creating community institutions that provide sustained communication services at the local level.

Some cultural and social reconciliation efforts have also included support for the establishment of radio stations in selected areas. One example is the Timor-

Leste Community Empowerment and Local Governance Project (CEP), which, in late 2002, helped to establish eight community radio stations and a supporting hub. CEP support for community radio included supplying broadcasting equipment; basic training to volunteer reporters, managers, and technicians; and some small initial operating funds. Though station sustainability has been challenging—managers and volunteers have struggled with funding shortages and weak operational and maintenance capacity—to date, all eight stations are still on the air. This sustainability is largely attributed to community ownership and their community-based boards, as well as to the sustained support of the government.

The World Bank further increased its engagement in the community radio sector by way of a multicountry Development Marketplace grant in 2002, which supported analyses of enabling environments for community radio development in Malawi, Zambia, Ghana, and Nigeria. This grant also supported the capacity-building of existing community radio stations on a pilot basis in these countries.

In 2003, the World Bank sponsored a workshop of community broadcasting experts and practitioners, which informed the design of additional pilot countries to extend community radio sector support linked to Bank lending and the design of a thematic Web site. For example, training for community radio reporters and roundtables to enhance networking among stations for community engagement in public issues were supported in Malawi and Benin. Program development for community radios on local public spending and social auditing took place in Peru, carrying out activities with indigenous peoples' radios with the assistance of Peru's national radio coordinator. During the ensuing years, and under the leadership of the World Bank Institute's Civic Engagement, Empowerment, and Respect for Diversity (CEERD) program,[5] further pilots were implemented within either community-driven development projects or policy-based operations in Timor-Leste (expanding on CEP support), Sri Lanka, Nigeria, Indonesia, Kenya, and Morocco.

BOX 4.2 Community Radio in Community-Driven Development Projects: Kenya, Ghana, and Sri Lanka

Kenya—In 2005, the World Bank initiated participatory development and the establishment of a community radio station in the Wajir District of Kenya under the Arid Lands Resource Management Project (ALRMP). After planning sessions in 2006, the stakeholders obtained a license from the government to establish the station; obtained use of land, a structure, and the specifications of equipment needed; mapped out the priorities for the initial content of their broadcasting; and planned the type of staffing and volunteers needed. The ALRMP project agreed to finance the costs of

BOX 4.2 Community Radio in Community-Driven Development Projects: Kenya, Ghana, and Sri Lanka (continued)

equipment, materials, and civil works on a cost-sharing basis, and finance the ongoing capacity development and initial operating costs of the station. The project is supporting community radio development because the critical bottlenecks to effective natural resource management in Kenya's arid and semiarid lands are social and administrative, rather than the absence of particular technologies in forestry or range management. Establishing community radio is expected to play a key role in addressing these challenges and promoting the empowerment of communities to achieve sustainable improvements in their standard of living.

Ghana—The Bank continues to address broadcasting policy and community radio development by helping develop the reform agenda for Ghana's broadcasting sector. The Bank supported the development of a groundbreaking study of Ghana's broadcasting sector with policy, legal, regulatory, and institutional recommendations to guide the reform process, and it guided foundational steps toward drafting important national broadcasting legislation. Further, the Bank supported technical collaboration with the Ghana Community Radio Network (GCRN) to stimulate the development of the community radio sector. Ghana has a well-conceived approach to community radio, reflecting global good practices in participatory planning and programming. However, the sector remains small because of ambiguities in the enabling environment, principally the absence of an effective broadcasting law, fragmentation in the regulatory framework, and unclear licensing procedures. The technical assistance activity began in 2004 and continues at the time of this publication. It focuses on showcasing the role of community radio within the Community-Based Rural Development Project to strengthen community empowerment and voice through community radio programming; developing a program to be embedded in the CDD project to engage communities in priority issues and generate opinion on improvements needed in local governance and public service delivery; and improving the enabling environment, particularly the regulatory framework for broadcasting and media development.

Sri Lanka—Work in Sri Lanka consisted of assessing the community radio–enabling environment. The activity was conducted in the context of the Community Development and Livelihood Improvement "Gemi Diriya" Project and consisted of collaboration with local experts on community radio planning and piloting to showcase its potential as a tool for poverty reduction, as well as to clarify regulatory impediments and negotiate changes. Participatory research and awareness building were completed in the communities of Uva and Southern provinces, and the resultant report, containing findings and recommendations, is under peer review.

In Timor-Leste, Sri Lanka, and Nigeria, participatory planning for community radio development has included the participation of women from the outset, and as a result, female reporters and producers have played a strong role. In these countries, many reporters, producers, and station managers have produced feature programs on women's issues, some of which invite listeners to submit questions that are answered on the air. National women's organizations and women's rights groups such as the Female Leadership Forum and Women Information Network in Nigeria are vocal advocates for community radio and work to ensure that community radio stations are vehicles for gender equity and rights.

The World Bank's support for community radio, along with partner donors, has extended to disaster management areas in Sri Lanka and Indonesia in the aftermath of the December 2004 tsunami. Though the Indonesia Kecamatan Development Program (KDP) had already been working with community radio to broadcast information about KDP and to strengthen community oversight at the local level, the establishment of community radio in post-tsunami Aceh was a crucial mechanism to help restore a sense of normalcy and to provide communities with local information, reconstruction news, and entertainment.

In July 2006, the World Bank Institute convened a stakeholder meeting in Nigeria, in collaboration with AMARC, to discuss the absence of community radio in

BOX 4.3 Community Radio and Women's Participation: Timor-Leste

In 2006 the World Bank, under the CEERD program and the East Asia and Pacific Region and with GENFUND (Integrating Gender Issues into the World Bank's Work) support, developed a capacity-building activity in Timor-Leste to support community radio as a vehicle for social expression and a tool to empower women throughout the country. The activity partnered with an external media training organization to train young women in community radio production, station management, and reporting techniques. Four workshops during a 12-week training session covered several topics, such as the role of women in politics, gender equality, and domestic violence. These workshops also examined how to sustain community radio stations, with in-depth analyses of fundraising techniques, marketing strategies, operational requirements, management approaches, and more. A key result of the activity was that 10 women journalists from community radio stations across the country collaborated to produce a six-part radio program series and a three-part drama series on the themes covered in the workshops. They also documented outcomes of the Second National East Timorese Women's Congress and its significance to women in media and communication.

BOX 4.4 Community Radio in Disaster Management: Aceh, Indonesia

With the support of the World Bank and partner agencies, the Aceh Emergency Radio Network (AERnet)[6] was established soon after the December 2004 tsunami to respond to the community's information and communications needs. This fledging network started with five community-run and -operated radio stations that promoted dialog and were staffed by both local and internally displaced people working as volunteers. Designed to give communities access to information about the reconstruction and rehabilitation efforts, the network's reporters also shared news with partnered networks, including Radio 68H, an independent public radio network, which syndicates local and national news and features. Renamed ARRnet[7] to reflect the transition from emergency to reconstruction, the network has been working to make a difference in many local communities. For example, after the tsunami, the airwaves in Aceh Besar District were virtually empty and few displaced people had access to radio sets. ARRnet's SeHa FM distributed radio sets in temporary camps and broadcast special programs for listeners, which provided entertainment and information.

This station quickly became popular, and still collects up to 200 song request coupons daily. Aside from music, the station also presents a range of regular programs such as interactive talk shows about health and religious topics, and reaches more than five subdistricts. ARRnet facilitated the establishment of 16 additional community radio stations in 2006 and plans to facilitate 26 more throughout the province, targeting tsunami-affected areas to promote a two-way exchange between victims, donors, and governments. This is being done through a network of Kecamatan Development Program information facilitators.

Nigeria, the role of community radio in general, and opportunities to support its development in Nigeria through the establishment of a clear government policy designed to support community radio development and investment support, starting under the Bank-financed Fadama Projects, the largest CDD projects in the country. In August 2006, the minister of information convened a joint government–civil society Community Radio Policy Committee, and by the end of 2006, they produced a draft Community Radio Policy Statement. This languished during the change of government in 2007, but as of 2008, it is being revived and, at the time of this publication, is expected to be institutionalized. The Fadama II Project is supporting the participatory planning of three pilot community radio stations, and Fadama III is expected to fund their establishment and the establishment and operations of a total of six pilot stations. This is being developed within Fadama's communications component, and in collaboration with Nigeria's stakeholder coalition for community radio, which includes over 120 local organizations.

Research and Analysis

Community radio can also be an important resource in the analytical work needed for development initiatives. In the area of voice and accountability, the World Bank is learning from its partners in the sector, providing the infrastructure for local and national networks in various developing countries, and exchanging knowledge and experience with counterparts on the ground. At the time of this writing, the Bank continues to support community radio development by supporting broadcasting sector policy and legal and regulatory reform in several developing countries, supporting the participatory development of prototype community radio stations in others, and prototyping the integration of community radio into CDD lending.

The World Bank's *Broadcasting, Voice and Accountability: A Public Interest Approach to Policy, Law and Regulation,* discussed in the Regulatory Environment section, is also a useful contribution. It is a concise and comprehensive overview of the enabling environment for information, voice, and media, with good practice examples from diverse countries.[8] It is designed to help stakeholders and development agencies to facilitate policy reviews and analyses in particular developing countries, identify areas for reform, and provide a framework for dialog and planning of reform efforts in appropriate contexts.

Community radio assessments are another important tool to supply basic knowledge about country context to improve institutional mechanisms and practices for making informed choices, local governance, and empowerment of poor communities. They also have an important role in promoting the value-added of community radios in donor-supported operations. In the last few years, community radio assessments were carried out in Benin, Indonesia, Sri Lanka, Mongolia, the Kyrgyz Republic, Morocco, and Ghana, among other countries.

Additionally, in 2007, a multicountry study was also carried out to clarify good practices in the development, operation, and maintenance of community radio stations, particularly on issues related to their effectiveness. This study was designed to encapsulate useful experiences from community broadcasters in the countries studied, to guide Bank project teams to design support programs for community radio development.[9]

Conclusion

Across many countries and in different regions, community radio stations foster community participation and create an appetite for transparent and accountable governance, even in challenging regulatory environments. Good governance and effective leadership, especially in impoverished communities, are collective processes, which depend on the development of an engaged, analytical, informed, and robust civil society. Community radio in particular has proved to be a sustainable and interactive medium for poor and marginalized populations to be heard and informed, shape knowledgeable opinions, learn the give-and-take of informed dialog, and become more decisive agents in their own development.

Good practice demonstrates that support for community radio includes the development of capacities in programming, credible local reporting, station management, and resource mobilization. A needs assessment must be undertaken before larger support programs for the community radio sector are developed. This preliminary assessment may help to clarify how best to support the participatory planning and establishment of community radio, how to enhance the capacities of its staff and volunteers, and the likelihood of station sustainability.

The World Bank's community broadcasting activities have been varied, with a focus on providing robust, ongoing vehicles for people—including the very poor—to influence decisions at local and national levels, to voice their individual (and community-based) concerns, and to hold government institutions accountable. There is also a strong focus on analysis of the enabling environment of policies and regulations for information and voice, to enable the Bank to support policy, legal, and regulatory improvements. Further areas of involvement include facilitating networking among community radio stations and support to national community networks, and provision of technical assistance to help station personnel produce better radio content, diversify their sources of revenue, interface with complementary ICTs, and play a proactive role in the development of the communities served.

Notes

1. Radios are effective mechanisms to increase access in the developing world because they are inexpensive, have broad coverage, and are battery-powered, and no literacy is required to operate them. At least 75 percent of the world's population is within "easy access" of some form of broadcast technology, primarily radios. See Alfonso Gumucio Dagron, *Making Waves: Stories of Participatory Communication for Social Change* (New York: The Rockefeller Foundation, 2001); Carter Eltzroth and Charles Kenny, *Broadcasting and Development: Options for the World Bank*, Working Paper 11 (World Bank, Washington, DC, 2003); L. W. Couch, ed., *Digital and Analog Communication Systems* (Upper Saddle River, NJ: Prentice Hall, 2001); and Steven Tripp and Warren Roby, "Auditory Presentations in Language Laboratories," in *Handbook of Research For Educational Communications and Technology,* ed. D. H. Jonassen (New York: Macmillan, 1996), 821–50.
2. See Steve Buckley, Kreszentia Duer, Toby Mendel, and Seán Ó Siochrú, *Broadcasting, Voice and Accountability: A Public Interest Approach to Policy, Law and Regulation* (copublication of the World Bank and the University of Michigan Press, 2008).
3. See Craig Hammer, Annex, in Buckley et al. (2008).

4. Examples include the Ghana Community Radio Network in Ghana and the National Community Radio Forum in South Africa.
5. The Civic Engagement, Empowerment, and Respect for Diversity (CEERD) program of the World Bank Institute supports the voice of poor communities in developing countries by promoting community radio development, and the development of a pluralistic broadcast sector that serves the public interest through informed, participatory development, and demand for good governance. The objectives of CEERD include building institutional capacity of community radios, enhancing community radio programming for citizens' engagement in public accountability, generating and sharing knowledge, and facilitating global networking of community radios. The CEERD program builds on the World Bank Institute's close collaboration with regional staff involved in communication, country and central staff supporting CDD projects, and regional and central staff involved in public sector reforms and good governance. The CEERD program also learns from the experiences of experts and practitioners in this field and works with organizations such as the World Association of Community Radio Broadcasters (AMARC); Ghana Community Radio Network; Search for Common Ground; national community radio networks in Asia, Africa, and Latin America; and others, to help strengthen the community broadcasting sector in developing countries.
6. Funded initially by Britain's Department for International Development and then the Japan Social Development Fund, ARRnet activities are implemented by the Combine Resource Institution. They are supported by JRKY (Jaringan Radio Komunitas Yogyakarta). The grant is managed by the Indonesia Kecamatan Development Project.
7. ARRnet is short for Aceh Reconstruction Radio Network and supersedes AERnet. It started in October 2005 and will run until March 2009, with funding from the Japan Social Development Fund.
8. *See* note 2.
9. This report, titled "Empowering Radio," will be available at the CEERD Web site: http://www.worldbank.org/CEERDwww.worldbank.org/CEERD.

4.4 Disability and Development: What Role for Communication?

Marco Nicoli and Katherine Guernsey†*

Why Disability and Development?

In order to alleviate poverty, economic development programs and policies and communication strategies must embrace an entire population, including groups at risk, such as those with disabilities. Without integrating the disabled population, poverty alleviation efforts are compromised, since disabled people and their entire families face a higher risk of poverty. Similarly, poor people experience a heightened rate of acquiring impairments that, in interaction with societal barriers, results in disability.

Disability is widely recognized as a development issue affecting the lives of more than 600 million people and their families.[1] The World Bank's overarching goal is poverty alleviation, and a development agenda inclusive of disabled people is necessary to achieve this goal. In this context, the concept of disability is consistent with the "social model," where the focus is on the interaction of people's functional limitations with societal barriers, including physical, attitudinal, legislative, informational, and other barriers.

The commitment to disability has come from the highest levels of the Bank, including a number of World Bank presidents. Former World Bank President James D. Wolfensohn indicated the importance of reaching out to, and collaborating with, disabled populations in developing countries: "Addressing disability is a significant part of reducing poverty. Bringing disabled people out of the corners and back alleys of society, and empowering them to thrive in the bustling center of national life, will do much to improve the lives of many from among the poorest of the poor around the world." "Inclusion—that is what development is all about—to bring into society people that have never been a part of it."[2]

The Role of Development Communication

Communication methods and techniques can play a crucial role in addressing needs and challenges for the inclusion of disabled people in the development agenda. Ini-

* Marco Nicoli is a former World Bank knowledge manager on disability and development, with previous experiences in the field of development communication.

† Katherine Guernsey is an international lawyer whose practice focuses on human rights, disability, and development.

tially, proper communication strategies and products are needed to raise awareness of what disability is and who disabled people are. Too often disability is overlooked, perceived as merely a health issue, or approached with pietism and largely misunderstood by people. The mainstream media can help to accustom the general public to the inclusion of people with disabilities in everyday life.

Communication campaigns are another important component as they form the basis for the education of society on disability prevention and on the affirmation of disability as one of the many different qualities of human diversity, such as sex, religion, culture, and so forth. Disability is neither a curse nor a blessing: it is a normal part of life and should be addressed as such. The more disabled people are shown in inclusive settings with their nondisabled peers, the more familiar society becomes with inclusion. In terms of prevention, disabled people and their nondisabled peers should be recognized as distinct audiences and the issue of prevention appropriately broached. While it is appropriate to engage in awareness-raising campaigns aimed at preventing injuries and the spread of communicable diseases, these campaigns must be accessible to people with disabilities and in no case should portray people with disabilities as objects of pity or "cautionary tales." For example, campaigns to improve driver and pedestrian safety should not use people injured by traffic accidents as "poster children" for what can happen when people do not heed the advice of the campaign.

In addition, communication strategies are instrumental for behavior change to fight stigma and prejudice with the goal of real social inclusion. Many persons with disabilities lead a life of exclusion not because of their own limitations, for everyone has personal limitations, but because of social norms that perceive them as outcasts, bewitched, sinners punished by God. This discrimination is often extended to family members or associates of disabled persons. Communication products can be very effective antidiscrimination tools. For example, communication campaigns have been used in post-conflict areas to reduce the fear and negative perception of various populations being reintegrated.[3] This fosters a positive behavioral change for the entire society.

Two-way communication processes are needed to include disabled people in any decisions concerning their civil, political, economic, social, and cultural rights. Development communication is not only about communicating and educating, but also about listening, sharing knowledge and opinions, and creating knowledge to address key issues successfully. Disabled people's contributions, needs, and perceptions should be articulated by them first and foremost, without external filters, in order to achieve more meaningful and sustainable results.

What Is the Role for World Bank Communication Professionals?

In order to deal effectively with these issues, communication professionals should include disability in their work. The following elements should provide the main scope of this work:

- Provide visibility—when relevant, the more often disability is linked with development issues, the more awareness is raised and it is normalized.
- Correct misinformation—communication should provide correct information and counter stereotypes.
- Reduce fear, increase familiarity—exposure to disability issues through communication products produces a progressive familiarization with the theme and therefore makes people more comfortable with the issue.
- Reduce stigma and shame—the leading/leadership role played by the World Bank in the development arena can have a domino effect on other organizations at national and local levels, thus reducing the stigma that affects disabled people.
- Give good examples through appropriate and accessible formats—in the design of communication strategies, when relevant, the communication practitioner should use a mix of accessible formats (large print, simplified language, accessible Web sites, Braille printing, and so forth); this will have a tangible effect on implementation. There is evidence that in countries where World Bank Public Information Centers (PICs) have been equipped with assistive technologies, some governments have adopted similar approaches for their own centers.
- Reinforce the notion of disability as a normal difference—rather than a misfortune.
- Include disabled persons organizations (DPOs)—be inclusive in the full range of the Bank's interaction with civil society, including communication assessments, consultations, trainings, and so forth.

Relevance of Disability and Development Work across Sectors

Disability-related interventions are relevant to most sectoral work. In this respect, communication professionals may encounter disability-related issues in many areas of their work and can rely on the cross-cutting nature of communication to deal effectively with those issues. Often, the Bank's work includes disabled people implicitly within the broad category of "vulnerable groups." It is important, however, to explicitly mention disabled people within the vulnerable groups list; otherwise they are often overlooked. Use of photos of disabled people in media products provides "visibility." The following are samples of good, inclusive media products on various themes, as well as their rationale:[4]

- Early childhood education—disabled children are included in "Education For All" but are still marginally reached.
- HIV/AIDS—disabled people are typically not reached by prevention campaigns and lack access to treatment.
- Gender—disabled women are subject to double discrimination.
- At-risk youth—both the cause of and subject to forms of disabilities because of at-risk behaviors (for example, crime and violence).

- Post-disaster and post-conflict—projects focus on rehabilitation and integration of disabled ex-combatants and civilians.
- Employment—the majority of disabled adults remain unemployed despite possessing employable skills.
- Infrastructure—make accessible transportation, water and sanitation, schools, and hospitals.
- ICT—new information and communication technologies are a great opportunity for inclusion and also a risk factor that can exacerbate the gap between disabled and nondisabled people if those technologies are not accessible.

Key Messages

Facts are very important when communicating key issues about disabled people. Facts, however, need to be "packaged" and transformed into usable information that is interesting and appealing to audiences. The following are some examples of basic information that can be "transformed" into messages and used to great effect when communicating issues related to disabilities:

- Approximately 400 million disabled people live in the developing world.[5]
- Among refugees, it is estimated that acute clinical depression and post-traumatic stress disorder (PTSD) affect between 40 and 70 percent.[6]
- The global GDP that is lost annually due to exclusion of disabled people from the employment sector is estimated to be between US$1.37 and US$1.94 trillion.[7]
- With estimates that 40 million of the 115 million children out of school have disabilities, it is difficult to reach universal primary education targets without including children with disabilities.
- Disabled people are excluded from economic and social life, and thus antipoverty initiatives often do not reach them.
- Exclusion affects not only people with disabilities, but also their families and communities.
- Disability and poverty form a vicious cycle. Poverty often leads to disability, which then traps people in poverty because of the societal barriers and exclusion faced by people with disabilities.[8]
- Disabled people are at increased risk of acquiring HIV/AIDS because of physical abuse, lack of intervention, and lack of appropriate preventive outreach.[9]
- The Convention on the Rights of Persons with Disabilities, adopted by the UN General Assembly on December 13, 2006, and with 117 signatory states as of October 10, 2007, sets the benchmark for the inclusion of disabled people in the development agenda.

To increase the awareness and knowledge on this issue, the World Bank has produced a number of communication and media products. They include the following:

- "Don't Shut Us Out," a 30-second public service announcement aired on several CNN networks (in English)[10]
- Disability and Development Issue Brief, posted on the Bank's external media site[11]
- *Development Outreach Magazine* on Disability and Development, July 2005[12]
- "From Exclusion to Inclusion," a 10-minute corporate video on the Bank's Disability and Development Work Web site[13]
- Staff and media training modules on communicating with proper terminology, and using the social inclusion paradigm[14]
- List of reporters and media networks whose focus is on disability issues[15]
- Disability Communication Manual[16]

Challenges for World Bank Communication Professionals

Development communication professionals often face a number of challenges when dealing with issues related to disabilities. For the most part, these challenges are similar to those encountered in other development communication approaches that seek to actively engage relevant stakeholder groups, especially those subject to marginalization. The main challenge usually is making sure that their voice is heard and accounted for. Primarily, communication should be a tool for empathy and understanding. While engaged in dialog and communication processes aimed at achieving mutual understanding, communication professionals dealing with disability should also pay attention to specific critical issues.

The lack of universal terms and definitions is often a major challenge. Because of cultural and language differences, little consistency exists on what is deemed to be the best usage of disability-related terminology between and even within countries. The word "handicapped," for example, is considered derogatory in the United States; however, it is the proper term in many Francophone countries. World Bank country office staff should speak directly with their local DPOs to determine what the appropriate cultural norms and related perceptions are in that country.[17]

The degree of disability diversity can be another issue to navigate. Disability involves not only different forms but also different degrees of impairments. Not all people with disabilities would self-identify with the term "impairment"; some would prefer "different ability" or other similar phrasing. The typical categories of impairment types include physical, cognitive or intellectual, sensory (vision and hearing), psychosocial, and learning. The different degrees range from mild to medium to severe, though again not all people with disabilities would necessarily identify with these descriptors. Two-way communication can effectively account for such differences in perceptions and types of disabilities.

The final major challenge can be referred to as the "knowledge gap." Communication professionals do not need to be disability specialists to properly cover and write about disability-related topics. As for any sector of intervention, however, it helps to have a basic understanding of the issues and sensitivity to them in order to devise effective strategies with a sound foundation. The best way to become familiar with disability issues is to start by consulting some of the basic material on the subject available on the Internet, such as the Convention on the Rights of Persons with Disabilities.[18]

Attending communication training on disability can be helpful, although these sessions are perhaps not as helpful as speaking directly with disability advocates and disabled individuals themselves, who are the best source of answers to the questions of communication practitioners. It is also important for the communication practitioner to familiarize herself or himself with the various tools and media that facilitate communication with disabled people. These include telephone TDY/TTY,[19] cell phone text messaging, instant messaging, closed and open captioning and sign language interpretation for hearing impaired persons; accessible formats of electronic files (for example, MS Word files and accessible Web sites), large print, high contrast and Braille printing for visually impaired people; and "plain language" for the benefit of all people, especially people with cognitive or intellectual disabilities.

Communication in the Convention on the Rights of Persons with Disabilities[20]

The Convention on the Rights of Persons with Disabilities (CRPD) is one of the few international conventions that make specific references to communication. The rationale for the active involvement of communication professionals is based on the reasonable expectation that development organizations, including the World Bank, will be called to provide technical assistance to client countries on how to implement the principles of the convention. Article 8 on "Awareness-raising," together with Article 9 on "Accessibility" and Article 32 on "International Cooperatio,n" should be key references for communication professionals.

Article 8 on awareness raising was included in the Convention in part to try to address the underlying causes of discrimination on the basis of disability—namely, the prevailing attitudes toward persons with disabilities in many societies. Even in countries where disability-related legislation exists (such as nondiscrimination legislation), the efficacy of such legislation is often hindered by public assumptions and stereotypes of persons with disabilities.

In order to enhance the implementation of domestic legislation and the CRPD, Article 8 sets forth the objectives for awareness-raising measures (for example, to foster respect for the rights and dignity of persons with disabilities),[21] as well as examples of such measures (for example, "encouraging all organs of the media to portray persons with disabilities in a manner consistent with the purpose of the present Convention").[22] Client countries that are States Parties to the CRPD may need Bank assistance in order to help implement their obligations under Article 8.

In addition, where other projects seek to be inclusive of persons with disabilities, engaging in some of the activities addressed in Article 8 may assist in enhancing the overall efficacy of such projects. For example, where an education project seeks to be inclusive of persons with disabilities, the addition of a public awareness-raising component to the project could be beneficial in helping to dispel stereotypes or inaccurate assumptions held by teachers and/or parents, regarding persons with disabilities in educational environments. Thus, compliance with Article 8 could be viewed as a tool for enhancing the achievement of wider development objectives.[23]

Article 9 on "Accessibility" addresses an overarching concern for the effective implementation of obligations for persons with disabilities—accessibility. In this regard it takes a broad approach to the issue, addressing not only physical accessibility but also accessibility of information. In addition, Article 9 captures both public and private actors, as it is applicable to either actor making their products or services "open or available to the public."

Although some delegations expressed concern about their capacity to uphold their obligations under Article 9, by the end of the negotiations there was general agreement that omitting the article would likely lead to accessibility issues being forgotten about in many planning activities, resulting in the inadvertent creation of further societal barriers for persons with disabilities. Given that it is almost always more cost-effective for such barriers to be avoided in the first place rather than removed at a later juncture, Article 9 came to be seen as a useful reminder to public and private actors of the need to address accessibility issues in an inclusive manner and early in planning processes.

Article 32 on "International Cooperation" was included because disability "is a major cross-cutting development issue for all development partners,"[24] and because international cooperation that is not inclusive of disability issues has the potential to lead to the inadvertent creation of long-term barriers for persons with disabilities. In terms of the obligations for States Parties under Article 32, it calls for "international cooperation, including international development programmes" to be "inclusive of and accessible to persons with disabilities."[25]

In this context the term "international cooperation" is interpreted broadly, including not only aid programmes but also the "exchange and sharing of information, experiences, training programmes and best practices."[26] Indeed, during the Ad Hoc Committee's[27] discussions it was noted on numerous occasions that developing countries have as much to learn from each other as from developed countries. Thus, not only can the Bank be of assistance to client countries in the inclusive implementation of projects, but there is also scope for the Bank to utilize its convening power and its communication capacities to help foster the sharing of information, expertise, and best practices between actors in this field.

Notes

1. For a list of other organizations that have adopted guidelines for inclusion of disabled people visit http://go.worldbank.org/IHINYN1EX0 (World Bank Intranet users only).
2. Disability Knowledge Toolkit: see http://go.worldbank.org/0GWEU0VOY0. See note 14.
3. Loretta Hieber, *Lifeline Media: Reaching Populations in Crisis* (Geneva: Media Action International, 2001).
4. Derived from the World Bank training, "Demystifying Disability through Communications" (World Bank, Washington, DC, 2004).
5. World Health Organization.
6. F. Baingana and I. Bannon *Integrating Mental Health and Psychosocial Interventions into World Bank Lending for Conflict-Affected Populations: A Toolkit* (Washington, DC: World Bank, 2004).
7. R. Metts, "Disability Issues, Trends and Recommendations for the World Bank" (Consultant report, Feb. 2000).
8. See DFID, "Disability, Poverty and Development" (UK Department for International Development, London, Feb. 2000).
9. *HIV/AIDS & Disability: Capturing Hidden Voices* (Washington, DC: World Bank/Yale University, 2004).
10. See the Global Partnership for Disability and Development site at http://www.worldbank.org/disability.
11. See News and Broadcast at www.worldbank.org.
12. See http://www1.worldbank.org/devoutreach/july05/index.asp.
13. See the Global Partnership for Disability and Development site at http://www.worldbank.org/disability.
14. A stand-alone training on the issue was developed and delivered in 2005: "Demystifying Disability Through Communication." Most of the content is available through the Disability and Development Team (HDNSP).
15. Contact the World Bank's Disability and Development Team, HDNSP, at http://go.worldbank.org/0GWEU0VOY0.
16. Claudia Werneck, *Manual on Disabilities and Inclusive Development for the Media and Social Communications Professionals* (Washington, DC: World Bank, 2005); http://siteresources.worldbank.org/DISABILITY/Resources.
17. See *World Bank Guidelines for Reporting and Writing about Disabilities.*
18. The World Bank Intranet contains a "disability toolkit," which also provides samples of good communication products.
19. These are electronic devices for text communication via a telephone line. They are used when one or more of the parties have hearing or speech difficulties.
20. Excerpted from by K. Guernsey, M. Nicoli and A. Ninio, "Convention on the Rights of

Persons with Disabilities: Its Implementation and the Relevance for the World Bank," Social Protection Discussion Paper No. 0712, (World Bank, Washington, DC, June 2007).

21. CRPD Article 8(1)(a).
22. CRPD Article 8(2)(c).
23. In this regard the Bank sector that could be of assistance is the Communication Network (CommNet). CommNet is the World Bank's professional association of communications staff working worldwide. CommNet has more than 300 members across the Bank Group (40 percent of whom are working outside Bank headquarters in 73 Bank country offices), who are engaged in a broad spectrum of communications and outreach activities.
24. Statement by José Antonio Ocampo, Under-Secretary-General for Economic and Social Affairs, UN General Assembly Ad Hoc Committee, 8th session, New York, December 5, 2006.
25. CRPD Article 32(1)(a).
26. CRPD Article 1(b).
27. The Ad Hoc Committee was a sub-body of the UN General Assembly, mandated to consider proposals for a new international convention on the human rights of persons with disabilities. It met at UN Headquarters in New York from 2002 to 2006, and included delegations from UN Member States, UN agencies, and intergovernmental organizations, as well as extensive participation by the international disability community.

4.5 How a Multilateral Institution Builds Capacity in Strategic Communication

*Cecilia Cabañero-Verzosa**

Introduction

Development communication includes different conceptual and operational modes and a wide range of approaches reflecting different needs, as discussed throughout the Sourcebook. Strategic communication employs a client-oriented approach, seeking to understand people's perceptions and motivations regarding specific issues in order to induce voluntary change and support the achievement of management objectives. This article illustrates how to build the institutional capacity in strategic communication in a major international organization. Strategic communication is one of the main approaches, usually linked to the diffusion perspective, adopted in development communication.

Strategic communication, as conceived and applied in World Bank operations, differs somewhat from the way it is often referred to in the relevant development literature. In this context, strategic communication is a way to promote voluntary change in people's attitudes and behaviors in order to achieve development objectives. This approach appears to be particularly valued by managers and decision makers who understand how strategic communication can often become a management tool, helping in the supervision and monitoring of the whole project, thus enhancing the chances of success and sustainability of the initiative.

For this reason, building capacity of managers of public sector programs to use strategic communication concepts in development work is a good idea. But good ideas are not enough to make development programs effective. These ideas need to be understood and embraced by many. These ideas need to be converted into new ways of doing development work. Knowledge, learning, and capacity-building programs help gain advocates and practitioners of good ideas. Building capacity of people to do something different from their usual practice requires a commitment to the long haul because the impact of capacity-building efforts is rarely evident in a short time.

In a large, multilateral institution like the World Bank, this capacity building can be a daunting endeavor. Results are slow to come by, but modest gains can pave the way to longer-term success. This is the story of how a knowledge, learning, and

• Cecilia Cabañero-Verzosa is the head of the Knowledge and Learning Unit, Development Communications Division, the World Bank.

capacity-building program on strategic communication was created and nurtured at the World Bank.

The paper highlights the program's diffusion process and what contributed to its successful launch. It shares lessons learned about the process of securing an authorizing environment; promoting the value of a learning, knowledge, and capacity-building program on strategic communication for the Bank's work; creating internal and external partnerships; and building organizational capacity for strategic communication. These reflections are not only on lessons learned but also on what can be done better by other organizations embarking on the same goal of developing a capacity-building program on strategic communication.

Why Is the World Bank in the Business of Knowledge, Learning, and Capacity-Building?

A fundamental idea guided the knowledge, learning, and capacity-building program on strategic communication. When World Bank staff and their development partners and developing country clients have strong communication and client engagement skills, development projects are more effective. The program's goal is to equip Bank staff, development partners, and developing country clients with the concepts, frameworks, and approaches that will enable them to design, implement, and supervise development projects centered on client needs rather than focused wholly on organizational goals. It is hoped that development projects would be designed in ways that provide project stakeholders and beneficiaries with the space to learn new information, acquire new attitudes, and adopt new practices that lead to effective development. The knowledge, learning, and capacity-building program would be characterized as audience-centered, comprehensive, and sustainable.[1]

The program is audience-centered because courses, knowledge-sharing sessions, and capacity-building efforts address current issues faced by various groups using robust concepts and frameworks that have been tested, used, and adapted to suit real-world conditions. Learning interventions are designed to be open-ended, with the World Bank offering strategic communication concepts, approaches, and tools, and the course participants providing subject matter content for these learning interventions. Thus, a team working on privatization projects reviews relevant communication approaches, assesses their utility for privatization issues, and adopts or adapts these communication concepts and tools to their own project needs. The strategic communication capacity-building program provides a framework for action learning: audiences bring the content of their projects into the discussion and the training team shares knowledge and experience on the use of strategic communication concepts and tools in these specific content areas. Together, as part of the learning intervention, both trainers and trainees develop an approach to strategic communication that addresses participants' concerns.

The program adopts a comprehensive approach. Rather than narrowly segmenting audiences for learning, DevComm takes a systems approach to audience selection by examining who works with whom on development projects. By identifying the learning needs of groups who work together, the learning program reaches a subsystem of audiences simultaneously, so learning inputs are mutually reinforcing. There are four critical groups for capacity-building interventions: World Bank operational staff, from the country director or manager to task team leaders, team members, and their administrative support staff; Bank clients in developing countries, including government officials, civil society, and media; communication specialists of the World Bank, who provide communication assistance to project teams and the World Bank's senior management; and the international donor community.

By addressing the learning needs of various groups simultaneously, participants had an opportunity to listen to varied perspectives on an issue. When Bank staff join their developing country clients, other donors, and civil society in learning programs, they collaborate on various tasks—communication strategy development, stakeholder mapping—and practice client engagement and negotiation skills, which simulate their joint work in the field for some real-time learning.

Finally, the program aims to become sustainable. By addressing learning needs of multiple audiences simultaneously, the strategic communication learning and capacity-building program is able to create a synergistic system that increases the probability of sustaining learning. An increasing number of client country government officials are requesting donors and multilateral and bilateral agencies to assist them in building their capacity and integrating communication in projects and policy reforms. Bank operational staff who listen to their client countries, in turn, look to the World Bank's communication specialists to provide relevant and timely communication support to projects supported by donor groups. Donors who appreciate the value of strategic communication to effectively enhance development projects readily offer financial and technical support for capacity-building and learning interventions and share experiences across regions and sectors.

Designing the Program

The ideas behind building capacity for strategic communication may be simple and straightforward, but it took 10 years for these core ideas to be accepted by many Bank staff and their managers. Developing country government officials and civil society organizations readily recognize the value of strategic communication, but they need the technical and financial support of donor organizations to translate these ideas into thriving programs. Hence, building institutional capacity for strategic communication has been a slow and painstaking process.

How is the capacity-building program designed and implemented? What are constraints to ready acceptance? What opportunities provide the impetus for the program to move forward? Many organizational issues hinder the building of capacity and the diffusion of strategic communication. There is the question of whether strategic communication is the Bank's business or that of the government. As the Bank promotes client country–driven development projects, why should the Bank be responsible for communicating about reforms? And when confronted with requests for technical support in the area of strategic communication, the Bank agonizes over the question of whether this is a domain where the Bank has comparative advantage in relation to other international institutions like the United Nations.

Strategic Communication: Mandated or Valued?

One of the ways that institutions promote internal reform is to mandate these new initiatives. This program decided against such a tactic for fear that Bank staff would comply in principle, but not in practice. Given the myriad tasks involved in project preparation, it was likely that Bank staff would be perfunctory in their performance of tasks related to strategic communication, without being committed to the essence of strategic communication that reorients the project preparation process from a technocratic approach to a client-centered perspective. Strategic communication may challenge the wisdom of the technical solution, and project teams feared they neither had time nor expertise to navigate the possible conflicts and disagreements with stakeholders on project issues.

To demonstrate value, the knowledge, learning, and capacity-building program provides an integrated service: learning interventions are coupled with technical support to developing country project teams. This twin approach is critical. Staff who learn concepts and approaches are able to apply these to their own project with technical support on the ground. Documented experiences in the use of strategic communication and other development communication approaches in cross-sectoral projects highlight what approaches work more effectively and why.

Addressing the Client's Client First

When Bank project staff and their managers were reluctant to embrace the practice of strategic communication, the program turned to their immediate clients, government officials, NGOs, media, and civil society. These groups were actively searching for help on strategic communication, because they were at the center of controversial reform programs in developing countries. They were quick to appreciate that a well-designed technical project was not going to succeed if stakeholders failed to understand the problems these reforms were meant to alleviate. Reforms were failing not because technical designs were flawed but because people did not understand the benefits they could gain from these reforms.

Fortunately, communication and learning technologies were functional and readily available. Two-way videoconferencing, online facilitated discussions, self-paced computerized learning modules—these tools expand our reach and enable us to conduct multicountry courses in Africa, Asia, Eastern Europe and Central Asia, and Latin America. These learning programs are designed to address the issues confronting participants in their real-world projects. Assignments prepared for classroom discussion are also the same documents clients use to develop projects submitted to donors for funding. Thus, through the training program, clients can access technical support from communication specialists, from academia, and from communication practitioners in international and developing country institutions. Course participants also benefit from discussions and the exchange of project experiences across countries.

Competitive Domains

In a large multilateral institution like the World Bank, where staff have expertise in a broad range of disciplines, one encounters the question of organizational mandate and turf. How does strategic communication affect the work of social development specialists who conduct social analysis and social assessments? When communication specialists conduct communication-based assessments[2] to identify opponents and supporters of public sector reforms and to mitigate political risk, how will this effort align with the political analysis that economists conduct? Should strategic communication concern itself primarily with widespread dissemination of information? Given limited time and funding to develop projects, how do project managers decide which set of specialists to involve in project preparation and supervision? Can sector experts attempt to do the communication-based assessment on their own rather than securing assistance of communication specialists?

The main drawback faced by the strategic communication capacity-building program was the lack of understanding by Bank staff about the science and art of development communication and, within it, of strategic communication. The program needed to find a niche in the organization. It had to build coalitions of support within and outside the institution to gain recognition for the theoretical framework and the professional practice of strategic communication.

Rather than portraying strategic communication as an isolated specialist tool, the program chose to work within the existing organizational processes to embed strategic communication into the learning programs of sectors (such as health, education, water and sanitation, infrastructure development, privatization). Program staff demonstrate how to use communication in sectoral projects. They work alongside project teams as they travel to developing countries to collaborate on the development of communication strategies to support reforms, conduct communication-based assessment, and conduct public opinion research to assess attitudes and perceptions of stakeholders and beneficiaries about reforms.

Gaining Support of Managers

But despite the growing support for development communication, including the strategic communication approach, among project teams and their developing country clients and donors, it has taken many years of fieldwork to capture managers' attention. Some sector managers are more receptive than others. Early interest in using communication to promote behavior change was evident to the human development sector, because it was obvious that people need to access health care and education services if human development goals are to be achieved. Early supporters also came from the environment sector, water and sanitation, and private sector development. Members of the Bank's Board of Executive Directors (including Italy and the Philippines) participated in strategic communication courses, which led to their increased interest in this program area. In 2005, strategic communication was included as a module in the two-week course for all newly appointed country directors and country managers. It continues to be a part of the follow-up learning program when these country directors and country managers have completed at least six months at their new posts.

But Where's the Money?

Finally, the question centers on resources, both for staff time and for financing communication activities in projects. To respond to this concern, DevComm, with the Africa region's sector specialists, coauthored a review of the health, nutrition, and population projects (HNP) in 36 African countries over more than 20 years.[3] A surprisingly high proportion (three-quarters) of the projects examined had a component of communication for behavior change. Communication component costs were about 8 percent of total costs.

Despite their marginal position in the HNP sector operations, communication components included a wide variety of interventions—mass media, traditional folk media, social marketing campaigns, community mobilization, education, women's literacy groups, and advocacy. Projects that focus on one or more diseases or health problems tended to have a communication component. In contrast, health reform projects were striking for their complete lack of a communication component despite the urgent need to build public support for these more controversial issues.

Other studies focused on the water sector and on private sector development. These studies confirmed the findings in the health, nutrition, and population project portfolio review: a large percentage of sectoral projects included a communication component. The question posed was the following: Were communication resources used to disseminate information, or were the resources used optimally to help project managers understand people's perceptions and motivations so that sectoral interventions can respond successfully to people's priorities?

What Worked

In the last decade, the knowledge, learning, and capacity-building program has reached some 8,500 participants worldwide, with some 200 courses and workshops using various training formats, including classroom delivery, blended courses, and computer-based, self-paced learning modules.

Strategic communication learning programs are cited as one of the most successful Bank-wide in terms of overall quality and usefulness in reports issued by the Bank's Knowledge and Learning Board. Over a three-year period, External Affairs (EXT) Strategic Communication Learning Program delivered courses that exceeded both the Bank's standards and American Society for Training and Development (ASTD) standards.[4]

In fiscal year 2007, the Bank's Knowledge and Learning Board consolidated all communication training under the management of External Affairs, with the goal of ensuring coherence in learning objectives and promoting a shared framework, concepts, and approaches on development communication. The EXT Strategic Communication Learning Program was given the mandate to design, deliver, and evaluate various types of communication courses—from interpersonal communication, to group and mass-mediated communication. Skill-building courses address a wide range of topics such as conducting communication-based assessments, mapping stakeholders, developing a communication strategy, mitigating political risk, building long-term relationships with critical stakeholders, engaging clients, and negotiating with multiple parties.

Courses offering two-way videoconferencing, computerized self-paced modules, and online facilitation were subjected to Level 2 and Level 3 evaluations going beyond the routine Level 1 evaluations conducted Bank-wide.[5] These research results proved that educational technologies provide meaningful learning outcomes, and there are alternatives to the traditional, and more expensive, classroom course.

The following timeline captures highlights of the diffusion process within the World Bank. The first formal course on strategic communication was conducted in the human development sector in 1993. But this effort was nurtured by External Affairs when then senior vice president of External Affairs, Mark Malloch Brown, created a new unit called Development Communication (EXTCD or DevComm) in 1998. DevComm has since led the Bank-wide learning program on a number of communication functions and approaches, including strategic communication.

In 2000, a distance-learning course on strategic communication was among the first set of courses launched Bank-wide through the newly created Global Development Learning Network, which provided two-way videoconferencing facilities to link headquarters with country offices. Distance-learning courses were delivered to Anglophone and Francophone Africa, Latin America, Eastern Europe, and Central Asia. With simultaneous translation facilities, DevComm conducted these courses in English, French, Spanish, and Russian.

Technology allowed DevComm to evolve the pure videoconference format with a blended course by 2005. Blended courses were of two types: a version including videoconferencing coupled with computer-based modules and online facilitation, and another version adding a face-to-face course within two to three months of completion of the videoconference and online facilitation.

In terms of sectoral responsiveness, following the early efforts of the human development sector, other sectors championed communication and partnered with DevComm in the design and delivery of communication courses, which also went beyond the strategic communication perspective to include others from the broader field of development communication. These included the social development sector (2003) that co-delivered a classroom course on stakeholder consultation and a distance-learning course on civic engagement for development effectiveness. In 2005, the Poverty Reduction and Economic Management (PREM) network and the Corporate Strategy Group partnered with DevComm in the co-delivery of the classroom course on managing political risk. In 2007, the Bank's strategy on governance and anticorruption included the provision that the Sustainable Development Network (which includes the social development sector) and EXT collaborate to develop and deliver a learning program for Bank staff and developing country clients on the demand side of governance.

Accelerate the Diffusion Process

Finding ways to accelerate the diffusion process is the key challenge for knowledge, learning, and capacity-building programs in strategic communication. There are three vital elements that define organizational strategy in the public sector: (1) the mission or purpose of the organization, (2) sources of support and legitimacy, and (3) capacity to achieve declared objectives.[6] This strategic triangle can be used to assess the pace of adoption of the program within the organization. Thus, if there is clear alignment in the mission, and there is an authorizing mandate for such a mission, with an organizational capacity to implement the program, it is highly likely that organizational members will more readily accept new ideas espoused by the program. If these three elements are not simultaneously present or are not in sync, the diffusion process will likely be slow. As in the case of the World Bank, the early efforts of the knowledge, learning, and capacity-building program focused on establishing legitimacy by demonstrating the value of strategic communication to development work.

Where There Is No Champion, Seek the Client's Client

When there was organizational resistance to strategic communication, the learning program focused on reaching the client's client first. This provided legitimacy and support for communication because the developing country project managers demanded technical support on strategic communication from the World Bank project teams.

Engage in Upward Communication

Communicating with managers was difficult but critical. Seeking support from a coalition of champions among managers of various sectors should be attempted as early as possible in the diffusion process. One approach used was to identify sectors that were more directly involved with services to people, such as health and education, water, and sanitation. These managers are confronted with the challenge of building support for policy reforms and creating a clientele for various health and educational infrastructure.

No Training without Technical Support; No Technical Support without Training

A two-part formula helps. Training provides structured knowledge, core concepts, and examples of good practice, as well as poor practice. Technical support to course participants enables these participants to apply the concepts and tools to their projects, thus deepening the learning experience.

Conclusion

A multilateral institution can build organizational capacity in strategic communication, as well as in other communication approaches for development purposes. This can be done by creating synergies between learning and technical support that allow participants to apply concepts learned to their own projects. It can be done with a small band of committed individuals ready to exploit organizational moments when the three elements of mission, legitimacy, and capability are in sync and the adoption of strategic communication is likely.

To mainstream strategic communication effectively, two key factors must be met: (1) a systematic approach integrating training and operational work within the organization, and (2) the demonstration of its value in operations. Strategic communication has a key role in the effective management of projects of various natures, especially when used in conjunction with other development communication approaches. As discussed in other sections of the Sourcebook, even if this article focuses on strategic communication, other fast-emerging perspectives and approaches, based on genuine two-way communication models, can, and should, be taken into account when building relevant communication capacities in development organizations.

Notes

1. Knowledge, learning, and capacity building refer to a set of activities aimed at providing a mechanism for acquiring new information and skills and creating an enabling environment so people can use newly acquired knowledge and skills in their work.
2. CBA is part of development communication. When applied for strategic communication initiatives, its use is limited by the monologic nature of the strategic communication approach.
3. E. A. Elmendorf, C. Cabañero-Verzosa, M. Lioy, and K. LaRusso. *Behavior Change Communication for Better Health Outcomes in Africa: Experience and Lessons Learned from World Bank-financed Health, Nutrition and Population Projects* (Washington, DC: World Bank, 2005).
4. Knowledge and Learning Board, *Annual Report* (Washington, DC: World Bank, 2005, 2006, 2007).
5. D. L. Kirkpatrick. *Evaluating Training Programs: The Four Levels* 2nd ed., San Francisco: Berrett-Koehler, 1998. The four levels measure the following: Level 1—Reaction; Level 2—Learning; Level 3—Behavior; and Level 4—Results.
6. M. H. Moore. *Creating Public Value: Strategic Management in Government* (Cambridge, MA: Harvard University Press, 1995), 70–71.

4.6 Assessing the Impact of Development Communication

*Paul Mitchell and Colleen Gorove**

Overview

The impact of development communication is far-reaching. Applied strategically and coherently to development objectives, communication activities help to achieve better results. This paper identifies positive development outcomes that can be attributed, in large part, to sound communication. In stating the case for development communication, this review draws primarily, though not exclusively, on lessons learned from the World Bank's experience. It synthesizes findings from a range of regions and programs with a particular focus on assessing results through case studies of development interventions at the country level.

The practice of development communication covers a wide range of activities that can be geared to support development outcomes. It encompasses a process that identifies the political, social, and cultural risks that could affect program sustainability and discovers measures to help mitigate those risks. Through communication, stakeholders are engaged in the development process and information is accessible to those who need it most. Stakeholder input informs project design, ensuring that planning and delivery meet needs and address demands. Communication measures help to build critical consensus, particularly where coalitions of support and the consent of citizens are needed for governance or reform efforts to succeed. From policy reform strategies to health and behavioral-change programs, effective communication is a vital part of the development process.

Measuring Demand for Development Communication

At an institutional level, development communication is increasingly mainstreamed. The World Bank's Operational Vice Presidencies recently suggested that all analytical and advisory work should contain a communication component. All Poverty Reduction Strategy Papers now include communication as part of the main activity in their design and implementation.[1] New policy approaches and reforms also include communication as part of the operation.[2]

• Paul Mitchell is a manager, and Colleen Gorove is a senior communication officer, both with the Development Communication Division of the World Bank.

In the present results-driven environment, one measure of the impact of development communication is in the demand for its services. From virtually no activity six years ago, substantive demand for services from the World Bank's Development Communication Division (DevComm) is registered now across regions. All regions are increasingly requesting development communication in their operations, and a number of World Bank sectors—such as urban, water, energy, and environment—have all mainstreamed communication. Countries such as Nigeria, Ghana, and Kenya have stated in their Country Assistance Strategy that all projects include a communication assessment. As of March 2006, DevComm is active in about 123 projects in a range of sectors (see figure 4.4).

The Costs of Not Communicating

Although communication requires up-front investment, the benefits usually outweigh the costs through more sustainable projects that achieve public buy-in and support. Indeed, the costs of not communicating are demonstrated time and time again through errant government and institutional efforts that fail to achieve their objectives. The costs are in time delays, monetary damages,[3] and project cancellations, not to mention immense intangible impacts on reputation, trust, and good will. The failure to obtain acceptance of any project means that all the design and project preparation costs are lost.

Figure 4.4 DevComm Portfolio by Sector in March 2006

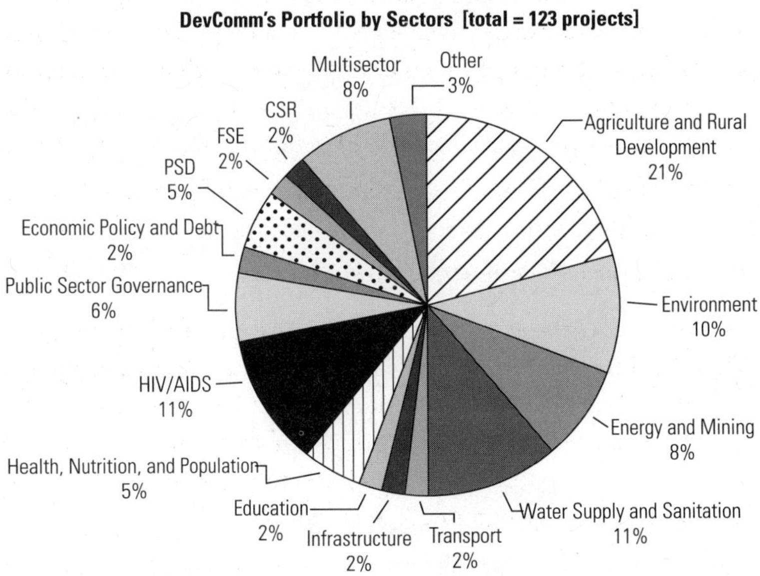

Source: DevComm statistics.

Note: PSD = Private Sector Development, FSE = Financial Sector Development, CSR = Corporate Social Responsibility.

4

As mentioned in module 3, the cost of the lack of adequate communication between Hydro-Quebec and the indigenous Cree community over hydroelectric projects in Canada led to litigation, delays, and new project components, adding approximately US$268 million to the project over the course of 30 years. In another example, the failure to undertake a communication analysis in the World Bank's Western China Poverty Reduction project led to an estimated additional cost of US$2 million.[4] In the end, the brunt of the cost is borne by the poor, who fail to receive the timely benefits of a well-functioning development program meant to help improve the quality of their lives.

A Methodology for Measuring Results

The impact of development communication is seen mainly at the project level, where the links between communication and outcomes can be made. Case-by-case examinations reveal—primarily through qualitative but also through some quantitative evidence—how communication influences project results. A review of this body of knowledge can serve as an evaluative methodology, because measurement of the impact of communication varies significantly at the project level, given the highly contextual nature of communication interventions and the lack of resources and guidelines in this arena.

The challenges inherent in measuring the impact of development communication are only exacerbated when researchers try to apply uniform criteria across a representative sampling of experiences. The following are four major challenges to developing a methodological framework.

- Separating the impact of communication from the impact of other activities is difficult, especially when communication predominates in early stages (leading to project approval), and then plays a supporting role. Furthermore, when the communication and risk analyses are done correctly, the result can be that nothing negative happens. World Bank's Operations Evaluation Department (OED) evaluations frequently mention projects failing because they did not incorporate good communication. Few reviews, however, explore the positive impact when objectives are achieved.
- Development communication impacts are little studied, making it difficult to develop longitudinal data across a range of programs over time. For example, a review of health projects in the Africa region revealed that more than 50 percent did not include indicators to measure the influence of their communication components for behavior change on actual health behaviors.[5]
- Task managers lack the knowledge, resources, and guidelines to measure the impact of communication within their projects. They are rarely able to undertake opinion research at the repeated intervals necessary to measure progress in behavior change.

- Given the specific context and dynamic nature of sociopolitical and nonfinancial risks, comparisons among projects are difficult to make. In addition, these kinds of risks can occur suddenly in reaction to unexpected changes in the sociopolitical system, making their assessment even more difficult.

Despite these challenges, there is a large body of case study evidence that demonstrates how communication affects development outcomes. Lessons learned from the analysis of such data can be used to inform an evaluation methodology to demonstrate the impact of communication on development.

The Impact of Communication on Development

Communication interventions in development programs produce four key results: reduced political risks, improved project design and performance, increased transparency, and enhanced voice and participation. Each of these results matters to development, and communication matters to achieving these results. Lessons learned from operations reviews indicate that communication applied strategically is essential to project success.

Reduced Political Risks

The reduction of political uncertainty is a significant result of good communication analysis and implementation. Many development failures—particularly those involving economic reform, utility reform, and large infrastructure projects—result from ignoring the political, social, and cultural context in which the development intervention takes place rather than from failing to propose the right technical solution. Analyzing República Bolivariana de Venezuela's economic reforms in the late 1980s, former Finance Minister Moises Naim concluded that the missing link was an effective communication strategy. He realized in retrospect that the government did not adequately appreciate the "need to grant public communication the same attention, resources, and seriousness as the other reforms it introduced."[6]

In the past, Bank projects suffered when critical aspects of the sociopolitical environment were disregarded. An OED review of the Bank's last decade of Country Assistance Strategy experiences stated, "Often economic reforms failed either because the government was not committed to them or because the government underestimated opposition to reforms and was unable to carry them through. An insufficient understanding of the political economy of reforms and the nature of the state may have led the Bank in some cases to push reforms that stood little chance of success."[7] A World Bank study concluded that in 10 projects in the Africa region the effectiveness of assistance was inextricably linked to domestic political commitment for change.[8] These findings are in line with other studies indicating that when political factors in lending operations are neglected the end result is failure.

Clear evidence of the role communication can play in building political will is exhibited in the Bangladesh Air Quality Project. The task managers recognized the potential for serious social conflict in this program to phase out two-stroke, three-wheeler taxis. The project concluded that "socially difficult environmental decisions can be executed if there is strong public support, and public support can be created by working with stakeholders and a continuous communication program. These difficult decisions are fundamentally the result of political will, which can be built, though technical issues are important."[9]

Lack of trust, consensus, and political support derails many development programs, and weaknesses in communication strategy exacerbate these problems.[10] Indeed, a Bank study on privatization in Africa determined that three of the top five recognized constraints—lack of consensus, lack of ownership, and political uncertainty—relate to the need for good communication.[11] Perceptions relating to reform and development issues cannot be taken for granted; high costs can be incurred when these issues are not addressed at the outset through development communication approaches.[12]

Failure to develop adequate communication mechanisms, particularly approaches for engaging stakeholders, is cited repeatedly in the World Bank's internal evaluative reviews. In fact, a World Bank study found that projects seeking beneficiaries' involvement achieved a 68 percent success rate, whereas projects not engaging beneficiaries had a success rate of only 10 percent.[13]

A review of power sector reforms in six states in India over a 10-year period outlines several key areas where communication to engage stakeholders alleviated political risks.[14] The review asserts the importance of addressing employees' natural fears and insecurities about reform. Gaining staff support and minimizing staff resistance required utilities' top management to establish proactive human resource and communication strategies at the outset of reform. As in the case of farmers and other consumer groups, the utility staff constitutes a vital stakeholder group, needing to be drawn into the reform process and thereby "owning" the problem.

This study of power reform looks at the relationship between political risk and communication. The author states, "In hindsight, the weakness of the Indian power reform program has been that while it has focused appropriately on sorting out distortions . . ., it has failed to carry credible assurances that this will improve the equation between the reformed utilities and their consumers. In addition, it has not factored in the mutual relationships between consumers, its claimed beneficiaries, and the politicians whose behavior it is ultimately seeking to change." The study emphasizes the central role of the politician and the legitimate concerns of the constituencies he or she represents, both poor and nonpoor. Initially, major stakeholders, including entrenched interest groups, would be established as owners of the issues, and then the emphasis would shift to seeking and negotiating solutions.

Development communication geared to building broad-based consensus among stakeholders and to creating coalitions for reform can be a powerful set of tools that mitigates change in political leadership and discourages politicians from disrupting or canceling ongoing projects. Establishing political support means not only engaging existing leaders but also gaining the support of opposing parties and other politically influential individuals. This is as important for the immediate benefit of passing reforms as it is for longer-term sustainability—so that as political winds change, the reforms remain. The resulting reduction in political risk also serves to increase interest among potential contractors for projects, especially in infrastructure, leading to more competitive markets.

Improved Project Design and Performance

When applied professionally from the start, improvement of project design and performance is a second key result of communication in development programs. Communication offers systematic listening tools (that is, public opinion research results, forums for two-way dialog with stakeholders, and so forth) that help to design and prioritize policy reforms in areas where there is a clear demand for change. Effective communication can focus on project interventions that respond to expressed needs of people. Involving stakeholders in design helps to identify obstacles to the reforms as originally conceived, informs the redesign process, generates ownership among those most affected, and leads to more responsive strategies and programs. Communication-assisted upstream analysis is critical to ensuring fewer downstream delays in project implementation.

Public opinion research is one of the main tools used for probing perceptions and attitudes of stakeholders. It objectively and independently uncovers opportunities, as well as red flags, obstacles, and risks. It informs the design of the project and assists in developing the supporting communication strategy. At times, consensus cannot be reached on government plans for reform. In such cases, results of public opinion research can help willing governments to consider approaches to address stakeholder concerns or to avoid implementation of programs having little to no chance of succeeding in the current environment.

The importance of using communication research early in the project cycle was illustrated in Mauritius in 2003. The context was an IFC[15] private sector participation initiative in the water sector. Opinion research showed citizens were hoping for better drinking water and sanitation services and, to a large extent, were aware that some sort of public-private partnership would be the best option to provide those services. They expressed, however, a significant level of mistrust in the ability of the government to carry out the process of reform properly. In particular, citizens were concerned about lack of transparency: the possibility that the government talk of private sector participation was in fact a desire to privatize the water utilities outright, leaving them in foreign hands.

Mauritians were concerned about corruption in the process and possible unfavorable deals done under the table. In addition, a majority of the population did not trust the government's capacity to ensure that a private operator would not raise the water tariffs to levels they could not afford. This absence of public trust was an important element in the government's determination that it lacked the sufficient political capital to move ahead with the reform at that time.[16]

Further evidence of the impact of communication on project design and performance is in a review done between 2002 and 2005 of 15 World Bank projects in the water and sanitation sector that contained communication programs.[17] In 33 percent of those projects, the communication program was credited with having a significant impact on project design—from redesign of the project to achieve consensus among stakeholders in Nigeria, to the splitting of a project in Albania into two distinct components so the less controversial portion could proceed without delay. Further, in 40 percent of the projects reviewed, communication programs were credited with building consensus and credibility that allowed the government to undertake the reform. Many of the projects studied involved private participation—a particularly sensitive and easily politicized issue.

Recently several project appraisal documents (PADs), including those of the West Africa Gas Pipeline and the Bumbuna Hydro projects, have included a new section titled "Political and Communication Assessment," in the risk and safeguard section, highlighting the importance of this work on project performance. In Bangladesh recent work on procurement reform began to focus not only on the administrative mechanisms needed but also on issues such as communication and behavior change as critical elements of the reform program. A report on the experience states, "From a continued procurement reform point of view, therefore, it is seen as crucial to include a social accountability component to the project accompanied by a clear communication strategy to assist in creating a change in behavior and assure compliance through the introduction of some enforcement mechanisms."[18]

Increased Transparency

Transparency and the increase of information flow make up the third key result of good communication. The 1999 *World Development Report on Knowledge for Development* emphasized the importance of addressing information failures. It argued that narrowing information gaps is central to economic growth and improved welfare: "Information problems lead to market failures and impede efficiency and growth (and) are often at the core of difficulties that poor people in developing countries encounter in their daily struggle to survive and improve their lives."[19]

Information asymmetries, especially those that affect the poor adversely, must be adequately addressed for the success of development programs. Efforts to improve forms of communicating information and knowledge through effective two-way flows between citizens and government are essential. As presented in a previous module, Uganda's experience in making information about its public sector expenditures in education more transparent provides a vivid illustration of good communication producing better development outcomes.

Transparency is a critical ingredient of improved governance, and good governance is a key development indicator for countries seeking better outcomes. In addition, transparency measures have the benefit of scaling up other results as well. Research by Daniel Kaufman indicates, "The coupling of progress on improving voice and participation—including through freedom of expression—with transparency reforms can be particularly effective."[20] Applying communication to increase transparency in the development process can also go a long way toward reducing opposition to reform, thus reducing political risks. This is particularly helpful with issues that are already the focus of a high degree of public distrust.

The various forms of media are major tools for information transparency. Media have a tremendous impact on the kind and amount of information people receive about reform plans and policies. Lessons show that proactive strategic communication reduces media campaigns focused on wrong or incomplete information.[21] Educating journalists on the full political and policy implications of reform in the short term has positive long-term effects on the depth and breadth of coverage, resulting in more and better reporting on the sector. Media workshops held early can help journalists to understand the technical, financial, economic, social, and political issues and the need for reform. Study tours for journalists have been used successfully on a number of occasions, including one by the government of Cape Verde as part of its "Let's Modernize Cape Verde" campaign, which included trips for journalists to other African countries undergoing infrastructure reforms.[22]

The transparency that media scrutiny brings to the development process also plays a critical role in reducing corruption. In September 2000, a local television station in Peru broadcast a video showing the national security chief bribing an opposition member of congress in return for voting for the incumbent government. The story spread rapidly in other publications, compounded by reports that the security chief was smuggling arms to Colombian guerrillas. The revelations led to his dismissal and, in November 2000, to the resignation of the president. Following these events, the newly elected president announced his intentions to fight corruption.

The above example illustrates how the media can alter the incentives for corruption for public officials. By providing the public with access to information, the media enhance the transparency of government actions and increase the risk that corruption will be exposed. The media also help build the public consensus required to fight corruption, fueling public disapproval that presses corrupt agents to resign and raising the penalties for corruption.[23]

Recently in Nigeria, the finance minister published, both in booklet form and through the media, all transfer of funds from the federal government to the state governments countrywide. Simply making this information public drew immense attention, forcing most state governments to make public much more information on their expenditures of these funds.

Enhanced Voice and Participation

Another key result of good communication is the enhanced voice and participation provided to citizens, particularly the poor, who are often excluded from the development processes that affect them. Bank research shows that better development outcomes correlate with improved voice and participation.[24] Two-way communication enhances voice and participation by establishing channels of dialog between governments and affected parties, as well as among stakeholders at large. Providing information is essential in addressing the needs of the poor; however, creating opportunities for the poor to voice their concerns is of equal importance.

In Georgia, the communication strategy for a Judicial Reform Project confirmed the urgency of engaging and educating stakeholders on the nature and scope of legal and judicial reforms, including their own rights as citizens. Lacking strategy for effective communication, Georgian authorities employed short-term tactics that proved ineffective in dealing with opposition and rumors that undermined reform efforts. The communication strategy answered with a multipronged, phased approach, starting with public education and information activities to create awareness and social consensus. This gradual effort to build local communication capacity contributed to the project's long-term objective of creating an independent, competent, and equitable judiciary.

Communication can provide the poor with a voice, thereby leveraging an increase in responsiveness by governments. Effective two-way channels of communication help the government to tailor programs and services to meet the needs of their constituents, particularly those who are most disadvantaged. Engaging all stakeholders in the planning and implementation of projects improves performance, enhances sustainability, builds local capacity, and educates people to articulate their needs.

The design of development communication approaches facilitates access to information, sustains participation, and, most important, translates information into knowledge that people find useful and agree to adopt. Building people's capacity to communicate enhances the quality of their participation, motivates them to take action, and empowers them to adopt behavior consistent with positive outcomes. Capacity building is an important concern for communication—both at the institutional and the grassroots level.

Conclusion

Communication interventions designed to build support for development objectives are among the most important tools available to policymakers. Analysis of development program experience makes a strong case for the application of strategic and coherent communication activities to development initiatives. A well-conceived and executed communication plan can help to bring about four critical development results: *reduced political risks, improved project design and performance, increased transparency, and enhanced voice and participation.* These outcomes are supported by a large body of case history, research, and World Bank evaluations that demonstrate the growing and positive impact of the use of communication in development interventions. The aggregate lessons of these experiences serve as an evaluative approach for assessing the impact of communication on development.

There is an increasing emphasis on producing and measuring results in World Bank operations. The overwhelming importance of mitigating political, social and cultural risks that affect program sustainability will stimulate increased attention to communication as a vital tool to improve development outcomes. To ensure a continued focus on achieving results and to improve and more systematically apply measurement techniques, development communication requires a sustained level of attention and resources from top management—combined with the will and ability of communication specialists. This leadership, in partnership with other development professionals, can sustain and increase the scope and effectiveness of communication interventions on global development results.

Notes

1. Masud Mozammel and Sina Odugbemi, *With the Support of Multitudes: Using Strategic Communication to Fight Poverty through PRSPs* (Washington, DC: World Bank, 2005).
2. OPCS, *Development Policy Good Practice Guidelines* (Operational Policy and Country Services, 2004).
3. John Paul Murdoch, Legal Counsel to the Grand Council of Crees, "Building Support and Enhancing Participation in Large Hydroelectric Projects - The Case of Strategic Communication," combined presentation at World Bank Energy Week, Washington, DC, March 14–18, 2005.
4. IADB, *China: Western Poverty Reduction Project, Inspection Panel Report* (Washington, DC: IADB, April 28, 2000).

5. A. E. Elmedor, C. Cabañero-Verzosa, M. Ling, and K. Larusso, *Behavior Change Communication for Better Health Outcomes in Africa: Experience and Lessons Learned from World Bank–Financed Health, Nutrition and Population Projects* (Washington, DC: World Bank, 2005).
6. Moises Naim, *Paper Tigers and Minotaurs: The Politics of Venezuela's Economic Reforms,* (Washington, DC: Carnegie Endowment for International Peace, 1993).
7. Operations Evaluation Department, World Bank, "What Have We Learned? Some Preliminary Lessons from OED's Review of Country Assistance Evaluations Over a Ten-Year Period," IEG Working Paper (World Bank, Washington, DC, Sept. 2004).
8. S. Devarajan, *Aid and Reform in Africa* (Washington, DC: World Bank, 2001).
9. J. Shaw et al., "Reducing Pollution From Two Stroke Three Wheelers," Better Air Quality Workshop, Manila, Philippines, December 17–19 (Clean Air Initiative—Asia, Pasig City, Philippines, 2003).
10. In the Yacyretá Dam Project, the Inspection Panel pointed out "the absence of an effective communication strategy between those implementing the Project and the affected population" as one of the many issues that plagued the project, which was delayed in controversies for decades. *Inspection Panel Report,* 1998.
11. Oliver C. White and Anita Bhatia, *Privatization in Africa* (Washington, DC: World Bank, 1998).
12. The Arun III project in Nepal started in the 1980s when the Bank's posture was "to not dignify criticisms with a response." A turning point came with an article in the *Washington Post* ("Monster of the Himalayas: The World Bank's Misconceived Mega-Project in the Heart of Nepal"), which described the project as "an environmental catastrophe." Without calculated communication and political risk interventions, the Bank was not prepared to respond to the *Washington Post* article and, perhaps worse, did not have the means to predict or preempt it. Ultimately the Bank decided not to proceed with the project. Annotated from EAP/EXT Case Studies, World Bank, Washington, DC, August 2005.
13. David Dollar and Lant Pritchett, *Assessing Aid: What Works, What Doesn't, and Why,* Policy Research Report (Washington, DC: World Bank, 1998).
14. Sumir Lal, "Can Good Economics Ever Be Good Politics? A Case Study of Power Reform in India," Working Paper No. 83 (World Bank, Washington, DC, 2006).
15. The International Finance Corporation (IFC) is a member of the World Bank Group.
16. Jose Manuel Bassat, Case Study: Mauritius Water Reform. Oct (2005). Unpublished.
17. Development Communication Division, Presentation on Communication Research in the Water Sector (World Bank, Washington, DC, June 2005).
18. Zafrul Islam, *Behavior Change and Social Accountability in Procurement Reform in Bangladesh* (Washington, DC: World Bank, 2005).
19. *World Development Report* (Washington, DC: World Bank, 1999).

20. Daniel Kaufman, "10 Myths about Governance and Corruption," *Finance and Development* (IMF) 42 (Sept. 2005). http://www.imf.org/external/pubs/ft/fandd/2005/09/basics.htm.
21. Development Communication Division, *Capacity Building Needs Assessment: Communicating Rural Power to Target Audience* (Washington, DC: World Bank, 2002).
22. Oliver C. White and Anita Bhatia, *Privatization in Africa* (Washington, DC: World Bank, 1998).
23. *World Development Report* (Washington, DC: World Bank, 2002).
24. *Voice and Accountability Indicators* (Washington, DC: World Bank, 2005).

Summary of Main Points in Module 4

- This module starts by presenting the three major service lines offered by the Development Communication Division—DevComm: (1) communication in operations, (2) public opinion research, and (3) knowledge and learning. The data presented indicate how DevComm's number and range of activities have increased steadily over time to address the growing demand for such services.
- The methodological framework that guides DevComm work in operations divides a communication program into four basic phases: (1) research or CBA, (2) strategy design, (3) implementation, and (4) monitoring and evaluation.
- The links between the phases of a communication program and those of the project cycle are illustrated graphically to highlight the value-added of communication in each specific phase.
- The first article discusses how development communication can assist in the preparation of Poverty Reduction Strategy Papers. It refers to specific cases to illustrate the shift from a focus on dissemination to integrated communication programs.
- The second article makes the case about the value of community radio as a way to give a voice to local communities, even the most marginalized ones, and involve them in providing inputs on decisions concerning their well-being.
- The third article provides insight on an issue too often neglected in development: disability. It provides relevant information and basic guidelines on how communication can help to raise awareness on this issue while also empowering persons with disabilities.
- The fourth article presents the role and challenges of building communication capacities in a multilateral institution, such as the World Bank, discussing some of the key elements needed to successfully enhance communication capacities, and focusing on the specific area of strategic communication.
- The final article is about evaluating the impacts of communication interventions. While acknowledging the difficulties in accurately assessing such impacts, the article also showcases the significant available evidence about the value of communication and advances a number of methodological suggestions on how impacts can be measured more accurately.

Appendix: The Rome Consensus

Communication for Development—A Major Pillar for Development and Change

Communication is essential to human, social, and economic development. At the heart of Communication for Development is participation and ownership by communities and individuals most affected by poverty and other development issues. There is a large and growing body of evidence demonstrating the value of Communication for Development.

Below are a few examples of that body of evidence presented at the WCCD:

- In 1959 a study of 145 rural radio fora in India found that forum members learned much more about the topics under discussion than non-forum members. In the words of the researcher, "Radio farm forum as an agent for transmission of knowledge has proved to be a success beyond expectation. Increase in knowledge in the forum villages between pre- and post-broadcasts was spectacular, whereas in the non-forum villages it was negligible. What little gain there was in non-forum villages, occurred mostly in those with radio" [Data presented by Dr. Bella Mody from Neurath, P. (1959), "Part Two: Evaluation and Results," in J. C. Mathur and P. Neurath (Eds.), *An Indian Experiment in Farm Radio Forums* (pp. 59–121), Paris: UNESCO].
- The participatory communication approach adopted in Senegal led to significant reductions in the practice of female genital cutting (FGC). Since 1997, 1,748 communities in Senegal have abandoned FGC. These represent 33 percent of the 5,000 communities that practiced FGC at that time [Tostan data, presented at the WCCD, 2006—http://www.tostan.org].
- In Uganda a national and local communication process related to the corruption of centrally allocated public funds for education at the local level in schools resulted in a very significant decrease in the level of funds that did not reach that local level—from 80 percent "lost" to only 20 percent lost [Reinikka, R., and J. Svensson, "The Power of Information," Policy Research Working Paper # 3239, 2004].
- Communication programs are linked to significant reductions in Acute Respiratory Infection—ARI—in Cambodia. Since the communication campaign started in 2004, awareness of ARI grew from 20 percent to 80 percent and the

reported incidence of ARI halved [BBC World Service Trust, Film on Health Communication, presented at the WCCD, 2006—http://www.bbc.co.uk/media selector/check/worldservice/meta/dps/2006/10/061027_health_wst?size=16x9&bg c=003399&lang=en-ws&nbram= 1&nbwm=1].

- Use of mobile phones and other communication techniques for farmers to obtain information on market prices in Tanzania resulted in farmers increasing the price they receive per ton of rice from US$100 to US$600. A $200,000 investment resulted in $1.8 million of gross income [The First Mile Project, presented at the WCCD, 2006—http://www.ifad.org/rural/firstmile/ FM_2.pdf].

Development Challenges

As of 2006, it is estimated that 1.3 billion people worldwide still live in absolute poverty. Even though many countries have experienced considerable economic development, far too many remain worse off in economic and social terms.

Nelson Mandela reminds us that "Poverty is not natural—it is man-made and it can be overcome and eradicated by the actions of human beings."

People's rights to equality and to communicate are protected and advanced in the Universal Declaration on Human Rights.

Related to poverty and rights there are other very considerable and related challenges. These are delineated in the Millennium Development Goals (MDGs), which are often the benchmark for decision making in civil society, national governments, and the international development community.

Achieving improved progress on these issues requires addressing some very sensitive and difficult challenges: respect for cultural diversity, self-determination of people, economic pressures, environment, gender relations, and political dynamics—among others. It also highlights the need to harmonize communication strategies and approaches, as indicated by the 9th UN Roundtable on Communication for Development and in other international fora.

These factors often complicate and threaten the success of overall development efforts in the local, national, and international arenas. It is the people-related issues that are the focus of Communication for Development.

Communication for Development

Communication for Development is a social process based on dialogue using a broad range of tools and methods. It is also about seeking change at different levels including listening, building trust, sharing knowledge and skills, building policies, debating and learning for sustained and meaningful change. It is not public relations or corporate communication.

Strategic Requirements

Development organizations must assign a much higher priority to the essential elements of the Communication for Development process, as shown by research and practice:

- The right and opportunity people have to participate in the decision-making processes that affect their lives
- Creating opportunities for sharing knowledge and skills
- Ensuring that people have access to communication tools so that they can themselves communicate within their communities and with the people making the decisions that affect them—for example, community radio and other community media
- The process of dialogue, debate, and engagement that builds public policies that are relevant, helpful and which have committed constituencies willing to implement them—for example, on responding to preserving the environment
- Recognizing and harnessing the communication trends that are taking place at local, national, and international levels for improved development action—from new media regulations and ICT trends to popular and traditional music
- Adopting an approach that is contextualized within cultures
- Related to all of the above, assigning priority to supporting the people most affected by the development issues in their communities and countries to have their say, to voice their perspectives, and to contribute and act on their ideas for improving their situation—for example, indigenous peoples and people living with HIV/AIDS

In order to be more effective in fighting poverty and meeting the other MDGs, the Communication for Development processes just outlined are required in greater scale and at more depth, making sure that the value-added of such initiatives is always properly monitored and evaluated.

Long-Term Foundation

These processes are not just about increasing the effectiveness of overall development efforts. They are also about creating sustainable social and economic processes. In particular:

- Strengthening Citizenship and Good Governance
- Deepening the communication links and processes within communities and societies

Those are essential pillars for any development issue.

Recommendations

Based on the arguments above, in order to make much more significant progress on the very difficult development challenges that we all face, we recommend that policy makers and funders do the following:

1. Overall national development policies should include specific Communication for Development components.
2. Development organizations should include Communication for Development as a central element at the inception of programs.
3. Strengthen the Communication for Development capacity within countries and organizations at all levels. This includes people in their communities, Communication for Development specialists, and other staff, including through the further development of training courses and academic programs.
4. Expand the level of financial investment to ensure adequate, coordinated financing of the core elements of Communication for Development as outlined under Strategic Requirements above. This includes budget line[s] for development communication.
5. Adopt and implement policies and legislation that provide an enabling environment for Communication for Development—including free and pluralistic media and the right to information and to communicate.
6. Development communication programs should be required to identify and include appropriate monitoring and evaluation indicators and methodologies throughout the process.
7. Strengthen partnerships and networks at international, national, and local levels to advance Communication for Development and improve development outcomes.
8. Move toward a rights-based approach to Communication for Development.

Conclusion

As Nelson Mandela highlighted, it is people that make the difference. Communication is about people. Communication for Development is essential to making the difference happen.

The Participants
World Congress on Communication for Development
Rome, Italy
October 27, 2006

Glossary

Capacity building. A complex concept increasingly referred to as capacity development. It refers to the strengthening of (communication) capacities at a personal, community, and institutional level.

Communication-based assessment (CBA). A flexible two-way communication research method (that is, one that can be carried out either in a few days or in a longer time period, depending on the circumstances) to investigate and assess key issues that can be relevant to any sector.

Communication for development. See the term "development communication."

Communication for social change. See the term "development communication."

Communication needs assessment (CNA). An investigative method to assess the situation related to such communication issues as audiences, media environments, communication institutional capacities, information flows, and networks.

Consultation. A way of involving stakeholders, even if in a limited way, in providing inputs to key aspects of the development initiative.

Development. A term with a broad and multifaceted meaning that can be broadly defined as the systematic attempt to support betterment of peoples' conditions, especially those of the poorest, at local, national, and international levels.

Development communication. Also referred to as communication for development, communication for social change, or development support communication, it is an interdisciplinary field dedicated to enhancing development initiatives through the professional use of dialogic and monologic approaches, methods, and media. Two basic definitions are presented in section 1.1.2.

Development communication specialist. A professional with specific knowledge and skills in the interdisciplinary field of development communication. Given the interdisciplinary nature of this field, a development communication specialist, in addition to mastering communication theory and practical applications, should also be familiar with the basic principles of other disciplines such as anthropology, communication research, marketing, adult education, and participatory practices.

Development support communication. See the term "development communication."

Dialog. The professional use of two-way communication methods and techniques to engage stakeholders in the investigation, assessment, and definitions of problems, needs, risks, opportunities, and priorities. Dialog is also used to ensure mutual understanding among stakeholders, reduce the likelihood of conflicts, and empower stakeholders.

Dialogic. A mode that is associated with the emerging participation paradigm. It is based on the horizontal, two-way model of communication that creates a constructive environment where stakeholders can participate in the definition of problems and solutions.

Diffusion mode. The perspective or modality rooted in the modernization paradigm that conceives communication as an agent for the dissemination of information and innovations. Based on the one-way, or monologic, communication model, diffusion approaches are based on the belief that effective dissemination of information can induce behavior change.

Empowerment. A process leading to individuals being able and willing to take part in decisions concerning their own lives. It can refer to a personal, community, or institutional level.

Information. A term often, and erroneously, used as a synonym for communication. This concept indicates only one of the functions of communication—to inform. Information is usually part of communication, but the opposite is not necessarily true.

Millennium Development Goals (MDGs). Basic guidelines, agreed to by most countries and international organizations, on eight specific goals to be achieved by 2015 in order to address the needs of the poorest of the world.

Monologic. This mode is associated with the diffusion model. As suggested by the name, it is basically describing a one-way linear communication model where a sender controls key decisions concerning what should be the message, how it should be transmitted, and for what purpose.

Multitrack communication. An innovative and integrated model of reference for applying communication in development operations. It is based on the assumption that an initial, two-communication assessment should always be done in all initiatives to actively engage stakeholders, thus minimizing risks and identifying best opportunities and solutions. On the basis of that assessment, a mix of communication tracks or approaches might be used according to the objectives to be reached.

Participation. Indicates the involvement of stakeholders in the decision-making and implementation process, which can occur at different levels and degrees (for example, from passive participation to full collaboration). Debated at length in the Sourcebook, this concept is at the core of the current development paradigm. In communication, the participation mode is linked with the two-way/dialogic model.

Participatory communication. A major approach within the dialogic or participatory mode. It combines participation and two-way communication methods, techniques, and tools to ensure mutual understanding, investigate key issues, minimize risks, and identify best options, and, most of all, to build broad consensus for change as defined by stakeholders.

Participatory Rural Communication Appraisal (PRCA). A flexible and participatory method for conducting communication action-research. Using a simple, easy-to-follow step-by-step methodology, this approach uses participatory communication to engage stakeholders in conducting the assessment of the situation and provide a significant input in the planning of the activities.

Strategic communication. DevComm defines strategic communication as the development of programs designed to influence the voluntary behavior of target audiences to achieve management objectives. Based on the one-way model, strategic communication is usually engaged in getting the right messages, to the right audiences, through the right media, to change intended behaviors.

Windows of Perceptions (WOPs). A tool that originated with the Participatory Rural Communication Appraisal, not only to analyze a problem and its causes, but also to contrast and compare the perceptions on the problem and all related issues among stakeholders' groups. WOPs was developed because of the realization that development project failures and obstacles often were not owing to structural or technical causes, but to misinterpretations and differences in perceptions.

Index